Camping and Backpacking with Children

Steven Boga

STACKPOLE BOOKS

Published by
STACKPOLE BOOKS
5067 Ritter Road
Mechanicsburg, PA 17055

Printed in the United States of America

Cover photo by William J. Boga
Cover design by Mark Olszewski
Illustrations by Karen Boga

First Edition

10 9 8 7 6 5 4

Library of Congress Cataloging-in-Publication Data

Boga, Steve, 1947–
    Camping and backpacking with children / Steven Boga.—1st ed.
      p. cm.
    ISBN 0–8117–2522–7
    1. Camping. 2. Backpacking. 3. Family recreation. I. Title.
GV191.7.B64 1994
795.54—dc20
                                        94-23013
                                          CIP

Contents

*Dedicated to my two remaining heroes, John Muir
and Henry David Thoreau, who through their
writings taught me about nature, and to my daughter,
Madeleine, who through her curiosity and enthusiasm
furthers my nature education.*

Acknowledgments

This book would not have been possible without the generous assistance of many happy campers.

Heartfelt thanks to the parents—Jeff Doran and Catherine Hallahan-Doran, Cindy Gronroos, Tim Hallahan and Ann Hansen, Jim Hamilton, and Bruce Maxwell and Ann Brice—and their kids—Sarah, Ben, and Jack Doran; Nick Gronroos; Brett Hallahan; Alistair Hamilton; and Tandy and Veery Maxwell.

Awestruck thanks to Mike Corbett and Ken Yager, who showed me that they could indeed get their young daughters, Ellie Tenaya Corbett and Hayley Sequoia Yager, to the top of Half Dome.

Respectful thanks to Jay Knick for the personal equipment seminars—and for allowing me to play with the gear at Sonoma Outfitters, his store in Santa Rosa, California.

Editorial thanks to Bruce Maxwell, Ann Brice, Tom and Jean Makris, Dan and Jan O'Connell, and my wife, Karen, who does a lot of the grunt work with only sporadic complaints.

Special thanks to my parents for putting me on trails and editing manuscripts, and especially to my dad, who endured backpacking trips with a perpetually adolescent son—and still found time to take pictures.

Preface

The mountains are calling, and I must go.
—John Muir

1958: We have been studying this weird guy John Muir in school. He used to hike around in the high mountains with only a blanket and a few biscuits, and today I got to see the trail that's named after him. Mom, Dad, and I are camping in Yosemite Valley, where Muir hung out a lot. This morning, Dad took me to Happy Isles, to the start (they call it the "trailhead") of the John Muir Trail. We stood there for what seemed like a long time, just staring at the trail sign, a big old iron thing with stenciled names and numbers that looked like it might have been around when that guy Muir first stood there. It listed nice-sounding places like Sunrise and Palisade Lakes, and incredible distances! "Mount Whitney: 212 miles." I can't imagine walking that far.

A couple of hikers carrying green backpacks and fishing gear came up from the parking lot. They stopped for a second to read the sign, then gave each other kind of strained smiles and headed up the trail with real determination. I watched them a long time. I couldn't help wondering, "Where are they going? How long will they be gone?"

When I looked at my father's face, I could tell he was thinking the same thing. Then he took my hand—which he never does—and led me to the other side of the sign. "There, you're on the John Muir Trail," he said. "We're at its lowest point—4,034 feet above sea level."

A few minutes later, while we were sitting on a rock eating some dried fruit and stale sandwiches, listening to the friendly roar of the Merced River, Dad said, "You know, I've always wanted to hike the whole trail, all 212 miles of it." It wasn't so much what he said but how he said it that got to me. He sounded full of regret, like he'd missed something really important. It made me feel kind of sad. And eating that stale sandwich he'd made, well, that just made me feel sadder. "I don't suppose I'll ever do it now. You have to put in food caches along the way. And you need a buddy to hike with." For a second, I thought I might cry. At that moment, I figured I probably liked him better than I ever had. I looked up at him and smiled, and he smiled back, and I could tell he was wondering if I could ever be that buddy. He looked so darn hopeful that I wanted to hug him and tell him, "Oh, sure you will, Dad. Someday we'll do it as a team."

But we just aren't that way together.

1960: Today we all hiked the first couple of miles of the John Muir Trail, to the top of Vernal Falls. Mom said it was the most beautiful hike she'd ever taken. The guidebook she keeps in her knapsack calls it "a steep climb through a mist-enshrouded, granite-walled amphitheater." That sounds about right to me.

It was a steep climb all right, but I was so excited that I kept hiking ahead, pretending I was John Muir. Then I'd run back down and hike with Mom and Dad for a while, before blasting ahead to see how many more tourists I could pass (final count: 234). Mom hikes slowly but does OK for her age, which must be right up there. Dad goes slowly to stay with her and to take pictures.

At the top, we sat on a rock and had lunch. The sun was reflecting brightly off the granite, so I put on my dark glasses, feeling really cool. It was hot enough for me to take off my shirt. The sun seemed awfully strong, like it was digging little craters into my back. I've noticed a change in my senses since we got to the mountains. For one thing, the sky looks a lot bluer than ever before; for another, the pine and spruce trees smell sweeter; and the sounds—the buzzing of insects, the chirping of birds and squirrels, the wind moving through the leaves—seem sweeter, too. My mother says I might be getting a jump on puberty.

When we wanted to talk, we had to shout above the roar of Vernal Falls, which sounded like thunder that wouldn't quit. Dad and I spent most of our time looking up the trail toward Nevada Falls, Muir Pass, Mount Whitney—wondering what was it like up there, what adventures awaited anyone going all the way to Whitney.

It's like Dad and I share a secret now.

1962: Dad and I are halfway through a two-week backpacking trip in Yosemite, a lot of it on the John Muir Trail. Our packs are way too heavy (Dad brought a hatchet and a heavy camera, and together we brought enough food to make John Muir throw up). And after a week alone, relations between us are sometimes about as chilly as the lakes we camp by.

Still, it has been an unforgettable trip and great in many ways. I have learned about boots, black bears, deer, mosquitoes, sleeping bags, pitching tents, building campfires, fishing, altitude, storms, glaciers, rock formations, crossing streams, white water, and the Belding ground squirrel. Though Dad has never concerned himself much with my urban survival skills, he takes an active interest in my wilderness education.

I have decided I like the hiking best, the mosquitoes least. Hiking trails with a pack on my back makes me feel powerful and self-sufficient. And it's something I feel good at. I wonder if I can get a job walking when I grow up.

> *"Beware of all enterprises that require new clothes."*
> *—Henry David Thoreau*

1988: A funny thing happened for a while today—I did nothing. I was sitting on a patch of spongy meadow at the edge of Magic Lake (our name) on a windless seventy-five-degree day, my back against a tree, at peace with the world. Jeff was off somewhere and it was mountain quiet, a deep, resounding silence broken only by the lapping of water against rocks and the happy hum of insects. Suddenly, it struck me that I had done nothing for maybe an hour. I hadn't read a book, written in my diary, or tried to catch a fish. My day pack, rod, and reel lay beside me, untouched.

In the city, where we all toil feverishly on treadmills of our own making, such contented repose is as rare as Belding ground squirrels.

Alone, ten thousand feet above sea level, it seems as natural as the environment. If I were a therapist, I would prescribe high-altitude camping for my wigged-out patients.

1994: As I enter my "middle years," kicking and screaming, I still have not hiked the length of the John Muir Trail. So what? I have my whole life to do that, and what better cause to devote one's life to? Actually, I have what seems like an attainable goal concerning the John Muir Trail. Three friends and I have a pact to hike the entire route in three installments. Starting next summer, we will hike about seventy miles on each ten-day trip.

Splitting the hike into three segments, carrying fancy tents—it's a bit cushier than the hike my father envisioned. But who is he to say? Today he does most of his walking on the golf course and it's not his dream anymore. It's mine. He gave it to me and I plan to keep it as long as I can.

Someday, maybe my daughter will inherit it from me.

1 How to Build Enthusiasm

*Wilderness helps children push new limits
and discover new things they can do and
achieve that they would otherwise never know.*
—Yvon Chouinard

Schools today offer a limited education with an arbitrary curriculum, and no subject is given shorter shrift than nature. Before college, students will hear little more than a mention of botany, geology, zoology, and natural history. Children grow up with few insights into the natural world or their place in it. From ignorance springs disrespect.

George Bernard Shaw liked to say that the only time his education was interrupted was when he was in school. Whether or not you agree with this sentiment, clearly much of what our children are asked to think about in school has only occasional relevance to what they *need* to think about.

Yet, it is wrong to blame teachers. They see our kids only briefly, in crowded classrooms severed from nature. It is parents who must expose children to the great outdoors. By educating our kids in nature's ways, we build respect, a precursor to love. In this way, we embolden a new generation of wilderness caretakers, Mother Nature's little helpers. We and the planet benefit.

"Nature is a part of our humanity, and without some awareness and experience of that divine mystery, man ceases to be man."

—Henry Beston

WHAT'S WORTH KNOWING

Pretend all of our schools' teaching was sucked into a giant whirlpool. It is your job to turn this into an opportunity. What would you do? I'd first teach children how to learn. This demands a curriculum based on questions rather than answers. Answers tend to terminate thinking. Questions, on the other hand, perpetuate the joy of learning. They tempt the learner to ask still more questions—to think. Here are some questions that seem to me worth answering:

- What does life need to survive? Plants? Animals? Humans?
- Which conditions are necessary for all life?
- What are the greatest threats to all life? To plants? Animals? Humans?
- What strategies do living things use to survive? Which are unique to plants? Animals? Humans?
- Which human survival strategies are similar to those of animals and plants? Which are different?
- What unique survival strategies does man's language permit him to develop?
- How might human survival change if we did not have language?

"I believe little learning actually occurs in classrooms, nor can it, nor should it. At best, the classroom, lecture hall, and laboratory are stimuli, provocations, offering something to be carried away—to the coffee shop, dream world, or whatever."

—Clark Brown, teacher

GAMES

This new learning system should rely heavily on educational games. "Game" is not usually associated with intellectual growth, but there are few concepts or skills that cannot be mastered through an educational game. Games are particularly effective in teaching outdoor skills.

Educational games do not rely on chance, although, as in life, chance plays a part. Many of these games are really simulations—role-playing—in which we simplify the universe and isolate certain skills. Ideally, we tout cooperation over competition, though the latter, if used deftly and in moderation, can add incentive.

The parent-teacher in this system plays the role of guide, coach, and flexible resource. After introducing the central problem and discussing the range of solutions, the parent-teacher turns the learners loose to discover the best alternative(s). A guide doesn't have to be an expert in every field, but he or she must be able to find solutions. The guide doesn't have to know who discovered America; only how to discover who discovered America.

Why are games effective learning tools? They make learning fun, spurring motivation. They also provide challenges that some kids are drawn to. Kalman J. Cohen, professor of economics at the Carnegie Institute of Technology, a games pioneer in the 1950s, concluded, "Games give students an opportunity to practice decision-making techniques. They force students to live with the consequences of their decisions, an experience hard to get in the classroom."

PARENT AS TEACHER

Your children's nature education can begin anytime, but the younger the better. Very young children are a blank slate upon which you can scribble. Here are some suggestions to help make your writing intelligent and sensitive.

Books

Make nature books available to your children. Start by introducing picture books about animals (plants will come later) and books about people confronting, or at least living in, nature. As they get older, pique their interest with outdoor adventure stories, such as *Call of the Wild* or *Robinson Crusoe*.

Look for used books at flea markets, garage sales, secondhand stores, and library sales. As your children outgrow or become tired of certain books, trade with friends or used book stores.

Activity books let kids become more physically involved in the learning process. Consider pop-up insect books, wildlife coloring books, and botanical connect-the-dot books.

Props

As your children focus their nature interests, fuel them by making available any or all of the following learning toys:

- binoculars
- camera
- constellation guide
- magnifying glass
- maps
- microscope
- rain gauge
- thermometer
- telescope

When it's time to buy your children a present, visit a nature store. Consider animal lotto, insect dominoes, mammal mobiles, butterfly gardens, and wildlife card games, T-shirts, and puzzles.

THE BACKYARD

Some people think you have to visit a regional, state, or national park to get close to nature. Actually, you need travel only as far as the closest lawn.

Have your kids lie on their stomachs in the center of the lawn. Tell them to put their nose close to the ground, to be still and quiet, and to see what they can see. Soon, they will see the wild kingdom, miniaturized. A microcosm of Earth life will be unveiled, a survival-of-the-fittest battle raging a few feet from your door: beetles locked in mortal combat, spiders on patrol, industrious ants, a wounded wasp, and so forth.

In his book *Tom Brown's Field Guide to Nature and Survival for Children*, the author wrote of the magical moment he first stuck his nose in the ground: "There was a whole world down there that I would not have believed could be so beautiful or intriguing. Tiny plants and fungi littered the grass forest floor. The very earth itself was a marvelous blend of tiny jewellike boulders, miniscule tracks, bits of plants, and sundry other mysterious items. The earth was littered with bits and pieces of the animal world: insect parts, hair, claws, whiskers, tiny teeth, bits of skulls."

There are so many adventures right in your backyard.

(PHOTO BY BRUCE MAXWELL)

ATTRACTING NATURE

You do not have to wait passively for nature to find you. Consider some active strategies for attracting plants and animals.

Bird Feeder.

A great way to attract wildlife to a yard is to install a bird feeder. You

*A budding birder.
It's never too early
to begin sparking
interest in your
children.*

(PHOTO BY ANN BRICE)

can put a slab of wood on a post, throw down some seed, and call it a bird feeder. Such a creation may attract a few birds, but if you want them to go out of their way to stop at your place, put in more than one kind of feeder—free-standing, hanging, platform—and make them look as natural as possible. Try to place them near brush, which offers birds security. Change their water often and keep it ice-free in winter.

Gardens

Let your children help with the planting of a vegetable garden, even a tiny one. This makes them caregivers and lets them run their hands through the dirt. It also gives kids a real sense of satisfaction when the crops start popping up. If your kids plant radishes, they will have a crop in about two weeks.

You can also plant a natural garden. Designate a corner of the yard for a "secret garden," complete with flowers, plants, and maybe a fake frog. Let the flora run amok. Such a garden can attract a variety of wildlife, especially if you add a pond.

Nesting Boxes
Find out which birds will nest in your area and what they like in a nesting box. Then set up boxes at the edge of your yard, as far away from human commotion as possible. Clean the boxes at the end of the season to get ready for the new tenants. Do this in early fall, in case any birds decide to winter there.

ENVIRONMENTAL AWARENESS
No more clams in the Chesapeake Bay; only a handful of grizzlies in the lower forty-eight states; whales for the killing. Most school kids are well aware of man's inhumanity (intentional or not) to wildlife. It doesn't take much to muster support, or at least sympathy, for seal pups that are being bludgeoned to death, but how do we instill a sensitivity to our nonbreathing natural resources? How do we provoke outrage over less glamorous matters like soil erosion and water pollution?

The following games can provide insights and alter perceptions:

Broken Soil
Have your children pick out a square foot of ground in the yard. Tell them you want to buy that land, but first you have to know what's on it and in it. Have them explore the land, from ground level down several inches below the surface. Have them discuss the interesting things they find in the soil.

When they are finished exploring, ask them to put the earth back exactly the way it was. Someone will point out that it's impossible. Impossible for people, you reply. Of course, nature can do it, but it will take a long time to repair what humans destroyed in seconds.

Broken Leaf
Have children tear a leaf in half, then give them some tape or glue and tell them to fix it. Even if they manage to attach the leaf parts, it will soon die. Again the lesson is that it is always easier to destroy than to create.

Oil Slick
Have your children pour a little motor oil into a container of water and shake it up. Next give them a sponge and an eye dropper, and have them

remove the oil. When they think they've removed most of it, have them feel and smell the water. Ask, "What do you think happens with a major oil spill?"

WALKING

Since hiking is the main wilderness transportation, your children must develop an affection—or at least a tolerance—for walking.

As soon as your baby is able to hold her head up, start carting her around in a child carrier, a kid backpack. The kid will enjoy the stimulation and the parent will benefit from the exercise. As your children get older, take walks in the neighborhood or the local park. Be a tour guide. Draw their attention to subtle points of interest—the first spring buds, a wasp's nest, or some volunteer flowers. Tune in to your breathing, feel the wind in your face, admire the shadowy patterns created by dappled sunlight—and gently share these moments.

W̶e are a fat nation—maybe the fattest in history—and growing all the time. Obesity soared during the 1980s, a decade known for advances in health consciousness. Most disturbing is the explosive weight gain among youth. A survey by the Fitness Products Council attributed the sorry state of American children to reductions in school exercise programs and increased attraction to TV, computers, and video games.

I believe our kids are eating more junk, watching more junk, and graduating to couch potato at an ever-younger age. Urbanization plays a part, too. A few years ago, Johnny was out helping Dad on the north forty; today, he's playing Nintendo till the cows come home.

We are aware of the problem but seem incapable of solving it. Consider that 90 percent of dieters quickly regain lost weight. But an effective diet, with permanent weight loss, is remarkably simple: Eat a high-carbohydrate, low-fat diet, and get regular exercise. Burn more calories than you consume and you will lose weight. You may not lose it as quickly as they do in the diet ads, but maintain good habits and the weight will stay off.

What's the best exercise? The first rule is, do what you love. Otherwise, you'll soon stop doing it. If you have a passion, go with it. But if you or your children are searching for healthful activity, walking offers a lot. It is outside, free, exploratory, aerobic, sensual, can be done right from your front door, and burns about one hundred calories per mile, regardless of pace.

The Senses

We live in a sight-oriented world, to the neglect of hearing, smell, taste, and touch. If your children are to take full advantage of nature, they will have to sharpen their senses. This they can do with various exercises.

Try this as a warm-up: Blindfold your children (which will automatically enhance the other senses) and have them sit quietly for a while. This in itself may be such a stunning accomplishment that you'll want to hand out prizes. At the end of the time limit—maybe two or three minutes—have the children write down what they heard, smelled, and felt.

Now let them try it again, this time telling them to be observant. Point out the differences in what the senses recorded when they knew they were supposed to be tuned in. After all, weren't the same things there the first time?

To help children develop their hearing, have them listen near and far, isolating specific sounds. Urge them to listen to the wind rustling leaves, the hum of insect wings, lapping water, and animal sounds. Play private detective games and trace sounds to their origin. Pretend you're a deer whose survival depends on acute hearing. Show children that by cupping their hands around their ears, making a "deer's ear," they can hear sounds they couldn't hear before.

Teach children that touch involves the whole body, not just the hands. Have them lie on the ground and "feel" the earth with as many parts of their body as they can. Have them sit up and close their eyes while you hand them objects to feel—moss, bark, and underwear they left on the floor for the fiftieth time. Have them feel the sun on their legs and the wind in their face. Take them to the fifty-yard line of the local football field, blindfold them, and ask them to walk to one of the goal lines, using only the sun and wind to guide them. Practice this skill.

Taste and smell are closely linked. Teach your children to eat slowly and savor their food, much as a wine taster savors a sip. Make a game out of trying to distinguish among tap water, bottled water, well water, and spring water. Make conscious efforts to smell nature's bouquet. Have them sniff the ground in various places and note the differences. When you're camping, have them smell the dens, trails, and runs of animals. Practice identifying which animal left its scent.

Sight can benefit from tune-ups, too. When you're hiking, encourage your children to look at something beyond their feet hitting the ground. Have them pick out colors, shapes, textures, and movements. Teach them to look closely at flowers, feathers, leaves, and spider webs. A magnifying glass permits closer scrutiny. Have them draw some of the things they see, which will demand their attention to detail. Have them alternate their gaze from the near to the far and back again, scanning the horizon for details, then quickly refocusing on, say, a tuft of lichen on a nearby log.

Above all, teach your kids to look at even the most familiar landscapes as if they are seeing them for the first time. Have them pick out any differences from the last time they had the same view. Add something new to their visual field and see if they notice it. Only by exercising all our senses can we expect to take the sensory ride that life has to offer.

Overnighter

When you feel your kids are ready, suggest a backyard camping trip. There you can introduce equipment—tents, sleeping bags, pads, maybe a stove for some after-dinner hot chocolate. Take advantage of any opportunities to chat about natural phenomena—constellations, animal sounds, and dew.

If your children enjoy their first night out, you can progress to car camping, car camping with day hikes, and backpacking.

RESOURCES

Magazines
Backpacker (Emmaus, PA: Rodale Press)
Subscription telephone: 1-800-666-3434
Outside (Chicago: Mariah Publications)
Subscription telephone: 1-800-678-1131
National Geographic (Washington, DC: National Geographic Society)

Books
Take a Hike! by Lynne Foster (1991: Sierra Club Books, San Francisco)
Soft Paths by Bruce Hampton and David Cole (1988: Stackpole Books, Harrisburg, PA)
Discover Nature Close to Home by Elizabeth P. Lawlor (1993: Stackpole Books, Harrisburg, PA)
Pleasure Packing by Robert S. Wood (1980: Ten Speed Press, Berkeley, CA)
Wilderness with Children by Michael Hodgson (1992: Stackpole Books, Harrisburg, PA)

2 How to Pick the Right Equipment

A three-year-old child is a being who gets almost as much fun out of a fifty-six dollar set of swings as it does out of finding a small green worm.
—Bill Vaughan

Always buy quality equipment from a reputable dealer. Quality gear will last longer and give you greater comfort than discount-store gear,

In utero, kids require very little equipment.

(Photo by Jim Hamilton)

especially when the going gets tough. Good gear is costly, but if you stay with camping and backpacking for the long haul, it will actually end up being cheaper.

The biggest equipment error I ever made was buying a cheap backpack the first time I went to Europe. I have a vision of that backpack that still haunts me. I see my $14 Kmart special emerging onto the airport conveyor belt in total disarray. The canvas pack is separated from its frame; personal items are missing or strewn along the belt. I am the laughingstock of Flight 379.

Clerks in reputable outdoor stores can update you on the latest technological innovations. In the meantime, here's a starter kit of information on the big-ticket items.

FOOTWEAR
Boots

The right boots and socks can make the difference between a glorious day of hiking and a miserable day of wet feet, blisters, and even falls. Compared with tennis shoes, hiking boots offer better durability, cushioning, ankle support, and protection from the elements.

One year, back in my macho adolescent days, I decided to forego boots and hike in tennis shoes. On the last day, we did a gradual fifteen-mile descent on a fairly rocky trail. Had I worn hiking boots, I would have suffered nothing more than the usual aches and pains. Wearing tennis shoes, however, I was temporarily crippled. The bottoms of my feet were sore to the touch and for an hour afterward all I could do was sit and moan. It was the last time I attempted a serious hike in anything but quality boots.

The first step in determining your children's footwear needs is to be realistic about their activity level. Consider what terrain they will be hiking. If it is sidewalks and cushy nature trails, tennis shoes will suffice. But if even once they will carry a backpack over rocky trails or cross-country, they need sturdy boots with lug soles.

Good boots cost money, and children, bless their ever-expanding little feet, will soon outgrow them. On the other hand, you want the best for your little darlings, and real boots are safer. One father spoke of the time his four-year-old daughter was racing down a steep granite slope toward an abyss. He yelled for her to stop, which she did, slamming down hard into her boots. "Any other shoes would have hopelessly buckled and skidded," he said, "but her Vasque boots gripped like steel-belted radials an inch from the edge."

Hiking boots, made of leather, nylon, or a combination, come in three basic types. Low boots are lightweight, have flexible soles and soft uppers, and look almost like regular athletic shoes. They are cool, quick-drying, and don't need much breaking in, but they may not hold up on rough terrain. High-top boots are heavier, have thicker soles, and offer more protection from impact and temperature extremes. High-top, off-trail boots are heavier still—sometimes more than five pounds—with rugged midsoles and maximum ankle support. They will support a hiker over most any terrain, but their weight will slow down most children. Buy the lightest boot that will serve your children's needs. In terms of leg wear, one pound on your feet is equivalent to twenty pounds on your back.

Right Fit

Proper fit is critical, no matter what your children hike in. Tight shoes limit the foot's natural elasticity during walking; loose shoes permit excessive foot movement inside the shoe, leading to blisters. Here are some tips for assuring the right fit:

• Shop for boots late in the day; feet tend to swell as the day goes on.

• To assure proper fit, take to the store the socks your children will wear on the trail. A good sock should be thick enough to provide cushioning.

• Consider boots as large as possible for your growing children. One way to lengthen boot life is to fit them when your children are wearing, say, three pairs of socks. Next year, two sock layers may do it; after that, one thin sock and one thick sock may achieve optimum snugness.

• Ask questions of clerks to narrow down the number of boots you need to try on.

• Check workmanship. Do you see loose threads or faulty glue? Slip your hand into the boot and feel for rough edges, ridges, or seams.

• Check for flexibility. You should be able to bend the sole fairly easily across its widest point, where the ball of the foot rests. Conversely, the boot should have a stable heel and a rigid shank (the narrow part of the sole beneath the instep).

• Keep the boots unlaced and have your children push first one foot, then the other, as far forward in the boot as possible. You should barely be able to fit your index finger between the heel and the back of the boot.

• Next, kick the heel against the floor. The back should feel snug but comfortable.

• Lace the boot snugly. Hold down the front of the boot. Your child should not be able to lift her heel within the shoe more than an eighth-inch.

• Using your thumb and forefinger to exert pressure, check that the widest part of foot rests in the widest part of the boot.

• Have your children walk around the store for at least fifteen minutes. Have them try slopes or stairs. Their feet should not slide around, though they should be able to wiggle their toes. If boots don't fit in the store, they won't fit in the outdoors, though heavy leather boots will gain flexibility.

• Don't buy children's hiking boots through a catalog unless the fit is guaranteed. You must be able to return a bad fit.

• By using multiple socks to adjust the fit, you might find used boots for children at flea markets, thrift shops, or garage sales. Because children usually outgrow boots before they wear them out, outdoor stores sometimes carry used boots for kids. They may even give you a trade-in.

• Allow everyone a week or two before a long hike to test their new boots and make sure they fit.

Boot Care
When you buy a pair of boots, find out the best waterproofing to use. As

soon as you get them home, apply the first coat. Do it again before the first hike. Silicone spray works best on split-leather and fabric boots.

Resist the temptation to dry boots in an oven or over an open flame. Air-dry them thoroughly away from direct heat. Stuff newspapers, socks, paper towels, or rags into the boots to soak up moisture. Change the wadding if boots stay wet. Store boots, unlaced and open, away from damp areas.

Get your children to clean their boots after a big hike. Meticulous care prolongs boot life.

F oot comfort depends on boots, socks, and hygiene. You and your children should wash your feet daily. Feet heat up and swell on long hikes and during the night. Aspirin and ibuprofen reduce swelling.

Keep everyone's feet dry with liberal sprinklings of baby powder, especially before long hikes. Feet sweat through about a quarter of a million pores.

Spray the inside of boots with a fungicide to discourage the growth of molds.

Attack hot spots with moleskin, Spenco 2nd Skin, or duct tape before they become blisters.

Sandals

The latest option in wilderness footwear is the sport sandal, which is light-weight, contoured, cushioned, and quick-drying. Its snug-fitting straps keep your feet securely in place, even on rocky trails, and high-traction outsoles can grip wet, slippery terrain.

Such high-tech features make the sport sandal a great second shoe on a backpacking trip. After imprisoning your feet in socks and boots for hours, airing them out in sandals is a slice of heaven.

Though sport sandals are touted as a hiking boot by some manufac-turers, many podiatrists disagree, especially if you have flat feet or any type of foot abnormality. Sandals lack ankle support and greatly increase the risk of stubbed toes. The heel in many sandals is lower than the ball of the foot, which, according to Dr. Harry Hlavac of the California College of Podiatric Medicine, can strain the arch and Achilles tendon.

That said, a good pair of sports sandals will work for a backpacker in a pinch. Backpacking in the High Sierra recently, my partner's new boots rubbed quarter-size blisters on his heel, convincing him to try hiking in sandals. They gave him instant relief and caused no problems, even on a rocky trail.

When buying sandals, test their fit by walking around the store for a few minutes. Make sure your feet are firmly centered and don't slide around. There should be about a quarter-inch from your foot to the edges of the sandal.

To check for adequate support, grab the ends of a sandal and try to bend it. If it bends anywhere but at the toe area, support is inadequate.

CLOTHING

Weather can change rapidly in the wilderness. A cloud drifting in front of the sun can drop the temperature several degrees. A gain in altitude can do the same. Sunny weather on a south-facing slope can become damp and cold on a nearby north-facing slope.

To prepare for such a climatic potpourri, dress your children in at least three layers. Because air is trapped and kept warm between each layer, two thin sweaters are more effective than one thick one. With several layers of warm clothing available, you can add or subtract to achieve the warmth needed. This provides maximum flexibility during weather fluctuations.

Taking off clothes during a warm spell is a minor inconvenience. Not having enough clothing when the temperature plummets can be a major disaster.

The inner layer should wick away moisture and offer protection from the sun. Cotton, a moisture absorber, is great in hot weather, not so great in cold weather. Wool retains its warmth when wet, but it can be unbearably scratchy. Synthetic fabrics like polypropylene, Thermax, or Caprilene are better for the inner sock and underwear layer. The middle, or insulative, layer can be a wool or fleece sweater. The outer layer should be rainproof and windproof. Gore-Tex laminated onto nylon allows perspiration to escape but does not allow rain in. A hood keeps rain out and heat in.

As needed, your children should add mittens (or gloves), a hat, and extra socks. In cold weather, consider shorts rather than long pants. Little heat is lost through the legs and few things are more disgusting than hiking in soggy pants.

Not every clothing item must be purchased at an elite outdoor store. You already own most of what you need, even for cold-weather camping. Look for missing items at flea markets, thrift shops, garage sales, and in your friends' closets. Seek hand-me-downs and, of course, recycle clothing through your own younger children.

When possible, select bright colors for your children. They are easier to spot from a distance. Also, sewing identification labels into your young children's clothing could help searchers if they ever get lost.

SLEEPING BAGS

> **R**ight now, while you're strong, write on a piece of paper, "I will not let my child sleep with me in my sleeping bag." Now follow that rule, at least if you care about a good night's sleep.

A sleeping bag is a shell, a nylon cocoon, filled with insulation. Your body provides the heat; a good bag merely retains it. How well a bag warms you depends primarily on its size, shape, type of insulation, and how it is contained in the bag.

Other variables you may find important include:

comfort rating	fill power	shell
fill weight	hood	zipper
loft	price	
stuffed size	weight	

You must first decide on down or synthetic fill. Down is the fluff growing next to the skin of waterfowl. Only goose and duck down are used in sleeping bags and goose down is considered superior. Maybe, but it would be by such a small margin, I believe, that other factors can tip the scales the other way. A good duck may be better than a bad goose.

For equal warmth, down is light, compact, and pricey. Synthetic fills (like Polarguard, Hollofil, and Quallofil) are comparatively heavy, bulky, and inexpensive. On the other hand, they maintain loft and warmth when wet and provide better ground insulation than down.

Although I have always owned down bags, I recommend synthetic bags for children, especially young ones who still may wet the bed. Synthetics are easy to wash and dry, and a damp bag still insulates well. Consider renting or borrowing bags before making a final decision.

Once you settle on type of fill, consider construction, size, and shape. Construction refers to the arrangement of baffles, the compartments inside the shell that hold the fill. Baffles distribute the fill evenly, keeping it from piling up at, say, your feet. Choices include slant tube, slant wall, slant box, and parallelogram baffles. Unless you are hiking from the equator to the top of Mount McKinley, don't fret about baffle construction. Loft and comfort rating are more important.

Avoid a quilted bargain-basement bag that is stitched straight through the top and bottom layers. Insulation along the stitching is near zero.

Sleeping bags come in three basic shapes: rectangular, semi-mummy, and mummy. Mummies are the lightest and warmest but are the most restrictive. Some are trimmer than others, but in most, if you turn over, your bag turns with you. Children especially may find this disturbing. I did. My only claustrophobia attack occurred when I was ten on a dark night in a tight mummy bag. My last mummy bag. Avoid this by having your child crawl in the prospective sleeping bag and do a snuggle test. Measure comfort by the number of ooohhs and aaahhs.

Most adult bags come in regular and long. Most manufacturers offer

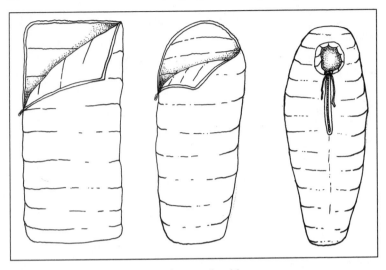

Bigger sleeping bags are roomier—and colder.

only one kids' size—"Junior." Why not put your children in adult bags? Because a bag that is too big for the occupant takes longer to heat up and loses heat faster. The excess space also adds needless weight to a load. On the other hand, a bag that is too small will be too cramped for a comfortable night's sleep.

• Comfort Rating. Sleeping bags are given a temperature rating, usually forty degrees above zero F. to minus forty degrees F., which is supposed to be the lowest temperature at which the bag will keep you warm. The first problem is that individual differences can affect how warmly you sleep. The second is that comfort ratings are supplied by manufacturers, who tend to shade the numbers in their favor. Consequently, they probably will not help you compare bags from different makers, though they will give you an idea where a bag fits in a particular manufacturer's line. Lower comfort ratings mean higher prices.

• Fill Power. This is the best measure of down quality. One ounce of down is placed in a tube and its volume is measured under a weight. The higher the result (cubic inches per ounce), the more efficient the down. A fill power of 550 is good; 650 is excellent.

• Fill Weight. This is how much the insulation inside the sleeping bag weighs. Fill weight and comfort rating are related.

• Hood. An enormous amount of heat is lost through the head and neck. A hood with a drawstring makes a sleeping bag versatile. In very cold weather, tighten down the hood so only a nose protrudes; on warmer nights, use the hood as a pillow.

• Loft. Gently shake and fluff your sleeping bag and lay it flat. The thickness of the insulation after fluffing is loft. More loft (eight inches is excellent) means more warm air trapped between you and the elements. As a rough gauge of warmth, figure about four inches of loft keeps you warm down to forty degrees, six inches to twenty degrees, and eight inches to zero.

• Price. Money is an object, of course. Bags are expensive, but they've inflated a lot less than hotel rooms. For quality down bags, expect to pay $150 to $300; for synthetic fill, you can do well for less than $200. You can find a kid's bag rated to fifteen degrees for less than $100. You can find used bags at flea markets, thrift shops, and garage sales, or you can adapt one out of a used adult bag. This works especially well with bags having less than full zippers. Amputate the bottom two feet and resew it.

• Shell. Cold air moving across the surface (shell) of a standard sleeping bag will draw warm air out of the insulation as you sleep. Laminating a nylon shell with rip stock Gore-Tex will substantially increase a bag's protection from moisture and heat loss without increasing weight.

• Stuffed Size. You should stuff quality sleeping bags, rather than roll them. Stuff sacks, usually coated nylon, come in a range of sizes. How small a bag will stuff is important for backpackers with limited space. Down is more compressible than synthetic fill, though the latter has narrowed the gap in the past few years. Compression stuff sacks with extra straps will make the package even smaller.

• Weight. This is more important for backpackers than car campers. Most kids' bags weigh less than three pounds; most adult ones less than five pounds.

• Zipper. Nylon coil zippers are better than tooth ones. No. 7 zippers are stronger than No. 5. A full zipper makes a bag versatile: unzip it part way and hang your leg outside; unzip it all the way and call it a blanket.

But that full zipper also creates tiny holes that can leak warm air. Good bags have the zipper covered to prevent this.

Another point is whether the zipper is on the right or left side. This is important if you want to zip one bag to another. If two bags have full zippers of the same size and type, with opposite configurations, they will zip together. This is often more important to adults than to children.

With care, a good sleeping bag will last for years. Store bags loose in a cool, dark, dry room. If you have space, hang them in a spare closet. Or use storage bags made of breathable cotton and roomy enough to avoid loft compression. Never store any sleeping bag, down or synthetic, compressed in a stuff sack or backpack.

You can sew two sheets together on three sides, insert your sleeping bag into the envelope, and use it on your bed as a quilt.

In camp, after pitching the tent, unstuff, unzip, and fluff all bags to allow them to regain full loft. Next morning, air-dry bags on a warm rock or line. That will evaporate perspiration that has condensed on the insulation fibers.

Bags are best machine washed. Use a commercial front-loader, not a home top-loader. Use mild soap and the "delicate" setting. Remove it carefully; if you yank from one end, you can tear the baffles. Tumble dry thoroughly on a very low setting. Never drape a soaking wet bag over a line.

To keep your children's sleeping bags clean, double a sheet, then sew the bottom and partway up the side to create a liner that can be taken out and washed.

SLEEPING PADS

A pad may be the most underrated piece of gear in the battle against a sleepless night. It is essential for an adult or child. It puts a layer of insulation between the body and the cold earth and cushions against roots and rocks. It also can be your life raft on a stormy night in a leaky tent.

Pads offer two basic choices—closed-cell and open-cell. The common material is foam. Closed-cell foam is a slab of tiny plastic bubbles, whole and unbroken (closed), so the pad won't absorb water. Open-cell foam is found in sponges, so it absorbs water well. Unlike closed-cell foam, all its polymer bubbles are burst (open) to form a honeycomb structure. With fewer solid walls, open-cell is lighter and more compressible.

For years, I used a closed-cell Ensolite pad. It was light, waterproof, and indestructible. Closed-cell pads come in various lengths and thicknesses. A three-eighth-inch-thick three-quarter length is sufficient for me, though I like a firm bed. I would still be sleeping on a closed-cell pad if I had not received a Therm-a-Rest mattress as a gift.

The Therm-a-Rest, made and patented by Cascade Designs, is the original self-inflating single-chamber air mattress. All eight models are open-cell foam bonded to a nylon shell. The only downside supposedly is the price, $40 to $100. However, I've had trouble with mine: first, microscopic holes developed that cause slow leaks; second, I have a disconcerting tendency to slide off its slippery surface. The Therm-a-Rest is cushier than closed-cell models, but I kind of miss my old Ensolite; I didn't need a patch kit and I knew where I'd wake up in the morning.

If you go with a self-inflating pad, be patient and let it inflate by itself. Blowing into it puts lots of moisture inside that can break down the foam. Store self-inflating pads in the usual cool, dry place. Leave them unrolled with the valve open, so moisture can escape. Use self-adhesive nylon tape for repairs. Fix pinholes with a dollop of seam sealer. Patch larger holes by cutting a rounded patch a half-inch larger than the hole. Clean the area with stove gas or denatured alcohol.

To decide which pad is right for you and your children, rank weight, warmth, bulk, comfort, durability, and cost in order of importance. Never lose sight of the ultimate goal: a good night's sleep for everyone, perhaps the most important element of a successful camping trip.

For children, who seem to be impervious to the rigors of sleeping on the ground, I recommend the cheaper closed-cell foam. A half-length pad might be just right for them.

SHELTERS
Your basic choices in camping shelters, from the primitive to the sophis-

ticated, are nothing, snow caves, tarps, tube tents, cabin-style tents, three-season tents, and four-season tents.

• Nothing. If conditions are right, nothing has much to offer, like billions of stars, most of which seem to be visible on a clear night in the backcountry. But let's say it's not a clear night. Let's say it's stormy or the bugs are swarming. Then, "nothing" doesn't cut it.

• Snow Cave. This is strictly for an emergency. Climbers caught on Mount McKinley might dig a snow cave; if you're camping with kids, you shouldn't be there.

• Tarp. You can buy a two-pound waterproof tarp, with grommets, for a fraction of the cost of a tent. A well-rigged tarp offers shelter from rain and sun but little protection from wind or insects and no privacy.

Practice in your backyard to learn what a tarp will and will not do. Since a tarp is flat, you must use rope and/or stakes and poles to hold it up and shape the material. With some creative rigging, many shapes are possible. With practice, you will be able to put up a tarp quickly in bad weather. You will want to do this because even five minutes is a long time if your children are cold, wet, tired, and hungry.

• Tube Tent. A tube tent isn't really a tent but an open-ended plastic or coated nylon sleeve. It's easily rigged by running a line through it and tying both ends to trees or car bumpers. It's cheap and light, but if the going gets tough, tube tenters invariably get wet. I traveled around Europe in 1970 carrying only a tube tent for shelter. Camping like that enabled me to live cheaply (and travel longer), but I spent many a sodden, sleepless night.

• Tents. Most kids love tents, perhaps because they remind them of forts. In their eyes, tent plus sleeping bag equals adventure. When I first started backpacking without my parents, I usually slept under the stars— just a blanket of frost on my sleeping bag. Part of me reflects on my impetuous youth with a sense of awe, a belief that I must have been one tough little cookie. But then I recall that John Muir used to traipse through the High Sierra carrying little more than a blanket and biscuits. *He* was tough.

At fortysomething, I always carry a tent and usually set it up. There are two overriding reasons for this: insects and weather. The cheapest tent, if it has a floor and no holes, will offer full protection against mosquitoes and even tinier no-see-ums. Most tents are adequate if the weather is mild and dry, but will they survive a weekend in the desert beneath an unrelenting sun? How about a snowstorm in the Rockies? Think of a tent as an insurance policy against the possible ravages of nature. You hope you don't need it, but you feel so much better if you have it.

Technology has made possible sturdy, light tents that sleep up to six (eight with kids). Unless you want to hold a square dance, there is no reason to carry those canvas behemoths that require three able people to set up.

Before you buy a tent, ask yourself big questions: Will you be backpacking or car camping? In winter? At high altitude? What about price? You must decide between three-season and four-season tents. For most people who camp from late spring through early fall, three-season tents are adequate. Four-season tents have extra features, like an internal guy system, that allow you to survive a winter storm at high altitude.

Even in three-season tents, there are several options to consider.

Weight-to-volume ratio. Tents range from one-person models, weighing less than three pounds and suitable for one anorexic bicyclist, to cabin-style models weighing more than forty pounds and suitable for bowling tournaments. If you are backpacking, your tent will usually be the heaviest item in your pack. My present tent, a dome, weighs about seven pounds. It is big enough to hold two adults, one child, and two backpacks. I could go to a smaller tent and drop a couple of pounds, but then I'd have to carry a tarp to cover the backpacks when it rains.

As with so many backpacking items, you have to balance the comfort of using a bigger model with the discomfort of carrying it. You should also figure how far you will be carrying it. If you are hiking the Pacific Crest Trail and have to lug every ounce of tent three thousand miles, you will place a disproportionate value on weight; if you are a casual weekend camper who carries the tent only from car to campsite, weight is nothing compared to spaciousness.

Spaciousness. Sierra Designs has a two-person tent that weighs only three pounds, thirteen ounces. With a floor space of thirty-two square feet, it is fine for one adult or two kids. Two full-sized adults could make it, but they had better be *very* friendly before trying to ride out a three-day squall in that shelter.

Most outdoor stores have pitched tents on display. When shopping for a tent, bring the whole family and crawl in. Assure yourselves that the mobile home you are buying is large enough to house you and your brood. If you are ordering from a catalog, determine the dimensions of the tent, then take a marker and an old sheet and draw the shape. Crawl onto the sheet and make sure it's big enough.

Packed size. This can be important even if you're not backpacking. Car trunks have gotten smaller, still another reason to eschew huge, bulky cabin tents for trim backpacking models. The packing size of good two-person tents ranges from about five by seventeen inches to seven by twenty-one inches. Even the largest quality six-person tent packs to about ten by thirty-one inches.

Ease of setup. This is an especially important feature if your kids will be helping you set up the tent or even if they might be shivering in the rain while you do it. Things to look for: How many poles? Are they all the same length? Are they shockcorded (linked by an internal elastic cord)? For good tents, the answers are two to four, yes, and yes.

Some of today's tents are easy enough for, yes, a child to put up. In 1991, North Face introduced the No-Hitch-Pitch system, with every pole preattached to one floor grommet and already threaded through the correct canopy rings. All the camper has to do is spread out the tent floor, push the poles into position, and snap the free ends into the remaining grommets.

Whatever tent you buy, always set it up at home before you head out into the wilderness. You don't want to be reading directions out there by flashlight. Besides, a single missing or broken pole can render your tent useless. I once broke a little nipple off one of my tent poles and, though it appeared insignificant, it was enough to disable my tent beyond use.

Shape. The A-frame is dead; long live the dome. Actually, a few A-

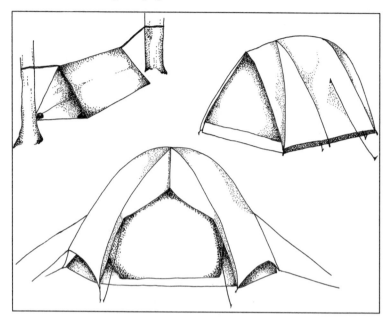

There's no place like dome.

frames endure, and many so-called domes aren't true domes. Now any self-standing tent is commonly called a "dome."

The greatest advantage of domes over flat-walled A-frames is usable space, especially headroom. Because the walls rise more or less vertically on all sides, domes have almost half again as much volume as an A-frame with the same floor area. You don't have to crawl on your belly or sit in the middle to avoid brushing against the sides of a dome. If you're tentbound for longer than a day, extra space can have a huge psychological impact.

Freestanding capabilities. Most good tents will stand on their own, using just the poles and no stakes. This means you can pick it up and move it after it has shape. You should still stake your tent, however, lest a sudden wind blow it into a nearby gorge.

Entrances. If there is only one door, it should be at the front or back, not on a side. The latter makes it inconvenient for the person farthest away.

Tautness. Quality tents are designed to be pitched tightly (although even the best tents need to be guyed in severe winds). Because cheap tents employ fewer poles and inferior fabric, they remain wrinkled even with the best pitch. That gives the wind something to bite into, and whenever there is flapping nylon, seams start to separate, fabric starts to tear, and nerves start to fray. To test tautness, toss a quarter on the canopy. It should bounce right off.

Poles. If you choose a dome, the poles should be light, flexible, hollow, and shockcorded. I prefer aluminum over fiberglass, as it's easy to break a fiberglass pole tip.

No-see-um mesh. Quality tents have at least one "screen" door or window; many now have two or more. Nylon mesh should be fine enough to keep out the tiniest no-see-ums while allowing you to see outside. More and more of today's tents have mesh windows, both on the sides and ceiling. Thus you retain that outdoor feeling while cowering inside your tent during the evening infestation of mosquitoes. If the weather is fine, you can remove the rain fly, improve air flow, and sleep under a canopy of stars.

Rain fly. The rain fly is vital to the moisture-control system. The most important thing a tent can do is control water movement. We are apt to focus on keeping rainwater out, but the biggest problem is removing condensation. During sleep, respiration and perspiration cause water vapor buildup that can condense on cool tent walls.

Top manufacturers beat the problem by providing two walls: an inner breathable canopy and an outer waterproof rain fly. With double walls, the inner canopy stays warmer than the fly and internal moisture passes through the canopy, condensing on the fly. It may drip back onto the tent canopy, but surface tension will prevent it from repenetrating and dripping onto you.

Insist on a full fly over your tent. Some inferior tents offer a tiny fly that sits atop the tent like a beanie. If the fly doesn't cover the entire tent, the nylon canopy must have a waterproof coating, which means interior moisture can't escape. This can make the inside of your tent feel like a swamp.

Vestibule. Many tents include a separate covered area for cooking or stowing gear. This is handy in bad weather.

I f your tent doesn't have a vestibule, you can make one out of a yard or so of coated rip stop nylon. Cut it in a triangle, with one side to fit the front of the fly near the door. Sear the cut edges with a flame, holding the fabric taut. Then sew Velcro strips along the edge of the fly and on the matching edge of the fabric.

Internal gear holders. Look for loops, pockets, and attics. The latest—elevated mesh shelves—are all the rage in today's tents.

Seams. Stitching creates tiny needle holes that offer still another entrance for moisture. Defend against this with a commercial seam sealer. Most are applied like a roll-on deodorant. Sealing tent seams may be a good job for your children.

Color. This could be important. If bad weather forces you to spend days in your tent, your sanity could be at stake. Three days of staring up at bright orange walls could send you screaming into the woods. Quality tents generally come in muted, natural hues.

Extras. These might include a netted roof vent or separate storage sacks for stakes, poles, and fabric; or a ground cloth sized to fit perfectly under your tent and prevent water from collecting around uneven edges.

Price. Price depends on materials, workmanship, design, features, and options. Costs vary dramatically and, as with most things, you generally get what you pay for. The range for quality two-person tents is $200 to $400. Four-person tents top out around $800. At the other end of the spectrum, you can find domes for less than $100 that seem like they might suffice. In fact, they might not last a weekend under a raging desert sun or a tropical deluge.

The most important consideration for most people is how well a tent protects in a driving rainstorm. That can be a tough call in a store. The worst tent in the world, assuming you can set it up properly, will be adequate when the weather is fine. Most tents will keep you dry in a sprinkle, a drizzle, and even a soft, steady rain. But a squall may reveal leaks you didn't know existed. At those times, quality takes on new importance.

Buying a Tent

• Find out if any local outdoor stores rent tents. If so, you can try one out before you buy.

• Ask friends, neighbors, and acquaintances about their successes and failures. You may even be able to borrow a tent for a test run.

• At the camping store, get in and out of demonstrator models several times. Now imagine yourself doing it in wind, rain, or snow. Check for good ventilation. See if closures are tight. Try the zippers to see if they work smoothly from outside as well as inside. Do they have storm flaps for protection against wind-driven rain?

• No matter how much you liked the demonstrator, inspect the tent you buy before you take it home. Make sure you have the stakes, poles, guy lines, and fly.

Pitching a Tent

• Try your tent out in the backyard first. Learn how to pitch it there before you try to do it in the wilderness.

• Pick a relatively level area that will drain. Avoid low spots.

• Choose an area soft enough to allow you to pound stakes into the ground. Granite, for example, fails this test.

• Stake your tent out tightly. Quality tents are designed to be pulled out taut. If you leave wrinkles, the wind will do a flap-dance on your tent.

• If the ground is soft, push the stakes in with the heel of your hand or the sole of your boot. If it's fairly hard, try gently pounding the stakes in with a rock or hammer; be careful not to bend them. If the ground is impenetrable, you can use extra nylon cord and tie the guy lines to rocks or trees or place a big rock on a tied stake lying on the ground. If the stakes pull out of soft ground or sand, you can tie the guy lines to a "deadman"—a stake, stick, or stuff sack filled with soil—and bury it perpendicular to the main pull.

• Pitch your tent out of direct sun when possible. Extended exposure will cause nylon to fade and break down, though the fly will help protect fragile netting and uncoated nylon.

Tent Care

• Before pitching a tent, lay down a ground cloth to protect the coated floor. A "space" blanket, weighing only a couple of ounces, works well.

• Before entering a tent, remove your shoes and leave them outside. Tracked-in debris rubs off the floor's protective coating.

• Before breaking down a tent, sweep it out, or, if it's a freestanding tent, pick it up and shake it out.

• Hand wash your tent. Set it up and sponge it with warm water and mild, nondetergent soap. Rinse thoroughly.

• Always clean and air-dry all components before storing. Never store a wet tent. If you must move on before your tent is dry, set it up again as soon as possible to let the seams dry.

• Never dry clean, machine wash, or machine dry a tent.

• Store in a dry place, out of sunlight and away from rodents and heat sources.

• If you're storing a tent for a long time, let it hang or leave it loosely packed.

• You can roll or stuff a tent, but rolling usually makes a smaller package. When rolling, leave the doors and windows open to allow air to escape. Fold the collapsed tent into a rectangle equaling the length of the folded poles. Place the poles at one end of the rectangle and roll the tent tightly, pushing air out with the poles. When you reach the end, hold the roll tightly and insert it into its bag.

• Repair small tears and punctures with nylon tape.

• When you have a seam leak but no sealer, try lip balm, candle wax, or snow seal. They will seal for a while.

STOVES

Backcountry overuse has led to campfire restrictions in many areas, so a stove has been upgraded from luxury to necessity. When car camping, you can use a two- or three-burner stove with a separate fuel tank. When backpacking, choose a lighter one-burner model.

Selling points include:

• Weight
• Compactness
• Ease of use
• Fuel capacity

- Burning time at maximum flame
- Flame adjustability
- Average boiling time
- Stability
- Effect of wind, cold, and altitude
- Safety features
- Ease of repair
- Availability of fuel
- Price

The big choice is between fuels, either liquids (gasoline or kerosene, sometimes both) or pressurized gas (propane or butane). No stove uses both, although some models will run on a variety of liquids.

The advantages of gasoline include easy availability, high heat output, moderate cost, and easy evaporation of spilled fuel. However, priming is required, the fuel is somewhat dangerous, the stove must be insulated from cold and snow, and a separate fuel bottle is required.

The advantages of kerosene include easy availability, spilled fuel will not readily ignite, high heat output, and there is no need to insulate the stove from cold and snow. However, priming is required and spilled kerosene is smelly and will not readily evaporate.

The advantages of butane or propane include no priming, immediate maximum heat output, a convenient no-spill fuel container, and easy lighting. However, butane and propane cartridges are heavy, and such stoves are inefficient when temperatures approach freezing, though the addition of 10 percent propane eases that drawback.

Roughly, one quart of liquid fuel should last one person a week. Double that if drinking water must be boiled or snow melted for water.

If you're low on fuel, conserve. Soak dried foods before lighting the stove, cover pots while cooking, and shut off the stove ten minutes early and let dinner sit in a covered pot to finish cooking.

Stove Safety Tips

• Read and follow instructions.

• Keep the stove clean and in good working order.

• Eliminate surprises by practicing with a new stove before beginning a trip.

• When carting the stove around, store the fuel separately.

• Fill your fuel tank using a filter funnel to keep debris out.

• Refuel stoves before each use so you don't run out in the middle of meal preparation.

• Never refuel a hot stove.

• Do not fill the fuel tank to the brim.

• Do not refuel a stove near flames.

• Do not pour fuel inside a tent.

• Replace the cap on the stove and the fuel bottle before lighting.

• Try a pot on the stove to check stability before lighting.

• For pressurized canister stoves, light the match and hold it next to the burner before turning on the gas. When replacing a canister, make sure gaskets are clean. The screw threads should be easy to turn—don't cross-thread the fitting. Once the canister is attached, listen for a hissing noise that could mean a leak. Never throw an "empty" canister in the fire.

• Do not light gas stoves in enclosed areas, such as tents. A burning stove consumes oxygen and gives off carbon monoxide. If you must cook inside the tent because of bad weather, light the stove outside, then carefully move it inside the vestibule or near the door. Keep the stove stable and the tent well ventilated.

• Do not light or operate a stove near spilled fuel.

• Mark fuel bottles clearly.

• For fuel storage, use only metal flasks or approved plastic containers (fuel dissolves some plastics).

• Do not closely surround a pressurized-gas cartridge with a windscreen; it could cause the cartridge to overheat and explode.

• Do not leave stoves unattended.

• If your stove has a removable key that adjusts the flame, remove it during operation so it doesn't get too hot.

• Carry spare parts, tools, and instructions for field repair. Clean holes and vents regularly.

BACKPACKS

Packs range from $10 fanny packs to $50 day packs to $500 expedition models. Fanny packs are belts with a pouch that sits against the small of your back. Day packs are small to medium-size backpacks, some of which have padded shoulder straps and waist belts.

There are two types of large backpacks—internal and external frame. The external frame, the best choice for older children, restricts movement but has a high center of gravity. The rigid frame can carry large, cumbersome loads comfortably. There are several points for securing gear to the outside of the pack, a real convenience when one parent is carrying a child and the other has everything else. External frames sit away from your back and thus are cooler in hot weather.

Internal-frame backpacks have the frame sewn right into the fabric. They offer a lower center of gravity and greater freedom of movement, but they do not handle large, unwieldy loads very well, especially if you must lash gear to the outside. They fit the contour of your back more closely, which makes them hotter but more secure.

I recommend that children younger than about eight carry only a frameless day pack with padded hip belt and shoulder straps. Later, if your children will be hiking mostly on trails, they can move up to a junior external-frame pack. Many companies make aluminum-frame backpacks that adjust as your children grow.

Proper fit in a pack can determine how much you enjoy the trip. Here are some tips.

• Patronize a store that specializes in camping and backpacking equipment. It will have the greatest selection and the most informed people.

• Listen to advice, but take nobody's word for which pack is best for your children. Run the tests yourself. Load weight into the model you are considering and have your children walk around the store, feeling for any rubbing, especially at the shoulders or lower back. Make sure most of the weight rests on hips and buttocks, not on shoulders.

• Compare the pack's fit range with your child's torso and hip/waist measurements. To determine torso length, measure from the highest point of the shoulder (where it meets the neck) to the top of the hipbone. The frame is too small when you can't get the hip belt and/or shoulder straps far enough apart or you can't let out the shoulder straps enough. It's too big when the top flops around or you are unable to tighten the shoulder straps or hip belt.

• Ensure that the hip belt fits snugly—it should rest on your child's hipbones, not around the waist—then adjust the shoulder straps. The straps should be set wide enough apart so they don't pinch the neck, but narrow enough so they don't slide off the shoulders. Getting the shoulder straps and hip belt to work in harmony solves 90 percent of fit problems.

• Make sure the horizontal bar anchoring the top of the shoulder straps is the right height. When the pack is loaded, it should be even with the top of your children's shoulders.

• Some stores rent packs, allowing you to sample various models before you buy.

Backpacker magazine recently surveyed 140 thru-hikers midway through their 2,100-mile walk of the entire Appalachian Trail. Two-thirds were using external-frame packs, but internal-frame owners were happier with what they had. Ninety percent said they would buy the same brand again, primarily Lowe, Gregory, and The North Face. The most popular externals were Camp Trails, Jansport, and Kelty.

Pack Care

When you come off the trail, unzip all the pockets and shake out the dirt, sand, and crumbs. If the pack is dirty, sponge it off with mild soap and water. Air-dry out of the sun, for ultraviolet rays can damage the nylon.

Store packs in a cool, dry, airy place to discourage mildew.

Before the next trip, inspect packs for loose seams or damaged hardware at major stress points around the shoulder straps and hip belt. Repair zippers. Stitch any rips with a heavy-duty needle and upholstery thread. Use silicone spray on external-frame squeaks.

3 How to Pack the Right Equipment

Nature uses as little as possible of anything.
—Johannes Kepler

Although I am not ordinarily a list maker, I make an exception before a camping or backpacking trip. In the backcountry, there are no Kmarts, and forgetting the silverware or the matches can be more than a little annoying.

Someone must make sure that everyone has the necessary gear before departure. If you are camping or backpacking with children, you are probably helping them make decisions as well. Let no one venture forth ill-equipped. My friend Jim, who for years has taken his sons and their friends backpacking, has left kids home who didn't have their equipment together. As he says, "If the weather turns bad and someone in the group doesn't have rain gear, or his pack breaks, much more is at stake than just one person's discomfort."

I'm not one to shave ounces by lopping off the end of my toothbrush or trimming the borders of my maps, but I do try to watch weight. Ounces add up to pounds, and pounds add up to discomfort. I regard each item critically, asking, "Can I do without it? Will something lighter do the job? Something I'm already carrying?" The portable shower is an easy call (it stays home), the fishing gear is more iffy, and the Swiss army knife makes every cut.

First, lay out all your gear. Compare what you have to what you need. Use a complete checklist (see below). The main categories are food, equipment, and clothing.

Some people keep their master checklist in their computer. That makes for easier revision each year to keep up with changing tastes and a growing family.

To calculate food purchases, first make a list of the total "people-meals" (number of people times number of meals). Then break it down into breakfast, lunch, and dinner. If you will be away from stores, buy food for an extra couple of days.

Equipment purchases include both new and replacement gear. Does the stove work? Will your sleeping bags make it another year? Do they need cleaning? Are they sufficient for the temperatures you'll be facing? How's the tent? Still big enough? Need seam sealing? What other items do you need? Candles? Fuel? Fishing gear? Frisbee? Book?

Car campers will usually take more equipment than backpackers, but with today's compact cars, you still must draw the line. The questions are somewhat different—Do we take an even dozen plastic trolls? Do the bicycles go or stay? How many whiffle balls are enough?—but some treasures still must stay behind.

Only you can decide what's essential and what's not. My rule is, if we're car camping and have space, I take the borderline item; backpacking, it stays home.

Use the ESSENTIALS mnemonic to help you categorize gear:

Emergencies	Sustenance	Shelter
Extras	Navigation	Toiletries
Incidentals	Attitude	Light

Something to carry it all in.

CHECKLIST AND COMMENTS

Emergencies
first-aid and snakebite kits
waterproof matches in a case
fire starter
whistle
signal mirror

Sustenance

stove	stove repair kit	windscreen
fuel	fuel container	lighter
frying pan	pot holder	silverware
plastic bags	large spoon	spatula
can opener	cups	plates
bowls	cooking grate	garbage bags
water container	ice chest	scrubbing pads
dishwashing soap	paper towels	dish towels
tablecloth	aluminum foil	spices
thermos	entrance rug	cutting board
tools	dry soups	packaged dinners
unleavened bread	grains	nuts
dried fruit	fruit juices	candy bars
dry milk	powdered drinks	food storage containers

nestled pots and pans, with lids
whisk broom and dustpan
water purification system (iodine, filter, or plenty of fuel)

Unless you're willing to eat nothing but cold food, you must carry a stove. Wood is scarce and fires are banned in many places, so you can no longer count on cooking over a campfire. Conveniently, my stove, a Coleman Peak 1, fits inside my cooking pot.

Select wide-mouth plastic water bottles. The wide opening makes it easier to fill, clean, and mix drinks.

An aluminum pie plate works as a lightweight pot lid.

Endurance will be maximized by a diet rich in carbohydrates and low in fat. My personal outdoor diet: granola and powdered milk in the morning; dried fruit, nuts, and unleavened bread for lunch; a freeze-dried entree, dry soup, and sometimes fish for dinner.

Ordinarily, you and your kids would be wise to avoid fatty candy bars, but hiking or backpacking several hours a day isn't an ordinary expenditure of energy. One per day is all right.

For backpackers, freeze-dried foods are a wonderful development, but you can still satisfy most food needs, cheaply and easily, at the local supermarket.

Steve Boga's Twelve Items to Bring Backpacking That Weigh Next to Nothing

1. Pillowcase. A jacket or sweater goes inside and—instant pillow!

2. Waterproof sunblock lip balm (can be used on ears and nose, too)

3. Katadyn Mini Filter—eight ounces, about the size of a hand, filters about a pint of water in a minute and a half

4. Foot bag (Hacky Sack)

5. Plastic garbage bags—protection of packs and equipment

6. Self-sealing plastic bags

7. Magnifying glass

8. Star guide

9. Space blanket

10. Whistle—for warning signals

11. Butane lighter

12. Dental floss

Shelter

    tarp (with rope, stakes, poles)
    tube tent (with rope, stakes)
    tent (with fly, poles, stakes)

ground cloth	garbage bags	mosquito netting
sleeping bags	stuff sacks	sleeping pads

hammock	pillows	pillowcases
underwear	long underwear	T-shirts
bandanna	wick-dry socks	wool socks
sweaters	shorts	long pants
stocking cap	baseball cap	mittens or gloves
rain suit	jacket	pants
gaiters	hiking boots	camp sneakers
sandals	thongs	swimsuit
sunglasses	bunting or pile jacket	
nylon windbreakers with hood		

Freshen sleeping bags and tents by hanging them on a line in the sun. Turn them frequently to prevent sun damage. At home, air them again. Avoid mildew by thoroughly drying tents and bags before stuffing them. Even if it didn't rain during your trip, they probably collected condensation. If you must stuff wet equipment, dry it at the first opportunity.

With care, a quality sleeping bag will last many years. Even if your child has a good bag, remember the sleeping pad. If you go with an open-cell pad like Therm-a-Rest, keep your old closed-cell pad, which has the following uses:

• Under your stove—a tiny piece of pad insulates from cold and snow.
• In your boots—a little piece can be an innersole or a heel pad.
• Around a water bottle—a medium-sized piece offers insulation.
• Under you—a big piece can be a seat pad.

Car campers can take their favorite pillows. Backpackers should bring a pillowcase and fill it at night with clothes. Down vests and jackets make ideal pillow fill.

A coated-nylon tarp is versatile. It can provide extra shelter or ground cover. In torrential rains, rig a tarp as an umbrella over your tent.

A tube tent is fine as long as there are no mosquitoes and it doesn't rain more than a drizzle. Space blankets are handy. Weighing about two ounces, they can be emergency shelters or reflectors and work as ground cloths. Consider putting one in every kid's day pack.

Large plastic garbage bags have myriad uses. Weighing almost nothing, one bag can protect your sleeping bag when you're crossing a stream, your pack in a storm, and your body in an emergency. Cut one open and use it as a dry emergency floor for your tent. Cut out neck and arm holes and fashion an emergency poncho. Use it as a liner inside your pack. Even use it for trash.

Extras

extra food	extra warm clothing
extra water	extra tent stakes

Water weighs about two pounds a quart, so carry no more than you need. If you are hiking next to a river or are near lakes, carry only a little.

Navigation

maps	compass
pencil and a straightedge	

Maps can be stored in a map case or resealable plastic bag. Fold a map to the section you will need that day on the trail. If you're hiking trails and have a topographic map, you probably won't need a compass. On the other hand, a compass is lightweight fun and a great learning tool.

Toiletries

toothbrush	toothpaste	dental floss
hairbrush	comb	sunblock
soap	toilet paper	moisturizing lotion
deodorant	insect repellent	small towel
towelettes	tampons	shaving kit
baking soda	trowel	lip balm, with sunblock

Baking soda can be used as toothpaste, boot deodorizer, foot soak, and even a fire extinguisher. In the mountains, where dry skin can be a problem, moisturizing lotion may make the leap from luxury to necessity. Sunglasses, too, are a wilderness necessity. The risk of skin and eye damage increases dramatically around granite or snow. Look for shades that block all ultraviolet rays. If you get caught without them, you can fashion crude eye shields from food boxes, a paperback book cover, or a toilet paper tube. Cut slits just large enough to see through.

Incidentals

rope	Frisbee	Hacky Sack
Nerf ball	volleyball	harmonica
kazoo	cards	books
constellation guide	coloring books	magnifying glass
binoculars	sketch pad	field guides
thermometer	camera	film
fishing license	fishing rod, reel, gear	

plastic collection containers
crayons, felt-tip pens, pencils
chess, checkers, backgammon sets

Bring plenty of rope. It can be used for clothesline, hanging food, rescue, lashing down, and cattle rustling. Don't forget the fishing license. Revenue-hungry states are increasing the fines, such as a whopping $650 in California. If you play Frisbee in fragile backcountry, take care not to scar meadows. Keep trampling to a minimum. Besides being a quiet toy, a Frisbee can serve as a plate, a platter, a cutting board, and a card table.

Attitude

buoyant, upbeat personality
patience
willingness to adjust to nature and to others trying to enjoy nature

A camping or backpacking trip requires packing lots of gear, but it also means preparing your children to embrace the wilderness. The ability to appreciate nature is as important as any hardware. An upbeat attitude is the ultimate essential.

Light

flashlight, with extra bulb and batteries	candles
lantern, with extra sock	candle lantern

There are dozens of flashlights to choose from, but always bring one with fresh batteries. To prevent your flashlight from accidentally being switched on in your pack and draining the batteries, use a rubber band or hair tie to hold the switch in the off position. Or simply reverse the batteries.

If you don't want to buy a candle lantern, make your own by softening the bottom of a candle and placing it in your cooking kit or an empty tuna can. With children in the tent, however, open flames are discouraged.

Something to Carry It All In

fanny pack	child carrier	day pack
internal- or external-frame backpack		waterproof pack cover
pack repair items (pins, rings)		

Don't save weight by leaving behind your day pack. Whenever you want to drop your backpack and venture from camp, a day pack is invaluable for carrying small items. Also, carrying repair items is a little like buying flight insurance. You hope you don't need them and most of the time you don't, but they provide peace of mind.

PACKING THE PACK

Now that you know what you're taking, where do you put it all? If you are car camping, probably in bags and boxes. If you are backpacking, develop a system for filling your pack and teach your kids to do likewise. Do it about the same way every time in a way that makes sense to you. You will grasp the need for systematic packing the first time you are caught in a storm and must madly rip through your pack in search of rain gear or a pesky tent stake.

Reserve space in the outside pockets of your pack for items needed most often on the trail: snacks, water, sunscreen, insect repellent, and maps. Place the heaviest items, like the stove and tent, up high and close to your back, putting the weight over your hips and feet. If you carry weight too low or too far back, you will tend to lean forward to compensate, stressing your lower back.

Pack medium-weight gear farther down in the pack to lower your center of gravity and add stability. Your sleeping bag is a good item for

The complete backpack: everything in its place and a place for everything.

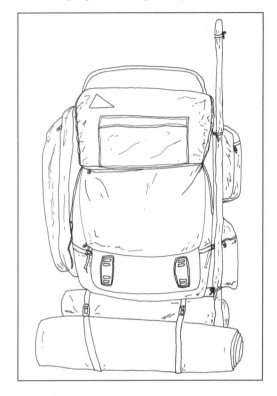

There's nothing like the feel of a well-packed pack.

(PHOTO BY JIM HAMILTON)

the bottom of your pack. Lash long items, like fishing rods and tent poles, to the outside of the pack. Pad sharp objects to keep them from poking you, especially if you have an internal-frame pack.

KNOWLEDGE

It's always good to take some of this along. Before you set off, give the kids who are old enough a wilderness test. Tell them you want to see if they are ready for the real thing. Make it fun.

Children will learn more if you let them do a little research, rather than just telling them the answers. Make it an open-book test and urge them to seek creative answers. You may have to adapt some of the questions to suit the younger set, but the following is a sample test with some interesting teaching points. Give your charges a set amount of time, say a week or two, to find the answers. Be prepared to guide them through the research. If they respond well to a test like this, create another one, but don't push too hard.

The answers are below and scattered throughout the book. If you run through these questions, make up your own, emphasizing the topics you believe are important. This will force you to do your research, too.

Sample Wilderness Test

1. True or false: Fast-moving water is always safe to drink.
2. True or false: Mosquitoes are attracted to dark colors.
3. Which clouds usually indicate rain?
    A. Cirrocumulus
    B. Altocumulus
    C. Cirrus
    D. Cumulonimbus
4. What's the major cause of death in national parks?
    A. Drowning
    B. Car accidents
    C. Bear attacks
    D. Falls
5. Choose the slowest runner:
    A. Grizzly bear
    B. Coyote

    C. Sprinter Carl Lewis

    D. Pronghorn antelope

6. Which piece of garbage takes the longest to decay?

    A. Candy wrapper

    B. Newspaper

    C. Tin can

    D. Glass bottle

7. What is DEET?

    A. Hiking organization

    B. Antihiking organization

    C. Poison found in certain mushrooms

    D. Chemical in insect repellent

8. What is *Giardia lamblia*?

    A. Waterborne parasite that makes you sick

    B. The fastest animal on earth

    C. Nerve tissue that is the first to be damaged by frostbite

    D. Italian soccer player

9. You're packing your pack. Which item weighs the most?

    A. Gallon of water

    B. Five-pound tent

    C. Large can of beans

    D. Down sleeping bag

10. Which animal kills the most people each year?

    A. Snake

    B. Deer

    C. Bear

    D. Dog

Answers

1. False. With an estimated sixteen million Americans infected at any time with the intestinal parasite *Giardia lamblia*, you can bet a lot of people answer yes to this question. We now know that drinking from turbulent water is actually riskier than partaking from pools, where the giardia bug tends to settle to the bottom.

    2. True. Mosquitoes also are attracted to heat, moisture, carbon dioxide, and whining. At least that's what I tell children.

3. D. Cumulonimbus clouds, the low-flying, dark, billowy ones, indicate rain is on the way. Find a weather book or the Boy Scout Handbook and study cloud formations.

4. A. According to 1991 figures reported in *Backpacker* magazine, sixty people drowned in national parks, thirty-four were killed in car accidents, twenty-five died in falls, and no one was killed by a bear.

5. Carl Lewis is pretty fast, up to twenty-seven miles per hour. But a grizzly has been clocked at thirty-two mph, coyotes at forty-three mph, and pronghorns at sixty mph.

6. D. *Backpacker* says the bottle will take up to 500,000 years to break down, the can 100 to 125 years, the candy wrapper two to three years, and the newspaper one to two years. That's why you carry out all trash.

7. D. DEET is the active ingredient in most mosquito repellents. It is certainly effective, but it's best to stay with concentrates of less than thirty percent.

8. A. *Giardia lamblia* is a waterborne intestinal protozoan. Virtually unknown before 1979, giardia now exists in so many of the world's waterways that you get half credit if you answered B—the world's fastest animal.

9. A. A gallon of water weighs 8.3 pounds, the tent five pounds, the sleeping bag three to six pounds, the can of beans two pounds. Carry no more water than you need to reach the next source.

10. B. Deer kill about 130 people per year, mostly by darting in front of cars. Bees are a distant second with about forty deaths; next come dogs with fourteen; bears are fifteenth on the list, with about one homicide every other year, lagging behind such acknowledged man killers as jellyfish and goats.

Getting out the door

Preliminaries completed, pack packed, test taken, you are now ready to set out on your excellent adventure. Leave someone a detailed description of where you plan to go and when you plan to get there. Include alternate routes you are considering. Make sure you leave this with people who actually care whether you return.

4 *How to Get There from Anywhere*

In America there are two classes of travel—
first class and with children.
—Robert Benchley

Whoever said "getting there is half the fun" never drove two hundred miles cooped up with kids. Backseat brouhahas mixed with tired, tense adults is a volatile combination.

Here are some tips for harmonious car travel. Most will have to do with the lighter side—toys, games, and songs—but harmony demands rules, too. The first one for me is No Screaming. Noise during a long automobile trip is cumulative; it builds up in your brain and, if unchecked, will cause your skull to explode.

To quell children, give them a roll of coins or Life Savers (for the very young, of course, candy is more valuable than money), and explain that they are not allowed to eat or use the roll until the car trip is over. Tell them that you will take back a coin or candy every time you have to warn them to be quiet. In this way, they determine the size of their reward.

The most important thing parents can bring on a trip is a childlike attitude. Excitement is contagious; so is melancholy and anger. Long-distance car travel is hard on everybody (sitting is bad for bodies), but it's important that you try to make the best of it. One person with a bad attitude can suck the joy right out of the car, poisoning the whole trip and making your children reluctant to return for more. On the other hand, if you create a joyful, child-centered atmosphere, your family might actually enjoy the travel time.

Don't skimp on breaks. Children need rest stops. Plan ahead. Many western interstates have rest stops complete with toilets, drinking water, grassy fields, and sometimes playgrounds. Just a few minutes of swings, slides, and tag can be a tonic for the whole family. In the East, rest stops include huge chain restaurants, gas stations, and sometimes grassy fields or playgrounds.

Explore points of interest off the main road. It's a good excuse for a break, gets you off the beaten path, and may be fun and educational.

Don't expect children to endure hours of confinement in a car and then to sit still another hour in a restaurant. If the weather is fine, eat outside. Pack meals at home or stop at a market or delicatessen and buy picnic fixings—it will be cheaper and healthier. Visit a fast-food place, preferably one with a playground. It may not be healthier, but at least you can be outside. Extend the break if it feels like it's the right thing to do. Play hide-and-seek or mother-may-I. Read a story. Watch your kids to determine when they are ready to hit the road.

Also, sitting all day in a car can constipate, so push fruits, vegetables, and grains. Make water the drink of choice—it's sugar-free and doesn't stain—though a small cooler inside the car is handy for soda and juice as well. Straws reduce spilling.

For breakfast on the road, cereal is ideal. It's cheap, convenient, and can be healthful. You can rinse your plastic bowls in a motel or rest-stop sink. Sandwiches and fruit work well for lunch. It's OK to eat between meals; just make the snacks healthful. Unless you pay attention, snacking can degenerate into a festival of junk foods. The dietary habits you instill in your children today will influence them their whole life.

If your car trip is long, consider breaking it up with a stay in a motel. Even a modest little place with a kidney-shaped pool, moderately clean sheets, and sixty-channel cable can be a welcome reward for being good travelers and not pulling daddy's hair when he's driving.

Speaking of driving, it is hard on the body. Behind the wheel, tension builds in the legs, neck, and lower back. Maintain good posture with a lumbar pillow or a rolled towel placed between the seat and your lower back. Take a break every hour, even if it's just a quick one for stretching. With two or more drivers, alternate duties. That way, those who aren't driving—and who have greater responsibility for entertaining the children—also get a break.

TOYS

Only you and your children can decide which toys make the trip. Keep in mind that someone who suffers from motion sickness may have trouble reading, writing, or playing cards.

With your supervision, children can pack their own car bag. It can be a paper bag, but it will feel more personal if it is a day pack.

Besides favorite dolls, blankies, or teddies, consider these popular items:

Magic slate. These waxy, erasable tablets are great for playing hangman and other word games.

Magnetic chess or checkers

Cards

Pipe cleaners. Bend them into creative shapes and play pretend.

Pillows and blankets.

Read-along cassette tapes and a player. Tapes can do a lot for you. Play them in a Walkman for silent, solitary fun; play them on the car stereo for family enjoyment, perhaps even a group sing. Books on tape can be mellow listening for the whole family.

Surprises. Acquire new toys and bring them out one by one, as needed.

GAMES

When toys lose their allure, try car games. However, you may have to delay playing games if conditions demand the driver's full concentration.

Cities and Towns

Any number can play this game. One player starts by naming any North American (or world) city. The next player names another city that begins with the last letter of the first city. The third player names a city beginning with the last letter of the second city. And so on.

For example, Reno could be answered with Oakland, followed by

Denver, followed by Raleigh. You lose if you repeat a city or can't think of an answer.

Name Making

When you go through a town or see one listed on a road sign, write down the name. See how many words each player can form from the letters in the name before coming to the next town.

Beetle

The idea is to be the first to see Volkswagens. A bus is worth three points, a Beetle is two points, any other model is one point. Or devise your own scoring system. Award points only when a VW is spotted through the windshield, so as not to penalize the driver.

License Plates

This game can continue from departure to return. Although it can be played with just pencil and paper, photocopying a list of states and Canadian provinces allows players to simply check off the plates as they see them. You can identify license plates on the highway, at rest stops, in camp-grounds, and in parking lots.

Personalized License Plates

Try to decode the personalized license plates you see on the road, like 2TH DR for "tooth doctor." Or encourage your children to invent their own. Ask, "If you were going to have a personalized license plate, what would it be?"

Travel I Spy

One player selects something—an oak tree, red barn, or painted mailbox—that everyone is supposed to look for. The first one to see the object calls, "I spy," and gets to pick the next object.

I Spy

One player silently picks something inside or outside the car that is visible for several minutes, then gives a color or shape clue. If everyone guesses incorrectly, he gives another clue, and so on until the item is guessed.

Distance Estimating

The driver picks a landmark ahead—a road sign, water tower, grain elevator, store, windmill, or road kill—and each player silently jots down a guess of the mileage to it. When everyone has written down their estimates, reveal what they are; this increases the drama. Secret ballots prevent a later player from guessing slightly above or slightly below an earlier one, thereby gaining an advantage.

The odometer reading should be noted as soon as the object is chosen, then again when the car reaches the object. A separate math prize can be awarded to players who correctly calculate the difference between the two readings.

Out of Reach

Ask your children to put one hand where the other cannot possibly touch it. Answer: When either hand is placed on an elbow, the other cannot possibly touch it.

Hangman

I got through more than one deadly college class by playing a lot of hangman. I justified it by saying that it improved my vocabulary and spelling.

It is best for two people, and you need only pencil and paper. Player A thinks of a word, then draws a gallows, below which he puts the number of spaces that correspond to the number of letters in his word. As player B guesses a letter that might be in A's word, A responds in one of two ways: (1) if the guess is correct, he writes the letter(s) on the appropriate line(s); (2) if the guess is incorrect, he writes the letter at the bottom of the page (a reminder of what letters have been asked) and draws a body part, starting with a head, of the little man he's trying to hang. Each wrong guess is penalized by adding another body part—torso, arms, legs—until either the word is completed (B wins) or the man is hanged (A wins).

Tip for B: Start guessing vowels. Tip for A: Before the game begins, establish how many missed guesses will be allowed before the man hangs.

Categories

One person picks a category, such as Muppets or famous bald people, and starts by naming an example. With bright kids and a broad category, you might get a mile up the trail before they realize how hard they've been working. Even choosing the category can be creative. Encourage your kids to take their time and put some thought into their answers.

Who Am I? (Twenty Questions)

The player who is "it" thinks of a character, alive or dead, real or fictional. Other players ask, say, twenty yes-or-no questions, trying to determine the identity of the character. For kids who have a better command of the language, the game can be structured to reward only "yes" answers; ten "no's" and they lose. Or you can abandon scoring and play until the character is identified. In either case, the game rewards logic and the ability to ask good questions. Discourage wild guesses, such as "Are you Gandhi?" on the third question.

Where Am I?

This is structured like Who Am I? One player begins by asking, "Where am I?" Other players try to find out by asking yes-or-no questions. The answer may be a very small place, such as atop the dashboard or in a trouser cuff, so players are encouraged to use their imaginations.

Ghost

This word game works best for two people, though more can play in a pinch. Alternate the start, with the first person stating a letter and the second person following with another letter, continuing in turn with each player having a particular word in mind. You lose if you inadvertently complete a word of three letters or more or if you are challenged and cannot state a legitimate word that you are spelling. Each loss earns a dreaded letter: G-H-O-S-T. First one to "T" loses.

I Went to the Store

This game may seem like nothing more than mind candy, but it's actually a good memory exercise.

Any number can play. The first player announces "I went to the store and bought _____," filling in the blank with just about any "A" word imaginable, say, "arachnid food." The second player repeats the "A" word, adding a "B" word of his own creation, as in, "I went to the store and bought arachnid food and bagels." Progress through the alphabet. A player who cannot repeat the litany of purchases is out and the others continue until only one player remains. Hearing the items repeated will facilitate recall, allowing the game to go on for a surprisingly long time.

Creative Problem Solving

Kids love solving problems. The following conundrums will enlighten as well as entertain. These problems can be posed and solved on the trail, but they will probably play better in camp, where it's easier to concentrate. If only two or three people are working on a problem, it will take a while to solve. Counsel patience.

State each situation, being careful not to say too much. Ask them to figure out "what's really going on." Allow yes-or-no questions only. Beyond that, it's up to you—allow unlimited questions or a set number. Older kids can be encouraged to word their questions so they strive for "yes" answers. Ten "no's" and they lose.

Problem 1. A man walks into a bar and asks for a drink of water. The bartender looks at him, reaches under the bar, pulls out a gun, and points it at him. The man thanks him and walks out of the bar.

What happened? The man had the hiccups. The bartender, seeing this, decided to scare the hiccups out of him. When it worked, the man thanked the bartender and left.

Problem 2. A man is lying face down beside a puddle of water in an otherwise empty room.

What happened? He stabbed himself with an icicle.

Problem 3. A man is trying to go home; another man, wearing a mask, is waiting there for him.

What is happening? The man is a baseball player trying to score; the other man is the catcher.

Magician

You can dazzle everyone with this one. Give the following instructions: "Silently pick a number between (and including) one and ten. Multiply that number by nine. If the answer is in two digits, add them; if it's in one digit, leave it as it is. Subtract five from the result. Locate the letter of the alphabet that corresponds to the number (A=1, B=2, C=3, D=4, etc.)

"Now think of a European country that begins with that letter. Next think of an animal that begins with the last letter of that country. Finally, think of a color that begins with the last letter of that animal."

Just as they are finishing their answer, hand them a piece of paper upon which you have written, "Orange kangaroo in Denmark."

After the "ooohs" and "aaahs" die down, explain how you did it—if you want. It worked because the number manipulation leads everyone to "D" (digits of the multiples of nine always add up to nine, and nine minus five is four, or "D") and Denmark is the only European country that begins with D. Kangaroo is the people's choice for a "K" animal, although some wise guys might tax your patience with krill or kudu. Once your patsy has chosen kangaroo, they're sure to pick orange.

Headwork

These are thought-provoking questions that don't really have one right answer. Here are some examples, but you can probably think of others.

- What noise might a dog make if it were in trouble?
- Why are the holes in a salt shaker bigger than the holes in a pepper shaker?
- If beings from another planet landed on Earth and wanted to see the most beautiful thing on our planet, what would you show them?
- Why are some beaches rockier than others?
- If you could eat only one food for the rest of your life, what would it be? Do you think you'd get tired of it?
- Name some things that can't be bought that are just as valuable as things that can.
- Why aren't human teeth as sharp as sharks' teeth?
- When is it helpful for people to yell at each other? When is it hurtful?
- Try to make up a story that begins, "I am the smallest person in the world."

Name That Tune

One player sings or hums a song and the others try to guess its name or the name of the movie or television show in which it originated.

5 How to Move along the Trail

> *Two roads diverged in a wood,*
> *and I—*
> *I took the one less travelled by*
> *And that has made all the difference.*
> *—Robert Frost*

PREPARATION

Preparation for a serious hike should begin months before you reach trailhead. Physical conditioning should include plenty of brisk walking and a diet rich in carbohydrates.

Include as many people from the group as possible at the planning session. Everyone appreciates the chance to offer an opinion, even if no one pays attention to it. Consider the condition of everyone in the group, particularly the weakest hiker. By looking at topographic maps, get a fix on total miles, hiking days, and difficulty of terrain. Then ask the tough questions. "Can she do it? Can he do it? Can you do it?" With younger children, less is usually better.

Before leaving home, test your equipment for comfort and condition. Lace on your hiking boots, load up and strap on your pack, and walk on uneven terrain. Adjust the pack straps and boot laces; find a comfortable fit and eliminate "hot spots" before you hit the trail. Adults and older children should carry no more than one quarter of body weight, younger children less than that, and the youngest only a token amount, say a day pack with a favorite toy inside. You want them to feel part of the action, but if you saddle your children with too much weight, you can turn the hike into a death march.

A walking stick is never a greater ally than when crossing white water.

At the trailhead, look for hiking sticks for everyone. You can buy fancy varnished staffs at outdoor stores, but why not use what nature provides? Besides amusement and image enhancement, a custom-fitted staff can help children balance on rocky terrain or while crossing streams, be a snake prober when stepping over rocks and logs, and be used to push aside brush encroaching on the trail. Children can even drive their stick into the ground and rest their pack against it.

If you are breaking in a hiker, it helps to know your route and destination. Then your voice will carry the proper authority when you inevitably say, "Not much farther to go." Encourage everyone to complain silently—maybe the impossible dream. One person's open negativity can sap the strength of the whole group.

Most kids are unprepared for "working through pain," but perhaps you can persuade them to use a little self-discipline. They should be able to grasp that the longer you fool around on the trail, the later you'll arrive in camp. I get good results with my daughter, Madeleine, by reminding her that in walking, everyone does her part and everyone carries her own weight. Since she is five and passionately establishing her independence, she accepts such thinking.

There are two schools of thought about limbering up before a hike. Tradition suggests you stretch your hamstrings, calves, feet, shoulders, and back; revisionists hold that just hiking slowly eliminates the need for elaborate warmup. Whether by philosophy or sheer laziness, I adhere to the second school. Children, being both undisciplined stretchers and youthfully limber, can usually begin walking with impunity.

You may have to teach your children how to walk, which they may find amusing or annoying. If this is their first time hiking on uneven ground with weight on their back, walking is a new sport with new problems. Tell your kids that walking uses about a hundred muscles; maybe that will boost their respect for the sport.

Advise children to seek a natural stride, swinging their legs from the hips rather than kicking out with the knees. By pivoting at the waist and leaning forward slightly, the stride will automatically lengthen. If the terrain is level, their feet should strike the ground heel first and roll forward, with a final push-off being delivered by the last bone of the big toe.

They should strive to keep their feet beneath their torso and planted firmly, stepping around rather than on obstacles that might teeter. Arms should dangle, swinging freely but not in an exaggerated way. Keep the head up and the shoulders relaxed, dropped back rather than hunched up. Avoid shuffling, which raises dust and wastes energy. Avoid slumping; it's easier to carry a load when walking fairly erect. If anyone walks bent over like Groucho Marx, find him a longer walking stick, which will help keep him erect.

Establish hiking rules early. Young children should stay in sight, older ones within earshot. As their voices grow stronger, they can go farther ahead. When I grew to be a better hiker than my parents, I used to soar ahead to the next trail junction, then hike back to them, soar ahead, and hike back. I was, for a time, out of earshot, but I never made a route decision without consulting my parents.

If you have agreed to break into smaller groups, arrange check-in points (often trail junctions) where everyone meets at certain intervals. Each group should have its own map.

Help members of your group see the big picture—the entire hike. It hinders your children to sprint the first half-mile in record time if the effort so exhausts them that they can't finish a three-mile trek. Better to expend energy evenly.

Give hiking, especially backpacking, the respect it deserves. It is an athletic event, not a stroll, and it can cause new injuries and aggravate old ones. Hiking too fast can cause muscle and tendon pulls, blisters, and burnout. Although children often seem impervious to muscle and tendon pulls, they are highly vulnerable to blisters and burnout.

"Ah, summer, what power you have to make us suffer and like it."   *—Russell Baker*

"Going to the woods and the wild place has little to do with recreation and much to do with creation."   *—Wendell Berry*

"The clearest way into the Universe is through a forest wilderness."   *—John Muir*

UPHILL

Teach your children to find and hold a steady pace on uphills. It will be slower than the pace they maintained on level ground, but it will require greater effort. Gunning it on hills costs a lot of energy. You should know—though perhaps not tell your children—that ascending a fourteen-degree slope (it rises fourteen feet in elevation for every one hundred feet in length) requires nearly four times the effort of walking on level ground. Add a backpack and the effort rises even more.

Don't lift the feet higher than necessary. Shorten the stride and lean forward slightly to keep the pack weight over the feet. Breathe deeply and rhythmically. On exceptionally difficult slopes, it is better to take six-inch steps and keep moving, no matter how slowly, than to take the frequent rest stops a faster pace would require. Starting and stopping consume extra energy. Perhaps it's time to tell the story of the tortoise and the hare.

On steep grades, you may have to walk on your toes. Toe stepping adds power and balance but soon fatigues calf muscles. Try alternating heel and toe steps to spread the load over different muscles.

When the climb is very steep or the load very heavy, try the "rest step" or "limp step" to flush away fatigue from the joints. There are two ways for the body to rest without appearing to stop. One, allow the lead leg to go limp just after that foot is placed for a new step and just before the weight is shifted to it. Two, relax the trailing leg just after you transfer weight to the lead leg. Most people prefer to let the trail leg go limp, and that is the easiest method to learn.

DOWNHILL

At first, downhill would seem easy, and though descending is easier on the lungs than climbing, it actually is twice as hard on hip, knee, and ankle joints. Putting on the brakes taxes the quadriceps, the big muscles in the front of the thigh. Downhill walking forces the foot to travel farther through the air with each step, so it's easier to slip and sprain an ankle on tippy rocks. Pounding downhill on your heels can jar your spine and make your whole body sore. On the other hand, if you put your weight forward, you may develop blisters on your toes. Cushion the shock of each downward step by rolling your hip forward and planting your foot with the knee slightly bent. As you transfer weight, allow the knee to flex so that it acts as a shock absorber.

CROSS COUNTRY

When you leave the security of a trail, you are traveling "cross country." Instead of relying on an established course, you must find your own way, often confronting swamps, deadfalls, and rocky ridges. Beware of backpacking cross country with children. With weight on your back, little inconveniences like scrambling over deadfalls or slipping between rock and river become hazards. Going cross country requires greater balance, strength, competence, and caution than traveling trails. Stick to the trails until you and your children are ready for more.

When I was thirteen, my father and I hiked to Emerick Lake in the High Sierra. The trail brought us to the side of the lake opposite the best campsites. For some reason, we walked around the north side of the lake, now known in my family as the "wrong side." The curvature of the shore prevented us from knowing what lay ahead. Large rocks became boulders; the terrain turned steep. We should have dropped our packs and explored our options, but we stubbornly pressed on. Scrambling up and sliding down those boulders took an hour; as we later found out, the other route would have taken us ten minutes.

FORDING STREAMS

Hiking in the spring may force you to cross water without a bridge. Look for rocks or fallen logs that might form a natural bridge or for narrows

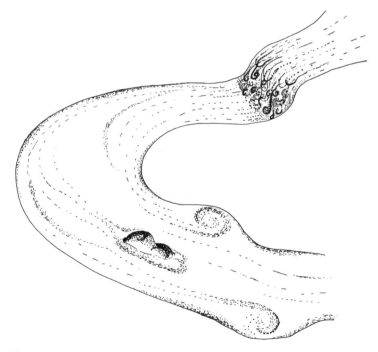

Crossing rivers deserves extra attention. Any idea where the best place to cross is?

you can bridge with a standing broad jump. Failing that, you may have to get wet.

Before you do, assess the situation. How deep is the water? How about the footing? Do you leave your boots on or go barefoot? If you leave them on, you protect your feet and get your boots wet. Barefoot? Maybe in calm water over a sandy bottom. Better to have the kids wear their extra tennis shoes and change into dry socks on the other side. Make sure their boots are secured in or on their packs, so they won't get lost if they fall in.

When wearing a pack on a dangerous crossing, loosen the shoulder straps and unbuckle the belly strap so that you can jettison the load and keep from drowning. Use your walking stick as a third leg for balance and for probing loose, slippery rocks.

If the water is swift and dangerous, send the strongest swimmer across first, roped but carrying no pack. Then tie off both ends of the rope. The taut line between trees on both sides will provide security and peace of mind. Choose a wide, shallow ford over a narrow, swift one. Start on the upstream side and angle downstream to minimize your battle against the current. Avoid crossing above a falls or other hazard.

WET WEATHER

When the weather turns foul, keep your often used items handy. Put your map, toilet paper, snacks, and water in a fanny pack or a side pocket of your pack for easy access. Store things that rain might harm, like a camera, in plastic bags.

Line your sleeping bag stuff sack with a garbage bag to make it more waterproof, especially if you carry your bag outside your pack. Carry a watch on overcast days when you can't gauge the time by the sun. Darkness can descend quickly, especially in the mountains.

Carry blister first aid, even if your boots are broken in. Prolonged rain softens even the most calloused skin, making it more vulnerable to blisters. If it's raining a lot, wring out your socks periodically during the day. Don't forget to towel-dry your feet and powder them. One way to prevent blisters is with duct tape. Carry it by wrapping several turns around the handle of your flashlight. When you apply it to your feet, smooth out all the wrinkles.

If you wear glasses, a baseball hat will shield them from the rain.

Don't reduce your eating and drinking just because it's cold and rainy. Chilly, wet weather demands that you take in even more fuel and fluids to ward off hypothermia. Hike in shorts, even in wet weather. Bare skin is preferable to clingy wet fabric.

PACE

At the trailhead, explain to your children that you have a destination. En route, you're going to explore, play games, and have fun, but you also have a goal—say, Lake Wobegone by dark—and that means you have to keep moving. Also, remind the fast starters to maintain a steady pace to the finish.

Most backpackers travel one-and-a-half to two-and-a-half miles per hour, but there are plenty of exceptions. Two fit twenty-year-olds hiking fairly level ground on good terrain may hit four miles an hour in spurts; a family with toddlers may not make four miles in a day.

Be prepared to amend (or abandon) your timetable. Urge kids along,

(Photo by Ann Brice)

Take frequent breaks to consult your field guides.

but don't insist they reach a destination by a certain time. Be flexible, especially with neophytes who you hope will return to the wilderness. Be prepared to accept defeat—bad weather, injury, illness, mosquitoes, or someone wimping out can alter your plans. Plan a bail-out route, just in case.

When I was fifteen, my parents took me to Yosemite to backpack in the high country. Just as we entered the park, our car's transmission went out. We were forced to abandon our backpacking plans and coast into Yosemite Valley for repairs. It's easier being flexible when the alternative is camping in Yosemite Valley, but you get the idea.

Hiking compatibility may be difficult because there are big differences in capabilities among children. It's a challenge to choreograph the movements of several hikers with different ideal paces. To get everybody from A to B, consider pacing, rest stops, maintaining energy, and foot care. If you plan to stay together, the slowest walker should begin in front, setting the pace. Later, you may want to rotate the lead, as most children are front-runners who get an energy boost when they lead. The responsibility makes them more open to learning about blazes, ducks, and other trail signs.

Have an adult bring up the rear to assure that no one wanders off the trail or calls a sit-down strike. From the caboose, you can help those who fall behind by readjusting their packs, pulling up their socks, and maybe showing them better ways to go over or around obstacles.

One way to slow down older, faster hikers is to keep adding gear to their packs.

If the troops begin losing their will to walk, it may be time for a serious break. Drop packs, relax, and explore. Go swim-

ming, fishing, or bug hunting. Side trips refresh some hikers,
making the final haul easier.

TRAIL ETHICS

Adults must teach children to stay on the trail. Erosion is a big problem
in the wilderness, and hikers contribute to it enough just by tromping on
trails in waffle-soled boots.

> *"The most important thing about Spaceship Earth: an
> instruction booklet didn't come with it."*
> —*Buckminster Fuller*

Impress upon children the need to avoid creating new trails next to
old ones. Not only should hikers stay on the path, but they should stay
near the middle to keep from caving in the sides. Instead of skirting that
mud, walk through it and clean your boots later. Good-fitting gaiters will
keep mud out of socks.

The most common trail abuse is cutting switchbacks, the S-curves that
enable hikers to ascend or descend a more gradual grade. Shortening the
route kills vegetation and forms a new path. With no vegetation, the topsoil soon washes away, forming a gully, a perfect sluice for storm water.
Nature has little chance to reclaim the land.

When you see an unauthorized shortcut, throw brush or
logs across it, blocking access to other hikers.

Pick up any trash left near the trail and carry it in an empty
bread bag.

When hiking in a group, allow a comfortable distance between you
and the hiker in front of you. Tailgating on the trail is just as annoying as
it is on the road and just as pointless. If you overtake hikers who don't
move over, ask politely if you may pass.

REST STOPS

Rest stops are important, particularly for young children, but prolonged stops can suck the momentum out of a hike. Breaks longer than five minutes are often counterproductive. Even on sunny days, long rest stops cause the body to cool, muscles to stiffen, and momentum to shred. Even a slight breeze can knife through sweat-damp clothing and start a child shivering. Carry a light windbreaker for such moments.

Make the most of stops. Take a breather, of course, but also do your chores. Peruse the map, find food or water in your pack, urinate, put on shorts, take off jackets, check feet, pull up socks, and adjust boots. I don't stop for a full-blown lunch. I prefer to eat a good breakfast—usually high-calorie granola—hit the trail soon after sunrise, fill everyone's pockets with nuts and dried fruit, keep a slower pace (if necessary), and hold rest stops to five minutes every half-hour or so.

One of the hardest lessons for children to learn is to maintain a slow, steady pace, minimizing the need for frequent stops. Kids are sprinters. Without killing their enthusiasm, you need to moderate their pace and stretch out their performance. On the other hand, you can't be too authoritarian with children. You will have to adjust stops and pace to your weakest hiker. If the hike is being interrupted by more stops than you would like, compromise. Persuade members of your group to rest with their packs on, lightening their load by leaning against a rock or a tree. This eliminates rehoisting the pack and getting used to the weight all over again.

When chatting with people you meet on the trail, move off-trail to avoid breaking down the edges and widening the path.

Rest stops also offer opportunities to savor the country. Try to stop beside a stream or lake, at the top of a slope, in the first shade after a shadeless stretch, where a tree or rock offers a seat, or anywhere the view is spectacular. If it is an extended stop, make it fun for your children. Go exploring; try to find something new; identify a snow plant, a bird's nest, or those animals wriggling in the water.

Remember to stop and smell the Spanish lavender.

(Photo by Ann Brice)

It's always nice to take a rest when you feel you've earned it. Promise your group a rest stop after, say, a hundred more steps. For variety and distraction, count backward. After a rest stop, you will once again have to reign in the fast starters, lest they burn out. My daughter has gone from sitting to sprinting to walking to trudging to stopping, all in less than a minute.

MOTIVATION

Motivating children to hike may demand ingenuity, patience, and more tricks than a circus sideshow. Which tricks you employ depends on the ages and dispositions of your children, but everything being equal, you'll be better off if you introduce them to nature early in life. When they are old enough to sit up, start carrying them on your back in a kid pack. Your baby will enjoy the stimulation of seeing new places, feeling the wind, and hearing the ambient sounds; you'll benefit from the exercise.

I recently hiked to the top of Yosemite's Half Dome with two dads, each of whom carried his daughter (ages two and three) on his back. It was a long eighteen-mile, eleven-hour hike with huge altitude gains and losses, but the kids reacted as though it were a stroll in the park. Neither ever complained. The reason: They live in Yosemite and have been on trails since they were infants.

There are kid carriers rated up to sixty pounds, but you probably won't want to schlep your second-grader around on your back. Your children will likely be pedestrians by age three or four. At that point, you can move on to short walks and backyard overnighters. Don't advance to car camping until you're sure your children are ready.

After car camping, if interest is high, try a short backpacking trip, say two days and one night. A short trip reduces the weight you have to carry and keeps you close to the trailhead in case problems arise. One hiking couple refers to ages two to five as "the lost years." Indeed, motivating my five-year-old to walk two miles is like pulling teeth with tweezers. With her sprinter's mentality and short attention span, nothing works every time or for very long. We count steps; play an alphabet game; sing; look for wildlife; identify leaves, rocks, wildflowers, and birds; offer praise for her progress; reward her with food—and find that we have covered about four hundred yards.

Some families find it effective just to talk. Increasing the chatter can distract kids from what their feet are doing and result in impressive physical feats.

Be a cheerleader, if necessary: "We're more than halfway." "Water

If you value your neck muscles, don't even think about carrying your child on your shoulders.

(PHOTO BY WILLIAM J. BOGA)

just ahead." "See that bird?" "You're doing great, a real mountain pace." Try to include a lake or river in your destination. Most children will be motivated to finish a hike if they know they can swim or throw rocks in the water at trail's end.

Daydreaming has a bad rap, but it can move kids along. When you round a bend and see your kids crumble at the sight of a steep, switchbacking trail leading to some distant pass that might as well be on Mars, tell them to start daydreaming. Tell them to think of something pleasant and absorbing and to embellish it until it takes over their thoughts. If all goes well, the hike will proceed on a kind of automatic pilot.

Try teaching your kids visualization, the first cousin of daydream-

Beware of tailgaters when you're hiking.

(Photo by William J. Boga)

ing. It's part imagination (a strong suit for children) and part concentration (not always a strong suit). This technique can be powerful. I have interviewed dozens of world-class adventure athletes—climbers, mountaineers, and hang-glider pilots—and most cite visualization as a key to their success.

Here are some visualization possibilities for hikers: Imagine you're a gazelle, cheetah, or some other fleet animal; you're tough, strong, graceful, and can go forever. Imagine crowds of people lining the course, cheering you on to greatness; we tend to do better when others are watching. Moving uphill, picture yourself suspended from helium balloons. Moving downhill, picture yourself as a liquid, flowing over rocks or roots. Moving on level ground, picture a giant's gentle hand at your back. Moving into the wind, imagine you are a bullet or knife slicing through the heavy air. Above all, see yourself relaxing.

When children tire of looking for birds' nests, squirrel burrows, and trees that resemble Aunt Ellen, introduce trail games (see below). When you run out of trail games, try bribery. Offer treats for so many steps, say a lemon drop or an M&M when they make it to the rock that looks like

A healthy imagination can lighten your step— and your spirits.

Uncle Ferg and another when they get to the next trail junction. If you're like most parents who monitor their children's candy consumption, you might try using nuts or dried fruit as rewards. But don't be surprised if they lack candy's motivational power.

Just about anything tastes good in the wilderness.

(PHOTO BY KEN YAGER)

If all else fails, accept the stops and the slower pace. Get into your kids' adventure, their microworld; let them drop their packs and explore something they've spotted off the trail. Pull out the binoculars or magnifying glass and check out that colorful bird or bug. Remember that your overriding goal is more ambitious than merely reaching Lake Muckamucka by lunchtime; it is to make the experience so much fun that your children will want to do it again.

ENTERTAINMENT

It's a rare child hiker who can provide her or his own entertainment on the trail. Young children have both a short attention span and a low boredom threshold. Those traits, combined with the common perception that hiking is drudgery, can result in a veritable whinefest if the entertainment slackens. Try to capitalize on children's imagination. Although your idea of fun may not be shuffling along the trail making choo-choo sounds, that may be just the ticket to keep your kids moving.

When Brett, son of my friend Tim, shows signs of trail meltdown, Tim plays a game of Treasure Map with him. With exaggerated solemnity, he pulls from his pocket a folded Kleenex, peers at it, and announces to his five-year-old, "Hey, I just found this treasure map. It says if you follow the directions, you'll find a great treasure. First, touch five tree trunks." Off goes Brett, miraculously rejuvenated. "Next, walk around a trail sign two times." Now Brett is skipping. "Then walk one hundred steps with your left hand on top of your head."

Games

Aesthetic appreciation seems to develop slowly in kids. Instead, many become obsessed with their physical condition. Be prepared to hear, *"My feet hurt." "This pack is too heavy." "I'm thirsty." "My mosquito bites itch." "Are we almost there?"*

To yank them out of themselves, consider playing some of the games in chapters 1, 4, and 6 while hiking. If matters become truly desperate, you can have children count their footsteps to the next boulder or trail sign. This works well if your kids are still at that delightful stage when counting is actually fun.

Trail Songs

Trail songs should be upbeat, energizing, and exploratory (almost anything with a banjo will do). Possibilities include "She'll Be Comin' 'Round the Mountain," "This Land Is Your Land," "Zippity Do Dah," "Heigh Ho," and "Little Miss Mack." Avoid songs like "One Hundred Bottles of Beer on the Wall."

In the end, your choice of songs will be dictated by the answers to these questions: Can you sing a lick? Do you know the words to any songs? What works with your special kids? In my case, Madeleine would probably hike to Mongolia if we would just keep singing her favorite ditty, "Row, Row, Row Your Boat."

Whatever strategies you employ—and you may employ them all— keep 'em hiking. We're planting seeds here and, if nurtured properly, they will someday blossom into a full-blown appreciation of hiking through nature. As long as we don't allow our adult goals to detract from their hiking experience, our children should be back for more.

6

How to Live in Camp

When I was a boy of fourteen, my father was so ignorant I could hardly stand to have the old man around. But when I got to be twenty-one, I was astonished at how much he had learned in seven years.
—Mark Twain

SELECTING A CAMPSITE IN THE WILDERNESS

After a hard day on the trail, settling into camp is refreshing for body and spirit. The ideal site has level spots for tents, water nearby, available deadwood, a beautiful view, protection from weather, and seclusion.

Upon arriving at your destination, drop your gear at the first campsite that looks good, then scout out other possible sites. If you keep your pack on, you'll tend to pick the first site just because you're tired. You'll be tempted to camp right on the shore of that stream or lake. Don't do it. You should camp at least two hundred feet from water; in many places, it's the law.

If insects are a problem, seek higher ground where breezes will keep them away.

The most important quality in a campsite is a relatively flat sleeping area. Kids like to help with the selection. After choosing what seems like the best spot for your tent, spread out a ground cloth and lie down. If there is an incline, lie with your head uphill. Close your eyes and imagine what it will feel like at four in the morning. Is it comfortable? Consider the terrain for nighttime potty duties. Is it safe? If not, search elsewhere.

This is a perfect time to start teaching your children "no-trace camping." When clearing the ground for the sleeping area—a first-rate chore

There are many qualities to look for in a campsite. How many can you spot here?

(PHOTO BY WILLIAM J. BOGA)

To children, tents are portable forts.

for kids—don't sweep it with your foot. Get down on all fours and re-move body-stabbing sticks, pine cones, and rocks; leave the leaves and needles for cushioning. In the morning, after you pack up and leave, the only evidence that you slept there should be some matted leaves, which will fluff up in a few hours.

Cut no living boughs for bedding or tent stakes. If you lose stakes, tie guy lines around heavy rocks. Don't dig trenches around the tent; they don't work anyway. Take nothing that belongs to the land; leave nothing that belongs to you. Even biodegradable matter takes years to biodegrade, and in the meantime others have to gaze upon your garbage. To compensate for the boorish brigade that doesn't see it that way, pick up after your neighbors.

Before pitching a tent, lay down a ground cloth to protect the water-proof coating of the floor. Make sure the edge of the ground cloth doesn't extend beyond the edge of the tent; otherwise, it will channel rain under the tent and soak the floor.

Store boots, socks, and wet gear in the vestibule. They are handy there but don't add to the condensation inside the tent.

ANIMALPROOFING

One of your first camp chores should be animalproofing your food. If you are car camping or in an area with lots of bears, you might find bear-proof boxes, steel hanging cables, or slippery poles with hanging hooks. If you're car camping in bear country with none of those amenities, store food in ice chests in your trunk. If you're still worried, slather stove fuel around the deck lid. No trunk and not enough ice chests? Cover the food so the bears can't see it. If you're backpacking and lack any man-made bear defenses, you must counterbalance your food in a tree.

First, gather together all food, toothpaste, lotions, shampoos, vitamins, and anything else a desperate animal might mistake for food. Divide the lot into two stuff sacks or garbage bags, roughly even in weight. Open all the pockets of your pack and do a final search. Leave the pockets open. That way, rodents can investigate without having to chew through the pack.

When I was a teenager and new to backpacking, I had my
canvas pack torn up by bears looking for three tasty
vitamin C tablets I'd forgotten to hang with the rest of the food.
It really put me off of tasty vitamins.

More recently, a couple I know, Dan and Jan, had two
delinquent five-hundred-pound bears rip through their Lake
Tahoe camp in the middle of the night. Even though all their
food was stored safely in the car, the bears vandalized their
camp, then did it again an hour later. During the second visit,
with the couple cowering in their tent and the bears sniffing and
snorting outside, Jan remembered that she had five Hershey
Kisses in her purse in the tent. "Although the bears eventually
left, it was nerve-wracking," Dan said.

When you are certain you have gathered all bear edibles, begin searching for the perfect limb. It will be a live, sturdy branch, at least ten feet
long, fifteen to twenty feet off the ground, and well away from other limbs.
It should be no more than four inches in diameter and narrow to no more
than one inch at its end. Tie one end of a rope around a baseball-size rock
and toss it over the limb, at least eight feet from the tree trunk. Did you
hang on to the other end of the rope? If not, try again. Can you reach both
ends of the rope? If not, try again.

Tie one end of the rope to the first sack. Pull on the other end of the
rope until the first sack hangs up near the limb. Now reach up as high as
you can on the rope and tie off the second sack. Tie a loop in the leftover
rope near the lip of the sack; that will allow you to reach up with a stick,
hook the loop, and pull down the bag. You can also use a stick to push
one bag up, thereby lowering the other one. When you're done, push the
lower bag high enough so that both sacks hang evenly. Your food sacks
should be at least twelve feet off the ground, ten feet from the tree trunk,
and five feet below the limb. If not, do it over.

In bear country, hanging your food is every bit as essential as finding water.

This food-hanging tip is from Kathy Benham of Richmond, Virginia: Tie a lightweight plastic hook onto one end of your rope and clip the hook to the food bag. "No more fiddling with knots in the rain or snow," she says.

SANITATION

"That's the great thing about the outdoors—it's one big toilet." —*Jeff Goldblum in "The Big Chill"*

Another important camping chore is choosing the location of the "toilet." In established campgrounds and high-use backcountry areas, it will be obvious—either an outhouse or a conventional cell-block model with indoor plumbing.

Latrines, with their dark, smelly holes that seem bottomless, can be unpleasant for adults and frightening for children. One researcher found that two-thirds of all visitors to heavily used Desolation Wilderness, near Lake Tahoe, shunned outhouses.

Some would say there are sound environmental reasons for rejecting latrines. They concentrate human waste; if not properly located, they can pollute water; they are a possible source of insect contamination; they create a large area of disturbed soil; and waste takes a long time to decompose, increasing the chance that animals will dig it up and scatter the remains. Still, latrines may be the best choice in fragile ecosystems with a limited number of disposal sites, or for large groups on long stays.

In most backcountry, the location of the toilet is left to you. There is no latrine, no hole in the ground, no rule book.

"All other things being equal, choose a john with a view."
—*Colin Fletcher*

There are two recommended means of human waste disposal. Your choice should depend on prevailing conditions.

1. In low-use areas, where risk of discovery is minimal, surface disposal of feces is recommended. Choose a dry, open exposure, above the spring high-water line, unlikely to be visited by others. Scatter feces with a stick to maximize exposure to sun and air.

2. In more popular areas, bury waste in catholes.

In either case, pack out your used toilet paper in plastic bags.

To give feces a decent burial, choose a fairly level spot well away from camp and waterways, above the spring high-water line, and unlikely to be visited by others. When traveling in a family-size group, it is usually best to disperse everyone's waste, not concentrate it.

To dig the perfect hole, use a stick or a lightweight backpacking trowel to dig down no more than six to eight inches. That's home to the microorganisms that most effectively break down excrement. When you've finished what you came to do, take a stick and mix soil with the feces for quicker decomposition. Then cover with a couple of inches of topsoil and camouflage the surface.

The decomposition rate of buried fecal matter varies widely, depending on soil type, texture, acidity, moisture content, slope of terrain, exposure, insect population, and temperature. Under the *best* conditions, human excrement can take more than a year to vanish. In desert conditions, it can take a lifetime or longer.

When disposing of human waste, keep in mind our three main objectives: minimizing the chance of water pollution, minimizing the chance of any human or animal finding the waste, maximizing the chance of rapid decomposition. As Kathleen Meyer writes in *How to Shit in the Woods*, "The objective in digging a hole is to inhibit the passing of disease-causing organisms by humans or animals or storm runoff into nearby surface waters and by flying insects back to food areas."

Because urine evaporates quickly and is relatively clean, it's not nearly the environmental and health hazard that solid waste is. Avoid urinating on sensitive flora and don't frequent one place, lest it begin to smell like a Bombay alleyway. In Grand Canyon National Park, the park service instructs people to urinate directly into the river or on the wet sand at the water's edge, and to avoid urinating on rocks and gravel, where the odor lingers.

For years, we were told to bury toilet paper. Turns out, though, the stuff is slow to decompose. Then we were told to burn it. But that caused the occasional forest fire, such as the 1985 blaze in Washington state. A group of campers, trying to practice minimum-impact camping, burned their toilet paper and along with it a half-million dollars worth of trees.

So now you can pack it out or use a natural alternative. If you choose the first, make available a plastic collection bag with a disinfectant-soaked sponge in it. Place it in a discreet location and notify everyone of its purpose. You can also station the toilet paper and trowel there.

There are many natural alternatives. The first and simplest is to you can wipe with hand and water, the method favored by billions of people worldwide. Take a cup of water to the toilet, pour small amounts on your fingertips and cleanse yourself. Afterward, wash your hands with soap and water. Or, you can use dead leaves, fallen bark, cones, or rocks.

Children who spend time in nature early in life tend to adjust quickly to outdoor toileting. But if they're four or older and have always used a flush toilet, they may rebel against these ideas. If so, be patient. Young children have only recently learned the routine of bowel and bladder control, and camping takes them out of their routine. Kids won't have trouble squatting, but try to make your child (and yourself) as comfortable as possible. Their squat spot should be relatively level, free of annoying underbrush. Some parents have tried to re-create the home toilet by setting two flat rocks close together but not touching. If problems persist, speak softly and soothingly; do not convey urgency. Praise all achievement. Until children are capable of going on their own, probably only one parent should accompany them. Shoo impatient siblings away.

> *"If a child lives with approval, he learns to live with himself."*
> —Dorothy Law Nolte

Try to avoid the mad dash to the toilet by taking your child regularly. Tell your child at regular intervals that it's time to go. If you backpack, your children will probably eat more fiber and drink more water than usual; this can mean looser stools and a harder time predicting potty needs. Stay alert.

Little girls—and little boys when they squat to defecate—can get their pants wet. You can take their pants off, but that's inconvenient. Another way is to cradle your child, one hand behind her neck and the other behind her knees, so that she is almost in a sitting position. At such an angle, she can go without spraying me or her clothes. It's a parent's love that makes it possible.

Every means of waste disposal in the backcountry has problems, but that's no excuse for carelessness. It is critical to avoid further contamination of wilderness waterways.

COOKING

If you camp somewhere that permits fires, show restraint (some areas permit fires but prohibit wood gathering). If you have to roam far and wide to find fallen wood, it's a sure sign the area is overused. If so, don't build a fire. Decaying wood is essential to healthy forests.

Even if you can build a fire, you should cook over a stove. It conserves wood, keeps your pots from getting black, and enables you to control a flame. It also makes camping with children safer and easier.

With a stove, you have hot water for soup or cocoa ready for your cold, tired pack in about ten minutes.

If you have to build a fire, the task can take forever.

Seek a stable plot for the stove, free of debris for at least five feet in all directions. Identify this area as the kitchen and forbid running and playing. Keep pots and utensils easily accessible.

Only you can decide whether your children are old enough to help with the stove. Even if they are too young to fill, pump, or light it, there are plenty of other chores to do. They can retrieve food, utensils, or water, open packages, measure, pour ingredients, stir (off the stove), or tend the stove.

(Photo by William J. Boga)

Never underestimate the importance of food breaks.

Never cook in your tent. Besides being a fire hazard, it coats the inside of your tent with condensation and creates fumes that can be fatal. In stormy weather, put the stove right outside the tent or in the vestibule.

Marshmallows roasting over an open fire—the one food young children can cook themselves.

(Photo by William J. Boga)

Remember that cooking time increases with elevation. As you climb, water boils at a lower temperature. Most backpacking food tells you to add five or so minutes at altitude. If you are cooking something other than dehydrated backpacking food, the added time may be significant. Plan for it.

WASHING

To use soap or not—ah, that is the question. When backpacking, I am a devout no-soaper, relying instead on sand for the dishes and daily brief dips in mountain lakes or streams to cleanse. I find soapless dips sufficient because nature's dirt is downright benign compared to city dirt, and mountain lakes, where I do most of my "swimming," are quite bracing, making me feel cleaner than I really am.

If you must take soap, use it sparingly and carry a biodegradable, nonphosphate type. Even with the right soap, never put it or toothpaste into

(PHOTO BY WILLIAM J. BOGA)

Washing dishes is a good camp chore for kids.

a water source. Both can upset the delicate balance of life in rivers and lakes.

Consider using soap on hands only after toileting and not at all on dishes or clothes. Scour pots with sand, rocks, or a pine cone. Do the dishes immediately after eating and before residue dries.

Rinse out those dirty socks and dusty trail clothes in soapless water away from the lake or stream. Besides its polluting effect, soap is difficult to remove from clothing without plenty of warm water, and residual soap can cause a rash.

Whether or not you insist on using soap, carry washing water in cooking pots or collapsible jugs at least two hundred feet from its source (and from any campsite) and wash there. This will allow the wastewater to filter through the soil and break down before seeping back into the water supply.

You can easily prepare no-dishwashing meals: Select foods that can be reconstituted with water. Grocery stores are filled with them, from potatoes to powdered milk. Re-package meals in quart-size, self-sealing plastic bags. Carry a quart-size plastic cup or bowl. At mealtime, boil water and pour it into the bag supported in the bowl. Most plastic bags are rated to 170 degrees Fahrenheit, but if supported they will hold boiling water. Stir the contents, zip the bag closed, and let sit for a few minutes. Cleanup consists of rinsing the spoon and dropping the used bag in the trash bag. Do the same with freeze-dried dinners. Because some of them take longer than five minutes to reconstitute, run them through a blender before you leave home. Smaller pieces will soak up water faster and reduce waiting time.

ODDS 'N' ENDS

Soon after you get to camp, take off your boots and put on running shoes or sandals. Your feet will go "aahhh" and you won't trample the camp area.

To fasten a rope to a tent or tarp lacking a grommet or loop, place a smooth pebble, an inch or so wide, on the underside of the fabric where the grommet should be. Gather the fabric into a hood around the pebble, holding it at the neck. Tie the rope around the neck to secure it.

To rig a no-peg clothesline, double your nylon cord and twist it repeatedly. Slide laundry in between twists, and it will hold even in the strongest wind. When hanging clotheslines or mirrors, don't drive a nail into a tree.

Heavy-duty garbage bags have multiple uses around camp. Reshaped with a knife and some duct tape, they work as a ground cloth for your tent, a pack cover, or a makeshift poncho.

Car campers can hang a sixteen-pocket shoe organizer for their odds and ends. You can stash water bottles, candle lanterns, flashlights, socks, gloves, pens, notepaper, and even shoes.

If you want to read in the tent, make a lantern by standing a flashlight on end and placing a wide-mouth quart water bottle over it.

As we've long suspected, smoke does follow us around the campfire. It's attracted to the vacuum formed by a large object like your body. If you build a small stone wall near the fire ring, the smoke will be drawn that way, leaving you in the clear. When drying clothes and gear by a fire, place nothing closer to the flames than you can comfortably hold your hand.

COLD WEATHER

Fluff everyone's sleeping bag before they crawl inside. Air trapped within the fibers will help retain body heat.

Plastic bags are remarkable foot warmers. Wear the bags between your liner socks and thick outer socks. Plastic produce bags make good mittens, though they make it harder to shuffle cards.

If you expect freezing temperatures, turn your water bottles upside down. Because water freezes from top to bottom, the mouths of the bottles will remain unclogged, unless it's cold enough to freeze the entire contents. Even colder? Sleep with your boots in your sleeping bag to keep them from freezing.

If your kids wake up cold, have them do muscular-tension exercises (isometrics) in their sleeping bags. Push palms together, hold for a few seconds, then repeat. The exertion will make them warmer.

> *"Never did we plan the morrow, for we had learned that in the wilderness some new and irresistible distraction is sure to turn up before breakfast."*   *—Aldo Leopold*

GAMES

When you eliminate the trappings of civilization, such as TV, telephone, and automobile, it's amazing how many more hours a day seems to hold. Unless you are moving camp every day, chores will consume only a tiny percentage of your kids' time. Although they may be quite capable of entertaining themselves, it will behoove you to have some ideas for the time you hear that plaintive cry, "There's nothing to do." Some suggestions:

Lost on the Moon

This is an ingenious decision-making exercise with an important survival lesson. It's fun to play, but to do it right, you need at least three people. The exercise poses the following problem to the group.

You are in a space crew originally scheduled to rendezvous with a mother ship on the light side of the moon. Technical difficulties have forced your ship to crash-land at a spot two hundred miles from the rendezvous point. The rough landing damaged much of the equipment aboard. Since survival depends on reaching the mother ship, the most critical items available must be chosen for the two-hundred-mile trip.

Below are the fifteen items left intact after landing. You must rank them in terms of their importance to your crew in its attempt to reach the rendezvous point. Place a 1 by the most important item, a 2 by the second-most important item, and so on through 15, the least important item.

Read the above two paragraphs aloud and supply each member of your group with the list below. If you have read this before leaving the trailhead, photocopy the list. You will need one copy for each individual in your group plus one for each group of three or more (adults and children can work together in the same group).

_____ Box of matches
_____ Food concentrate
_____ Fifty feet of nylon rope
_____ Parachute silk
_____ Portable heating unit
_____ Two .45-caliber pistols
_____ One case dehydrated milk
_____ Two one-hundred-pound tanks of oxygen
_____ Map of the moon's constellations
_____ Life raft
_____ Magnetic compass
_____ Five gallons of water
_____ Signal flares
_____ First-aid kit with syringes
_____ Solar-powered two-way radio

In part one, everyone does the exercise solo, without sharing answers. In part two, participants form groups of three or four. Ask each group first to appoint a recording secretary, then to take a few notes to discuss the problem and list one ranking that represents the decision of the group. Explain that decisions should be based on logic and fact rather than personal preference and should reflect common agreement rather than majority vote or one-person dominance. While the discussion rages, make the following chart:

Group #	Average Individual Score	Range High-Low	Group Score	Net Change

Scoring individual and group sheets involves subtraction. Simply take the difference between the given answer and the correct answer. For example, the correct answer for "box of matches," as provided by the National Aeronautics and Space Administration, is 15; if someone answers 7, have them take the difference (8), write it next to the item, and circle it. When all fifteen answers have been read, add up the circled numbers. The lower the score, the better. You or one of the participants can score the group sheet.

The correct answers:

(15) Box of matches—limited use on a moon with little atmosphere.

(4) Food concentrate—important food source.

(6) Fifty feet of nylon rope—climbing tool.

(8) Parachute silk—shelter from sun's rays.

(13) Portable heating unit—useful only on light side of the moon.

(11) Two 45-caliber pistols—possible self-propulsion devices.

(12) One case of dehydrated milk—food mixed with water.

(1) Two one-hundred-pound tanks of oxygen—for breathing.

(3) Map of the moon's constellations—for navigation.

(9) Life raft—inflation bottles for self-propulsion across chasms and so forth.

(14) Magnetic compass—useless with no magnetized poles.

(2) Five gallons of water—more important than food.

(10) Signal flares—for distress calls.

(7) First-aid kit with syringes—for medicine.

(5) Solar-powered two-way radio—for possible communication with the mother ship.

If the results turn out as they often do, the group score will be better (lower) than the best individual score. When that happens, the lesson is clear: Even if you have Captain Kirk on your team, you are better off discussing the matter rather than just allowing one person to dictate. Perhaps this lesson might spill over into other areas of life.

Sample Questions
- Did the group do better than the average individual? Why?
- Did some members have more influence than others?
- How did your group reach agreement?
- How did you feel working in the group?
- What are the advantages and disadvantages of working in a group?

Kim's Game

Rudyard Kipling's *Kim* was a story about a boy who developed great powers of observation through practice. Kim's Game has its origins in that book. Any number can play. Place twenty or more common objects—

knife, compass, spoon, etc.—on a table, allow the players to study them for one minute, then cover them with a cloth. Each player then lists as many objects as he or she can recall. Remove the cloth. Score one point for each item correctly remembered and subtract two points for each item listed that's not on the table.

In one variation, everyone studies the objects for one minute as before, then they turn their backs while you move six or eight objects around the table. The players have thirty seconds more to study the table, then list the moved objects.

In another variation, you remove six or eight objects. The players then look for thirty seconds and list the objects that were removed.

Aniverbs

Human behavior can sometimes be described vividly by using a verb derived from the animal kingdom. Have your kids list as many as they can. Below are eleven that come to mind.

1. Ape—to mimic

   The small child will sometimes *ape* his parents' worst mannerisms.

2. Badger—to pester

   The mother *badgered* her daughter to clean her room by putting her dirty clothes in her bed.

3. Dog—to trail persistently.

   Whenever he appears in public, Michael Jordan is *dogged* by fans.

4. Fox—to deceive by ingenuity

   For years the fugitive out*foxed* the police.

5. Horse—to engage in rowdy play

   The kids *horsed* around until they were tired enough for bed.

6. Monkey—to play or tamper with something

   The boys *monkeyed* with their bicycle lock until it came loose.

7. Snake—to move or crawl like a snake

   The soldier escaped by *snaking* through the bushes.

8. Weasel—to evade

   The student *weasled* out of explaining why he was late to school.

9. Whale—to thrash

   She *whaled* on her brother for using her toys without permission.

10. Wolf—to eat voraciously

The boy *wolfed* down lunch so he could get back to the baseball game.

11. Bull—to crash into or through

The fullback *bulled* over left tackle for a first down.

Rock, Scissors, Paper

This classic can provide a diversion for two or more people as well as help decide who is going to do the dishes or filter the water.

Each child holds the left hand out, palm up; the right hand is clenched into a fist, and, with a rhythmic count of "one, two," each player hits his fist into his palm. Synchronized with "three," the fists become rock (keep the fist), paper (flat hand), or scissors (two fingers extended). The scoring is simple: Paper covers rock, rock breaks scissors, and scissors cut paper. Play the best of seven . . . or ninety-seven.

Make a Square

Ideal for two players, this game requires only a sheet of paper and a pencil. It takes time to set up; if it's a favorite with your kids, you might want to photocopy several "game boards." They look like this:

```
.  .  .  .  .
.  .  .  .  .
.  .  .  .  .
.  .  .  .  .
.  .  .  .  .
```

Just about any number of dots will work, but you might try ten rows and ten columns to start, giving you one hundred possible squares that can be filled in.

The object is to complete as many squares as possible. The first player connects any two horizontal or vertical (not diagonal) dots. The second player connects two more dots. They can be completely separate from the first or join the line the first player made. The first player then connects another pair of dots, being careful not to form the third side of a developing square. If player 1 does just that, player 2 can complete the square in his turn. When you complete a square, you get to put your initials inside and draw another line. Thus you can complete multiple squares during a turn. The winner is the player with the most squares.

Cross Out

I don't know what this game is called, so I call it Cross Out. A game for two players, it can be played with pencil and paper or with twigs in the dirt.

Place the twigs (or draw the lines) in a pattern like this:

I I I I I
I I I
I

Players take turns removing (or crossing out) one or more twigs (lines) in any single row. The object is to leave the last twig for the other player.

Dual Triangles

Since you already have twigs (make sure they're at least a couple of inches long), ask the children to form two triangles with five of them. (Clue: the two triangles share a common base.)

Quintuple Triangles

Same game, except this time participants are asked to form five triangles with six sticks of varying length. (Answer: One triangle is inside the other, upside down, its vertex touching the midpoint of the outer triangle's base.)

Trick Sticks

Don't throw those sticks away. The problem this time is to make three and a half-dozen, using only six sticks. As the name suggests, there is a trick to this one. In order to get it, participants must know their Roman numerals.

III   VI

You may have to provide hints, but this exercise certainly rewards creative thinking.

Tic Tac Toe

You know this one. It's for two players, one using X, the other O. The board is created by the two horizontal and two vertical lines shown below, creating nine boxes. Players take turns placing their symbol in a box. Three X's or three O's up, down, or diagonally win.

Tongue Twisters

These are phrases that are hard to repeat without making a mistake, usually ones that cause you to trip over your tongue and others to dissolve into gales of laughter.

Each person tries to repeat the twister quickly, or in the case of long ones, just say it once. You can keep score or not.

Some examples:

- *Toy boat, toy boat, toy boat.*
- *Rubber baby buggy bumpers.*
- *She sells seashells by the seashore.*
- *Peter Piper picked a peck of pickled peppers,*
  A peck of pickled peppers Peter Piper picked.
  If Peter Piper picked a peck of pickled peppers,
  Where's the peck of pickled peppers Peter Piper picked?
- *How much wood could a woodchuck chuck*
  If a woodchuck could chuck wood?
- *A cup of coffee in a copper coffee cup.*
- *Ten thin tin things.*

Hot or Cold

This game should be played in either a noisy campground or in complete solitude; otherwise, the tumult might drive your neighbors crazy.

One player is "it"; we'll call her Daisy. Daisy leaves the group. During her absence, the group chooses one object for her to touch. Daisy is called back, and as she approaches, the group begins rhythmic clapping to indicate how close she is to the object. The louder the applause, the closer she is; the softer the applause, the farther away. When the object is touched, pick a new "it."

Charades

Again, play this game only when noise won't disturb others around you.

In the simplest form, each willing person stands before the group and acts out a book, movie, or famous character, using body language and hand gestures but no words, while members of the group shout out their guesses. The actor can attempt to convey the big picture (example: acting out a man crossing a desert for *Lawrence of Arabia*) or do it word by word (as you might for *Little Big Man*). It is not in the spirit of the game to try to spell the title by shaping letters with your fingers.

In an uninhibited group, charades can produce riotous laughter, directed at both the actor and some of the off-the-wall blurtations from the audience.

If only a few are playing, you can take volunteers to be on stage. If you have a lot of people, you may prefer to form teams and compete against the clock. If sensitive or insecure kids are playing, reassure them that you are laughing *with* them, not *at* them.

Crazy, Mixed-Up Kids

With everyone seated, players slap their knees twice, clap their hands twice, and then grab their right ear with their left hand and their nose with their right hand. On signal, they slap and clap again, but reverse positions—right hand to left ear and left hand to nose. Repeat the routine, getting faster and faster until everyone is laughing and completely mixed up.

Huckle, Buckle, Beanstock

Place a common object in a visible but not obvious place. The players, who know what's been stashed, walk around looking for it. The first one to spot it sits down, looks away from the object, and says—you guessed it—"Huckle, buckle, beanstock," then waits for the others to find it.

Gossip (Telephone)

You need several people to play this game. Start by whispering a message in the ear of someone, who then attempts to whisper the message to the next person, and so on. Typically, by the time the message comes around to the first player, it bears little resemblance to the original, which makes everybody laugh like lovable idiots.

Sames and Differences

Have your charges look at an object of their choice—leaf, rock, tree, or cloud—then encourage them to discover another object that is similar in some way. Ask, "In what ways is it the same? In what ways is it different?" Urge them to be specific, emphasizing the five senses. If they need more guidance, give them an example, like a branch of a tree and a branch of a river. What's the same about those two things? Shape? Name? What's different? Texture? Size? Movement?

Cards

Even if you're backpacking, a deck of cards is worth its weight. Most of my card playing in the past twenty years has been in the wilderness. I first learned to play solitaire as a young camper. My daughter has been playing Fish since she was three. Young children also love Old Maid, Crazy Eights, and War. Older kids can play rummy, gin rummy, casino, canasta, hearts, solitaire, or poker, using twigs or moose droppings for money.

Chess and Checkers

You can find tiny chess and checkers sets that fold up and weigh next to nothing. Your children might not take to the mental rigors of chess (then again, they might), but most kids like checkers, which can also be played by drawing a board in the dirt with a stick and using black and white rocks for checkers.

Water Quiz

If your children have a working knowledge of math, especially percentages, give them the Gee Whiz Water Quiz. They won't get many answers exactly right, but it should increase their understanding of where water goes and of the need for conservation.

    1. How much of Earth's water is fresh?

    2. How much of Earth's total fresh water is available for human use?

    3. Where is the greatest amount of fresh water on Earth?

4. How much water does the average American use a day?

5. What percent of a living tree is water?

6. What percent of your brain is water?

7. How much of an adult body is water?

8. How much water is needed to produce a Sunday newspaper?

9. How much water is needed to produce an American car, including tires?

10. How much water is used to produce a fast-food meal, including hamburger, fries, and soft drink?

ANSWERS

1. 3 percent; 2. 1 percent; 3. The polar ice caps, which contain six million square miles of water—enough to feed all the world's rivers for a hundred years; 4. 200 gallons; 5. 75 percent; 6. 75 percent; 7. 65 to 70 percent; 8. 150 gallons; 9. 39,000 gallons; 10. 1,400 gallons

ACTIVITIES

Although I am a teacher and a strong supporter of public education, I believe that the wilderness consistently beats the classroom as a learning laboratory. Being in nature lends relevance to the study of astronomy, botany, biology, medicine, mineralogy, geology, meteorology, ornithology, entomology, ichthyology, zoology, map reading, navigation, and a host of survival skills. Although it's inevitable that you and your children will be interested in some subjects more than others, they all will be more compelling in the wilderness than in the classroom. Some examples:

Ornithology (Birds)

Birds seem to have a special hold on children. My daughter's third word (after "mama" and "dadda") was "doot," which was infant talk for "bird." What is it about birds that draws kids? They are active and attractive; they are diverse and ubiquitous; they sing songs, build nests, and come to feeders; and best of all, they fly. Arctic terns may rack up 22,000 frequent-flyer miles a year; some swifts reach speeds of up to two hundred miles per hour; short-tailed shearwaters migrate in flocks up to 400,000 strong; homing pigeons can find their way home from a thousand miles away.

Although their numbers vary from place to place and season to season, birds are just about everywhere. More than 650 species are regular breeders or frequent visitors north of the Mexican border. Birds nest on sandy beaches and rocky cliffs, in marshes and deserts, along city streets and country roads, and in garages and barns.

In order to observe birds, keep quiet. Walk slowly and steadily, or not at all. Don't wear bright clothes. Get an early start, especially if you're looking for land birds in spring. They are noisiest and most active from dawn to midmorning.

Birding can be done alone or in a group. Many birders enjoy the solitude of an early morning walk or a restful hour near a pond or stream. On the other hand, a group provides companionship, extra pairs of eyes, and, if there is at least one experienced observer along, a steeper learning curve. Many areas of the country have bird clubs (often a local chapter of the Audubon Society) where you can meet other birders. Try calling the biology department of the local high school or college or the nearest natural history museum to find out about such clubs.

To identify birds, you need to develop an eye for detail. Learn to concentrate on certain features:

• Posture and movement: The way a bird perches or moves often reveals its identity. Wrens cock their tails; woodpeckers and goldfinches have an undulating pattern of flight. Field guide illustrations don't always convey this type of information; that's why it's valuable to have along an experienced birder.

• Size and proportions: When you see a bird you don't recognize, compare its size with a bird you do know—say, a robin or a crow. Note whether the bird is slender or robust, and whether its legs or bill are unusually long.

• Songs and calls: Birds have two sets of vocal cords, and some have been recorded singing two songs at once. Recognizing a bird by sound is often easier than identifying it by sight, especially with small birds in deep foliage. Of course, you have to learn the sounds. You can listen to recordings, but for beginners, it's better to apprentice with someone who has a good ear for bird calls. Singing is usually most persistent in the morning, although some species don't seem to care what time it is. One researcher recorded a male red-eyed vireo repeating his refrain 22,197 times between dawn and dark.

• Color and markings: These attributes most strikingly reveal a bird's identity, although some species change colors depending on season, sex, or age. With experience, you will be able to absorb more and more information in a quick glance and will learn the special characteristics that separate closely related species—say, the bill color of a tern or the wing bars of a vireo.

• Nest and eggs: With a little practice, you will be able to identify the nest and the eggs of many species. Field guides describe the variations in both. Do not disturb nests or steal eggs.

Whether your kids are compiling a life list (of species seen and identified) or just like watching birds, you will want a decent pair of binoculars. Also, supply young birders with a pocket-size field guide, a pen, and

Seeing a beautiful bird like an egret can take your breath away.

(Photo by William J. Boga)

a notebook. If you are backpacking and counting ounces, you may opt for pocket-size binoculars. They're fine when the sun is high, but full-size ones deliver a brighter image, which is important in low light.

The key to evaluating binoculars is the numbers marked on every pair: typically 8x24 or 10x25 on compacts, 7x42 or 7x50 on full-size glasses. The second number is the diameter, in millimeters, of the binocular's objective lenses. Doubling the diameter, say from 25 to 50, quadruples its light-gathering capacity. Cheap binoculars are available for less than $50. At the other end of the spectrum, the Leica 7x42 BA, compact and waterproof, weighing thirty-two ounces, costs $1,650.

Entomology (Insects)

When you go camping, you'll likely share your accommodations with a variety of insects. About three-quarters of the animal species on Earth, about 700,000, are insects. There are more than 100,000 insect species in North America. Although delicate walkingsticks and bright butterflies get rave reviews, the vast majority of people say they don't like insects. Actually, they have much to recommend them. They fill vital ecological niches, supply humans with medicine, keep other insects in check, and play an important role in the reproduction of flowering plants.

They also expand our awe of the miracle of life. Consider the ways insects defend themselves. The walkingstick uses camouflage, mosquitoes bite, and some caterpillars have stinging nettlelike hairs. Or take note of the species' deceptive complexity. The eye of a dragonfly has a thousand parts; an ant society is amazingly sophisticated.

Forty-three species of ants were found in a single tree in a Peruvian rain forest.

Most children are innately fascinated by creepy crawlers. Madeleine has been going on "roly-poly hunts" since she was two. If your child shares this interest, make available an insect field guide and a lightweight magnifying glass. Most nature stores have a meshed, cylindrical bug house, a fairly benign way to inspect insects before they crawl or fly away.

We can hope that our children will refrain from killing insects and even put them back where they found them, but this runs counter to the instincts of many young people. The hope is that with knowledge comes respect.

Fishing

> *"Fishing is an excellent way to relax and contemplate the*
> *beauty of nature and get in touch with your inner self and*
> *maim and kill fish."*　　　　　　　　　　*Dave Barry*

Fishing is a good activity for your kids—if they're interested. It's active, involves them in nature (albeit in an adversarial way), teaches them new skills, and reinforces important qualities, such as the patience to wait, oh, two days for a nibble. Oh, yes, it can also be a source of food. However, you can't just pass out rods and reels and expect beginners to perform flawlessly. If they are going to become proficient, they will need careful, patient instruction and lots of practice. That is especially true if they are learning to fly-fish.

I have fished for trout since I was eight years old. In the ensuing thirty-eight years, I have broken rods, cast lures into treetops, snagged old boots, lost my reel from my rod, snarled my line into something more complex than Rubik's Cube, and struck out in hundreds of lakes around the world. In short, I have paid my dues.

Soon after I became a competent fisherman, I became an apathetic one. I still occasionally fish for trout above nine thousand feet, but my heart is no longer in it. I've lost that killer instinct. Every year, it gets harder for me to murder little animals—and the fish I catch do tend toward the petite. On the other hand, fresh-caught mountain trout is perhaps the finest eating on the planet.

If you fish in high-impact areas, you should scatter entrails and leftovers far and wide, at least two hundred feet from water and campsite. In alpine backcountry areas, don't throw the remains back into lakes or streams; chilly mountain waters act like a refrigerator, preventing rapid decomposition. Guts slowly rotting in an otherwise pristine lake are a slap in the face of the wilderness backpacker.

Day Hiking

There is nothing quite like replacing backpack with day pack and setting off over hill and dale, by trail or cross country, many pounds lighter in spirit and load. Hiking is marvelous exercise and great for the soul, but caution is needed. Never hike alone; people of all ages should have a partner every time they leave camp. (Obviously, that rule has been broken by lots of otherwise responsible people, John Muir and Henry David Thoreau, to name two.) If anyone in your group leaves camp alone, insist upon an itinerary. Look at a map and discuss details.

Hiking Mother Ann Brice's Day Hike Necessities

1. Water
2. Snacks
3. Sunscreen
4. Swiss Army knife
5. Magnifying lens—for looking at specimens
6. Notepad
7. Baggies—for collectibles
8. Band-Aids and moleskin
9. Tissue/toilet paper
10. Field guides
11. Maps
12. Mosquito repellant

Husband Bruce Maxwell's Day Hike Necessities

1. Mosquito repellant
2. Sunscreen
3. Snacks

Night Hiking

At night, we lose much of our dominance over nature. Our eyes, through which we gather most of our information, become all but useless, forcing us to rely on other senses. We tend to think of nighttime as cold and empty ("the dead of night"), but actually the night is filled not only with stars but also with the pulse and hum of life itself.

Writer W. H. Hudson liked to prove this to his dinner guests. He would lead them into the dark forest that adjoined his estate and ask them to stand quietly. When all was still, he would fire a revolver he'd hidden beneath his coat and suddenly the air would be filled with a mad chorus of howls and shrieks, with animals crashing through brush to flee the noise. "The wild outcry," he called it. "The extraordinary hullabaloo."

Such a hullabaloo is possible because 85 percent of the world's mammals are active at night, or at least around dawn and dusk. Sixty percent of carnivores hunt at night. Only humans, apes, monkeys, some birds, and a few other species prefer daytime.

Night creatures have complex eyes with a mirrorlike membrane that reflects light to the retina twice, giving the brain two chances to make it out. It's that reflection that we see in our headlights—white for a coyote, yellow for a raccoon, red for a woodcock.

Take your children to visit a place at night that you saw during the day. If it's cold, dress warmly and take pads to sit on. Carry a flashlight if necessary, but then turn it off and sit quietly. Hug a tree, stroke a flower, sniff, listen. If you must talk, whisper. Later, ask questions: How did it feel? What's different now that it's night? Did the other senses come into play? Hearing? Touch? Smell? Why do you think so many animals are more active during the night?

Mineralogy

As I write this, people are sleeping on the sidewalks of Los Angeles, displaced by a devastating earthquake. It displaced quite a few rocks, too. Scientists estimate that the nearby San Gabriel Mountains will be three to six feet higher because of that temblor. Rocks on the move.

The point is that rocks have a life story. They are "born," they move around, and they change size. Some have beautiful colors and others have interesting shapes. Although most adults take rocks for granted, children seem to have a special intimacy with them.

Here are a couple of exercises for your rock-loving kids. Start by asking, "What is dirt?" After listening patiently to the inevitable wild answers, urge them to find out for themselves. Have them pick up a handful and examine it. What do they see? Rather than just one thing, dirt is really made up of myriad plant bits, seeds, dead insects, and tiny rocks.

Next, have them put together a row of rocks of descending size. They can begin with one about the diameter of a thumbnail, lining up smaller and smaller pebbles until they are too small to pick up. When they reach that point, have them add a pinch of sand to the end of the row. Ask questions like, "How are rocks and sand alike? (Hint: hard mineral matter.) Why are they round or close to it? (Erosion of corners.) How did sand become so small? (Water erosion.) If your children are mature enough, build up to the big question: How did rocks get here?

Geologists divide rocks into three types based on their origin:

• Sedimentary rock is the easiest to understand. The mud and decaying plant and animal material that drifts to the bottom of a lake is sediment. The layers of gunk at the bottom are pressed tightly together by the weight of ensuing layers (this may take millions of years) until they become hard as rock. Then perhaps the lake disappears, the land is tilted by earthquake, and the sedimentary rock is exposed. Sandstone, which is reddish and sometimes embedded with fossils, is a common sedimentary rock. Compared to other rocks, sedimentary is soft and easy to break up.

• Metamorphic rock has had its form altered. For example, proper conditions and intense pressure will change shale (a soft, flaky, sedimentary rock made up of compressed mud) into slate (a hard, dark metamorphic rock used in blackboards).

• Igneous rock is born deep in the Earth, where everything is hot and liquid. As molten igneous material slowly slides toward the cooler surface of the Earth, it solidifies into rock. Igneous rock is also formed when a volcano erupts. Molten lava spews onto the surface, eventually cooling and solidifying. This type of rock is usually extra hard. Granite and obsidian are igneous.

Photography

Great photography is a complex mix that includes composition, subject matter, lighting, and other variables.

Having said that, it's easy to teach your children how to take good pictures that are fun to look at. Photography is one of the first recreational skills a child can learn, especially with today's point-and-shoot cameras. Emphasize the following points:

- Remember to remove the lens cap.
- Hold the camera steady.
- Don't shoot into the sun.
- Keep fingers away from the lens opening.
- Take a deep breath and hold.
- Slowly squeeze the shutter button.

Pictures of people should:
- Have a center of interest.
- Have contrast.
- Show action, though not too fast.

Pictures of scenery should:
- Lead the viewer's eye to the center of interest.
- Have good background.
- Be framed, perhaps by two trees.

Young children must understand that photography requires delayed gratification. The real enjoyment comes days or weeks later when you pick up the pictures and your children feel the accomplishment of being able to say, "I took that!"

Scatology

This is the study and collection of mammal droppings. While it's not for everybody (nor is it the stuff of dinner conversation), scat does offer excellent clues about animals in the area. Serious scatologists can determine the range of an animal, seasonal changes in diet, and population density.

Back in the lab, samples can be scrutinized for parasites and indications of disease.

Scat is indeed a valuable learning tool. In Great Smoky Mountains National Park, black bear researchers from the University of Tennessee have injected animals with a harmless isotope that shows up in their scat for up to three years. It allows them to identify individual animals and gather information without recapturing or even seeing the bear.

But you don't have to be a scientist to appreciate good scat. Every young child I've ever hiked with has delighted in pointing out trail poop. By examining droppings for the basic characteristics of size, shape, and content, even laypeople can often identify the responsible animal. Deer, which drop little pellets thirteen to twenty-two times a day, are easily distinguished from moose but may be confused with rabbits. Bobcats and mountain lions, like house cats, try to bury their scat, so look for scratches in the soil. In fact, scat is often only one of many clues. Look for tracks or fur caught on branches. Flies are a sure sign of fresh scat.

One wildlife researcher, Olaus Murie, has a collection of 1200 scat specimens, dried, varnished, labeled, and wrapped in plastic bags. Murie's collection is in constant demand for classes and seminars. Imagine how proud his mother must be.

Star Gazing

For thousands of years, people have grouped the stars into figures called constellations. Legends and myths have been passed down about them. It's fun to learn the myths and pass them on to your children while pointing out the star clusters in the sky. Visit your library for a book about legends of the constellations.

A good starting point is the Big Dipper, probably the most visible constellation in the northern sky. Four stars make up the cup and three bright ones seem to complete the handle. Actually, the handle's midpoint is composed of two stars. Can you see them? Indians, who called these two stars the squaw and the papoose, used them to test the eyesight of young braves.

The two stars that form the side of the bowl farthest from the handle are called the pointers; if you follow their line upward, they take you to the North Star, which, because it is almost in a direct line with the axis of the Earth, doesn't seem to move as the Earth turns. All other stars seem to rotate around the North Star.

The North Star is also the first star in the handle of the Little Dipper, which is fainter than the Big Dipper. If you follow a line from the middle star of the handle of the Big Dipper through the North Star, you'll come to a big "W," which is Cassiopeia, the Lady in the Chair.

Acquire a star chart for your latitude and continue to "connect the dots" and identify constellations.

Storytelling

If not a lost art, storytelling is certainly an endangered one. (I blame TV, as I do for most trends I don't like.) But when sitting around a campfire or lying in a sleeping bag, storytelling is a natural entertainment. All you need is patience and a modest gift of gab.

Well, maybe a bit more. Here are a few tips for the beginning storyteller:

• Don't try to make up stories from scratch at first. Read adventure, mystery, or history stories in books and magazines, and retell them in your own words.

• Avoid unsuitable stories, overly sentimental ones, talking down to your audience, stories in dialect, and mumbling. For younger children, avoid off-color, sarcastic, and very scary stories.

• Look and feel relaxed; if not, your audience will sense your discomfort and uncertainty.

• Be enthusiastic, conveying emotion by changes in volume and tone. Children can detect indifference like a Geiger counter detects uranium.

• Have the framework of the story established before you start. Don't forget that a good story has a definite beginning, middle, and end.

• Start strongly; try to catch your listeners' attention from the first words.

• Make the details clear, especially in the events, characters, and setting of the story.

• Include vivid action. Emphasize verbs over adjectives and adverbs.

• Make the narration "visible" to the audience. Include sensory experiences besides sight. In other words, don't tell them, show them: hear the wind howl through the trees or smell the pine needles on a crisp fall morning.

• Sprinkle in humor, but don't overdue it unless your kids are so young they can't recognize corn. Mix with dramatic inflection and pauses.

• Remember that "brevity is the soul of wit." If you are telling a long story, condense it into five to fifteen minutes. If it is a sure winner, you can tell it in installments, keeping your audience hanging until the next chapter.

J oseph Pulitzer, writer and newspaper owner, used to advise his reporters to write their stories:

Briefly, so readers will read it

Clearly, so they will understand it

Forcibly, so they will appreciate it

Picturesquely, so they will remember it; and above all,

Accurately, so they will be guided by its light.

Change "read" to "listen to" in the first line, and it's good advice for the storyteller.

Here's a traditional campfire story to get you started.

"One time, I had a real scary encounter with a grizzly bear" (adding quickly, "Of course, there are no grizzlies around here"). "I managed to climb a nearby tree just ahead of the bear's snapping jaws. Seated on a branch, I watched in terror as the enraged bear clawed and chewed at the trunk. Then he shook it in an attempt to knock me from my perch. But the tree was too big and soon the bear gave up and disappeared into the woods.

"I started climbing down the tree, but before I got very far, the bear returned, this time with another bear. Together they chewed and clawed and shoved at the tree, but the tree was too strong. They too disappeared for a time but were soon back, this time with a third bear. It was no use— the tree was too big for the three bears, and when they finally disappeared into the forest, a wave of relief washed over me.

"I again started down the tree. But to my horror, the three bears came back! This time, though, each of them was carrying a beaver."

Bear stories are usually well received, as long as they're not too scary. This one really happened:

A woman who had just bought a new camera, complete with tele- photo lens, was determined to get a good bear picture on her visit to Great Smoky Mountain National Park. When a black bear scrounging for hand- outs wandered into her campground, the woman moved closer and raised the camera. The suddenly magnified image of the bear scared her out of her wits. Turning to run, she collided with a tree and knocked herself unconscious. The curious bear ambled over for a look.

When the woman regained consciousness, the bear was gone. A fel- low camper, trying to be friendly, handed her a Polaroid photo he'd taken of the bear standing over her, licking her face while she was out. Seeing that, she fainted.

One way to get others involved is to play a storytelling game. In one version, a player starts by stating aloud the opening sentence of the story. The second player adds another sentence and so on into nonsense land. In another version, you supply a list of common words that the players are supposed to work into the story.

If you feel ill-equipped to tell a story, consider reading a story to your charges. The possibilities are unlimited, but here are a few of my favorites:

• *The Jungle Book,* by Rudyard Kipling
• *Alice's Adventures in Wonderland*, by Lewis Carroll (though some kids will incorrectly think they are too old for this one)
• *The Wind in the Willows*, by Kenneth Grahame
• *The Hobbit*, by J. R. R. Tolkien
• *The Merry Adventures of Robin Hood*, by Howard Pyle

- *Twenty Thousand Leagues under the Sea*, by Jules Verne
- *Treasure Island*, by Robert Louis Stevenson

Swimming

Children love water. The focal point of many vacations is a lake, river, ocean, or swimming pool. But every year in the United States more than a thousand children fourteen and younger drown, the second most common cause of accidental death in children (after car accidents). Teach your kids to swim and watch them well. Beyond that, enforce the following safety rules:

- Adapt slowly to extremely cold water.
- Don't go in the water when overheated, overtired, or after eating a meal. Mom had that one right.
- Beware of unfamiliar swimming holes. Know that a place is safe.
- Don't swim above waterfalls. (The closest I've ever come to meeting Neptune was diving into a deceptively fast-moving stream above a thirty-foot waterfall.)
- Teach children to investigate the depth of any pool into which they intend to dive or jump. (I've known two teenagers who, because they ignored that, are permanently disabled.)
- Don't be macho in the water by overestimating your ability to stay underwater or swim long distances.
- Be sensitive to the safety of others.
- As a parent, don't rely blindly on waterwings or flotation devices to save your children.

Tracking

Maybe more than any other skill, identifying tracks will make your children feel like wilderness mavens. The study of tracks, besides being fun, is great awareness training. It forces children to tune into their surroundings, to look critically at nature, and to play in the dirt. As outdoorsman Tom Brown says, "Each track, no matter how old, is like a window to the past, enabling one to understand a page, a part, or a chapter of an animal's life."

Track pack. If you intend to be even moderately serious about studying tracks, make a track pack for each child. Small enough to fit on a belt

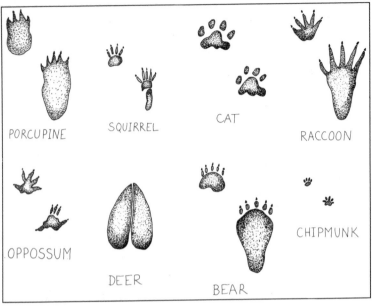

PORCUPINE   SQUIRREL   CAT   RACCOON

OPPOSSUM   DEER   BEAR   CHIPMUNK

Studying tracks is a fun way to learn more about animals.

and weighing almost nothing, a track pack contains all the equipment children should need. It includes the following:

- Notebook and pencil, for drawing tracks and collecting evidence
- Tape measure or ruler, for measuring length, width, and stride
- Magnifying glass, for scrutiny of tracks
- Clear tape, for securing other bits of evidence in a notebook
- Popsicle sticks, for marking tracks to revisit
- Tweezers, for removing evidence
- Plastic sandwich bags, for collecting evidence

Track classification. Tom Brown presents a simple classification system you can easily teach your kids. Hand them a three-by-five-inch file card containing the following information:

4 x 4 x no claws = cat family

4 x 4 x claws = dog family

4 x 4 x claws + huge rear feet = rabbit and hare family

5 x 5 x claws + small heel pads = raccoons, opossum, bear
4 x 5 x claws = rodent family
2 x 2 x hooves = deer family

Explain that the first figure represents the number of toes on the front paws and the second is toes on the rear, followed by distinguishing characteristics. Until your children have memorized their cards, they should keep them handy. You can also copy the page in this book that depicts some common animal tracks. Protect it all in a plastic bag.

Field Trip. Once everyone has a file card and a track pack, head out as a group to a nature area. The best time to look for tracks is evening or early morning, when the sun is low. With good shadows, the ground will seem to come to life. Keep the tracks between you and the source of light. Look for transition zones or fringe areas called ecotones, where animals are most likely to be found. Guide your children to soft soil, such as mudflats, sandbars, and waterways.

When you find tracks, try to match them to a family on the file card. Have your children measure the length and width of each track and record the data in their notebooks. Both measurements are taken at the longest part of the track, not counting the claw marks. If you are teaching tracking (as opposed to track identification), have your charges measure the *stride*, the distance from the heel of one print to the heel of the opposite print, and *the straddle*, the distance from the inside of the heel of one print to the inside heel of the opposite print.

After measurements are taken, have everyone sketch the track in his or her notebook. This will aid identification and speed learning. If you intend to come back to this spot, mark it by pushing a Popsicle stick into the ground nearby.

Sign identification. Besides tracks, there are other bits of evidence, called signs, that point to the past presence of animals. Learning to read these signs is the other part of tracking. Show your children examples of the following signs:

• Trails. Animals, like people, prefer to take the easiest route of travel, unless pursued.

• Runs. Less worn than trails, runs are the backroads of the transition areas that carry animals to watering, feeding, and bedding areas.

• Beds. Animal bedding areas are usually found in thick brush, which offers maximum protection from predators and weather.

• Scratches. Animals leave scratches when they dig for food, climb trees, and dig burrows. The easiest to spot might be the scratches of squirrels climbing trees.

• Gnawings. This occurs when animals attempt to gnaw through vegetation, wood, or even bone. The classic example is the cone-shaped tree stump left by a beaver.

• Rubs. When animals must pass under or next to an obstruction in their path, they may inadvertently rub against it. If this happens repeatedly, the obstruction will become slightly polished or worn. The most dramatic example is a tree trunk used by a bear as a back scratcher.

• Broken vegetation. As animals push through vegetation, they leave visible breaks, tears, and tramples.

• Hair and feathers. Looking closely, children can easily find these signs, which can be taped in their notebooks.

Tree Identification

North America has the world's tallest, oldest, and most massive trees. It is home to nearly sixty oaks, thirty-five pines, and more than a dozen maples. About 750 species of trees grow wild north of Mexico.

Some trees have leaves; others have needles (really just long, narrow leaves). Both contain chlorophyll, the green pigment required for photosynthesis. Some species, like giant sequoias and weeping willows, are immediately familiar; others must be identified through a process of elimination. With a field guide, consider the following variables when trying to identify a tree:

Leaves. Pinpoint the general type of leaf—needlelike, scalelike, or broad and flat—then look at the size, shape, texture, color, and arrangement. Most broad leaves alternate on the twig (maples with paired leaves are a major exception).

Flowers. Blossom size, shape, and color can help you determine to which group a tree belongs.

Fruits. Closely related trees bear similar fruits. Acorns are oak fruit and cones are conifer fruit.

Bark. In winter, when deciduous trees lose their leaves, bark may offer the best chance of identifying a species. Consider color, pattern, and texture.

Shape. This involves height, crown width, arrangement of branches, and other variables. Shape varies with location. A forest tree will be taller and its crown narrower than the same species growing in the open.

There is a simple way to calculate the height of a standing tree, and your children can probably do it from start to finish.

You just need a piece of cardboard and a tape measure. The ground around the tree must be reasonably level with enough space to allow you to make your observations.

Cut a right triangle from the cardboard, with sides of one foot (the long side, or hypotenuse, will be about seventeen inches). Walk away from the tree until you are standing about where you think the tree will land if it falls. Face the tree and hold the triangle so that the base is parallel to the ground and the height is parallel to the tree. Put the base at eye level and sight along the long side as though it were a gun sight. If you are too close to the tree, you will be sighting into the branches; too far away and you will see sky. Move back and forth until you see the tip of the tree in your "sight." Remember to keep the base of the triangle parallel to the ground.

With the tape measure, measure the distance from the base of the tree to the spot where the correct sighting took place. Then measure the distance from your eye to the ground. Add those figures and you have the approximate height of the tree.

Wildflower Identification

A wildflower is any flowering plant that isn't cultivated and is neither a tree nor a tall shrub. More than 15,000 such species grow north of Mexico.

Identifying a few can be fun for children. Consider bringing along a field guide to flowers. Nature stores sell wildflower coloring books.

The vast array of flower colors, shapes, textures, and scents serve only one function: to produce the seed for a new generation. Every flower contains egg-producing female organs (pistils), pollen-producing male organs (stamens), or both.

Since flowers seldom pollinate themselves, most species need the help of an outside agent to transfer pollen from the stamen of one flower to the pistil of another. Many grasses and weeds rely on the wind; others depend on insects or birds, attracting them with color or smell. In exchange for distributing its seed, the flower may supply nectar to its animal allies.

Flowers have long provided food and medicine to man, but some are poisonous. Do not randomly eat flowers.

BEDTIME

After games and activities and before it gets dark, gather and arrange the items you might need during the night and first thing in the morning. Place them strategically in the tent or near your bed so that you can find them in the dark. You might include diapers, toilet paper, wipes, tissues, flashlight, books, water bottle, or rain gear.

Do your tent time—reading books, telling stories, singing songs—then kiss your children good night and leave. Chances are, your kids will get less sleep than they do at home. In the evenings, they tend to be energized by their new surroundings; in the mornings, there is no shortage of sleep disturbers, from the sounds of nature to dawn's early light.

Parents of young children are often ready to turn in when their kids do, but first you must batten down the hatches. The last adult to crawl in should make sure that:

• All food and garbage is safe from animals.

• The fire is safely contained.

• Pack pockets are open and packs are secure from the weather, if necessary.

• The path from tent to toilet is clear.

"People who say they sleep like a baby usually don't have one."
                                                            —Leo J. Burke

"The persons hardest to convince they're at the retirement age are children at bedtime." —Shannon Fife

LEAVING CAMP

Before final departure, police your campsite. Check for trash and forgotten articles. Pick up other people's mistakes. Check not only the ground but the trees. Did you get your clothesline? Food-hanging rope? Douse all fires until they are dead, then douse them again. Do some landscaping, smoothing out heavily trodden areas and filling in any holes or trenches your party dug.

Ease campsite damage by traveling in small groups, camping away from the water, and being kind to the land. Urge your children to leave the campsite in better shape than it was when you arrived. Be guided by the adage, "Take only photos; leave only footprints."

7 *How to Weather the Outdoors*

> *Some are weatherwise,*
> *but most are otherwise.*
> *—Benjamin Franklin*

One way to make school more relevant is to offer classes in weather (meteorology). What could be more practical? We deal with weather every day. And a comprehensive weather class could include the study of basic geography, geology, botany, zoology, physics, chemistry, and even sociology. You heard it here first.

People are fascinated by weather, though few understand much about it. It has long been the No. 1 ice breaker. As an awkward teenager, I once sidled up to a girl I was sweet on. "Large weather we're having," I cooed.

> *"There is only one thing we can be sure of about the weather—there will be plenty of it."* —Mark Twain

Kids have a natural affinity for weather because it's very here-and-now, so feed that interest early. There are several ways to do this:

• Keep an eye on the sky and talk about what you see. Practice identifying clouds and interpreting their significance. Become conscious of the winds. Point out changes in temperature and humidity. Encourage discussions on anything that falls from the sky or billows up from the ground. If you are tongue-tied when your child asks, "What are clouds?" get to a library.

• Buy some weather gadgets and make observations at about the same times every day. Cheap tools include an indoor/outdoor (or minimum-maximum) thermometer, a rain gauge, and possibly an anemometer, which measures wind speed. Chart your rainfall and your daily high and low temperatures. Practice converting Celsius temperatures to Fahrenheit and vice versa; the formula is $F = \frac{9}{5}C + 32$; the Fahrenheit temperature equals nine-fifths the Celsius temperature plus 32.

• Have your children keep a log or diary. Help them see trends. Try making forecasts of the weather in twelve and twenty-four hours. Discuss why the forecast was right or wrong.

• Peruse the weather page of your newspaper. Note the weather in other parts of the world. *USA Today* has an eye-catching weather page, and most local newspapers have expanded their weather coverage in the past few years.

• Watch television weather, complete with graphics and satellite photos. If you subscribe to cable TV, you probably have access to twenty-four-hour weather information.

• Use a computer and an on-line network to obtain information from the National Weather Service.

• Listen to the radio. The National Oceanic and Atmospheric Administration (the parent organization of the National Weather Service) maintains a network of 380 radio stations across the United States that broadcasts on the VHF FM band in the 162.40 to 162.55 MHz range.

• Take a barometer or altimeter into the wilderness. Used for measuring air pressure (the altimeter translates that pressure into elevation), both can help the backcountry weather prognosticator. Also, be alert to incidental signs of dropping barometric pressure: a "trick" knee, headache, sleepiness, birds roosting, or bees returning to the hive.

• Challenge your children with discussion questions. Write a question on a piece of paper and give them a week or so to find the answer. For example:

1. Why is it summer in Australia when it's winter here? (hint: the tilt of the Earth)

2. What causes winds? (differential heating of the Earth)

3. Why are there clouds? (condensation of water vapor)

4. Why is the sky blue? (refraction of light)

5. How is temperature measured? (with mercury in a thermometer by degrees)

Weather knowledge is valuable to wilderness campers. For backpackers, weather prediction can be a life-or-death matter. Decisions like "Do we pitch the tent or make a stab at the summit?" often hinge on weather forecasts.

Unless your hiking partner is a professional forecaster, you'll have to make do when you're backpacking. Even when you're car camping, you may be beyond the reach of radio stations and newspapers. If so, you will have to be your own forecaster. Remember, though, that weather is never absolutely predictable. Keep in mind a few principles:

1. Air expands and rises when warmed. As the sun warms the Earth's surface, "bubbles" of air rise. As long as a bubble is warmer than the sur-

(PHOTO BY BRUCE MAXWELL)

Weather can affect local water sources.

rounding air, it will continue to rise. As it rises, nearby air moves in horizontally to take the place it vacated. That horizontal movement is called wind.

2. As warm air rises, it cools. If a humid mass of air is cooled enough, the water vapor in it condenses into water droplets that reflect light, forming a cloud. Cool those droplets even more and they get heavier, eventually falling as precipitation.

3. Mountains tend to create updrafts, resulting in high precipitation on the windward slopes and dry conditions on the lee side. The dry air that continues flowing down the lee side compresses and becomes warmer. Most of the deserts of North America lie in the so-called "rain shadow" (usually east side) of a mountain range.

4. During stormy weather, locations many miles distant will have similar temperatures, humidities, and winds. When skies are clear, however, local conditions may vary a lot. Microclimates form. Local winds develop in response to differences in surface heating. An understanding of microclimates can be a big help when you have to break for lunch or pitch a tent.

5. Wind speed increases with elevation, so that any time of the day it's windier on the mountaintop than down below. However, wind speed near sea level usually increases as the day goes on, while on the mountaintop it decreases. At night, as the ground cools and conditions stabilize, winds decrease at lower levels and increase on a mountain.

6. In apparent contradiction of the principle that warm air rises, it is often colder at the bottom of a depression (like beside a mountain lake) than up on a slope. At night, the ground cools, as does any air around it. The cool air near the slope's surface flows downhill and collects in the valley bottom. That pushes the warmer air hanging over the middle of the valley up and outward. On a clear, calm night, the temperature in a small depression may be twenty degrees lower than on a nearby slope.

Air can't be weighed, but its pressure can be measured with a barometer, calibrated in "inches of mercury." At sea level, a barometer should register close to the standard pressure of 29.92 inches of mercury. If it's significantly higher or lower, an area of high or low pressure is nearby. Take note of dramatic barometric changes. If the reading suddenly plummets, a major low-pressure area is fast approaching. Prepare for a storm, possibly a severe one.

You also must take climate into consideration. This is the long-term prevailing weather conditions of a region. If you know the climate where you'll be camping, you can make educated guesses about its weather. Climate is influenced by several factors. Latitude determines the amount of sun an area receives. Hiking near the equator? You'll get lots; at the poles, you'll go six months with almost none.

Elevation affects both temperature and precipitation. Mountain camping? Expect cooler and wetter climes. Proximity to an ocean or large body of water moderates temperatures. Continental areas are generally drier, with greater temperature extremes.

The slope of the land is important. In the Northern Hemisphere, south- and west-facing slopes will be warmer than north- and east-facing ones. At noon on a sunny day, a south-facing slope may be ten or more degrees warmer than a nearby north-facing slope.

Dark, rough surfaces absorb more of the sun's rays than light, smooth ones. Other things being equal (they seldom are), dark, rough surfaces will be warmer than smooth, light ones.

Some climates are easier to forecast than others. In the tropics, you can expect humid heat. Near the other end of the spectrum, a hiker doing the Appalachian Trail in winter can count on cold followed by snow followed by cold. If you hike the High Sierra's John Muir Trail in summer, be prepared for hot days and cold nights, a possibility of rain, with snow unlikely. Conditions can change quickly and dramatically.

Campers and hikers should watch out for weather fronts, which are the contact points where two air masses clash. A warm front means that the leading edge of a moving air mass is warmer than the air mass it is overtaking and replacing. Stratus clouds are usually associated with this type of front. A cold front means that cold air is replacing relatively warmer air. The result is anvil-shaped cumulonimbus clouds moving in from the west or northwest, bringing violent, though brief, thunderstorms.

The mean temperature is technically the average of all temperatures day and night. More typically, it is the average high and low temperature for the day or month. If you are planning a camping vacation, check out month-by-month mean temperature and precipitation totals for your prospective destinations.

I did a lot of backpacking in New Zealand a few years ago. On my way home, I visited the island of Moorea, near Tahiti. I knew the average high temperature in January was eighty-nine degrees. What I didn't know was Moorea's mean rainfall, which, as it turns out, is a whopping 13.2 inches in January.

Precipitation or rainfall, measured in inches, is often listed as an annual total. For the camping family, it's more valuable to know the month-by-month totals. In California's Mediterranean climate, for example, you can count on almost no sea-level rainfall in the summer. But when I was planning a backpacking trip to Europe, I discovered that Ireland receives approximately the same amount of rain (lots) every month of the year.

Wind can be destructive. So could a complete lack of wind. Remove all the forces that propel the winds, theorizes one meteorologist, and air movement would die in nine to twelve days. With almost no exchange of heat, the tropics would fry and the upper latitudes would freeze. Eventually, human life would be erased from Earth.

Pay attention to the direction and intensity of winds, important clues in the prediction of weather. Wind also plays an important role in our well-being. Windchill is a measure of the cooling power of temperature and wind on your skin. Moving air has a chilling effect on the human body that makes the thermometer temperature seem lower. On a hot day, the cooling effect of air brushing against our bodies is pleasant. As the temperature drops, however, windchill can be dangerous. For example, a temperature of 5 degrees Fahrenheit (F.) combined with a light breeze of ten miles per hour equals a windchill temperature of -15 degrees F. This is a potentially critical drop (and one not measured by a conventional thermometer), for frostbite occurs much sooner at -15 F.

Clouds offer important clues to what weather will do. Cirrus clouds are the highest in the sky. They are indistinct, fuzzy clouds, composed of ice crystals, and are associated with fair weather, but only temporarily. Appearing as much as a thousand miles ahead of a front, they typically provide a few hours to two days' warning of an approaching storm. If you see cirrus clouds, keep an eye on the sky for signs of cloud buildup.

Stratus clouds come in waves, layers, or bands. When the waves are smooth and regular, expect fair, cool, weather; when the waves become irregular or break up into a buttermilk sky, a storm is probably brewing.

Cumulus clouds are lumpy and billowy with flat bottoms and puffy tops. Normally, they indicate fair weather. If, however, they billow upward, mass together, and darken into towering, anvil-shaped cumulonimbus clouds, a thunderstorm is imminent.

You can often forecast the weather by watching the evolution and progression of clouds.

Become a cloud watcher, if you aren't already. This is easy to do with young children. Their active imaginations make them expert players of the game called "What does that cloud look like?"

The temperature at which water vapor in the air condenses and dew (drops of water) begins to form is called the dew point. Air can hold only a certain amount of water vapor at a given temperature. When the temperature falls, excess vapor condenses onto everything from plants to cars. Because dew forms on cold, clear nights, it is a sign of fair weather.

Another factor to watch is the relative humidity, or the amount of moisture (water vapor) in the air compared with the total amount it can hold. Because warm air holds more water vapor than cold air, a relative humidity of 75 percent on a warm day is moister than a relative humidity of 75 percent on a cold day.

Humidity can affect activities and health. When the humidity approaches 100 percent, it may be difficult to get small twigs to burn. On the other hand, relative humidity below 20 percent can make dead grass highly flammable. High humidity saps strength ("it's not the heat, it's the humidity"), and some experts believe dryness may promote the growth of certain viruses. A moderate level, say 30 percent to 50 percent, is thought to be the most healthful and comfortable.

Finally, spend time with your children perusing a weather map. Learn the symbols and discuss what they mean. Compare yesterday's weather map with tomorrow's and next week's.

"Everybody talks about the weather, but nobody does anything about it." —Charles Dudley Warner

According to Don Haggerty, author of *Rhymes to Predict the Weather*, the most important variables to watch in predicting weather are barometer reading, cloud progression (rising or lowering ceiling), and wind shifts (veering or backing). It also doesn't hurt to know a few weather rhymes and what they mean:

1. *Red sky in the morning, sailor take warning; red sky at night, sailor's delight.* Fair weather involves high-pressure cells that are composed of dry, stagnant air filled with dust and haze. When the sun is low

in the sky, the dust causes light to be refracted (bent), making visible the red end of the spectrum. If the sunset is fiery, then a high-pressure pocket of air lies hundreds of miles to the west (the direction of the prevailing winds in the Northern Hemisphere) and has yet to arrive. A scarlet dawn indicates that high-pressure air has passed eastward, increasing the chances that the following weather will be wet.

2. *Hen's scratchings and mare's tails make tall ships carry low sails.* "Hen's scratchings and mare's tails" refers to those wispy high-altitude cirrus clouds, which typically follow tranquil weather and often indicate a low-pressure air mass is on its way. Watch the sky and, if a lower, thicker mass of clouds rolls in behind the mare's tails, remember that *"the lower they get, the nearer the wet."*

3. *A backing wind says storms are nigh. A veering wind will clear the sky.* A "backing wind" is one that is shifting counterclockwise (say, from westerly to southwesterly), while a "veering wind" is one that is shifting clockwise (southwesterly to westerly). In the Northern Hemisphere, prevailing fair-weather winds tend to blow from the west or north, foul-weather winds from the south, southeast, or east. If you notice the wind backing, expect worsening weather. In evaluating winds, trust cloud movement more than ground air.

4. *If with your nose you smell the day, stormy weather's on the way.* You hear people say, "Smells like rain today." Extra humidity helps transmit smells, and plants give off oils that are absorbed by soil, then released into the air when humidity exceeds 80 percent.

5. *Smoke rising high, clears the sky. When smoke descends, good weather ends.* Air gets colder with elevation. (The rate at which it gets colder is called the lapse rate.) If the area is dominated by a high-pressure system (lapse rate is high), the temperature will drop quickly with elevation and smoke will rise nicely. Low-pressure air has a low lapse rate. Smoke starts to rise, but the low lapse rate fails to propel it neatly upward. It flattens out, spreading like a blanket over the ground.

6. *When the dew is on the grass, rain will never come to pass.* A clear night will lower temperatures enough for humidity to condense as dew. If you find morning dew on the plants, expect fair weather. But *"when*

grass is dry before the morning light, look for rain before night." This is especially true if the warming trend is caused by increasing cloud cover.

7. *Ring around the moon, rain by noon. Ring around the sun, rain before night is done.* The most common halos are high cirrus clouds, which portend bad weather twelve to eighteen hours hence.

8. *When stars begin to muddle, the Earth becomes a puddle.* If your view of the stars becomes blurred, you either need glasses or bad weather is likely. Excessive twinkling, particularly if the stars appear blue, suggests increased humidity and/or high winds disturbing the upper atmosphere. Humid air absorbs red and green light but lets shorter-wavelength blue pass through.

9. *When the air gets light, the glass falls low. Batten down tight, for the winds will blow.* The "glass," of course, is a barometer, which measures air pressure. Stormy weather arrives in low-pressure air masses, resulting in a lower barometer reading.

10. *Rainbow to windward, foul fares the day. Rainbow to leeward, damp runs away.* With the damp air of a rainbow upwind, what you see is what you will get. When it is leeward, you've already got it and the storm may have passed.

11. *Swallows flying way up high means there's no rain in the sky.* In the high air pressure that accompanies fair weather, insects are carried aloft, as are the swallows that feed upon them.

RESOURCES

Rhymes to Predict the Weather by Don Haggerty (1985: Spring-Meadow Publishing, Seattle, WA)

The Weather Companion by Gary Lockhart (1988: John Wiley and Sons, New York)

8 How to Treat Wildlife like You'd Like to Be Treated

> *Animals have these advantages over man:*
> *they never hear the clock strike, they die without*
> *any idea of death, they have no theologians to*
> *instruct them, their last moments are not disturbed*
> *by unpleasant and unwelcome ceremonies,*
> *their funerals cost them nothing,*
> *and no one starts lawsuits over their wills.*
> *—Voltaire*

Children are fascinated by animals. They have animal dolls, animal games, animal heroes, and imaginary animal pals. They worship at the shrine of Kermit, Yogi, Bugs, Mickey, and Miss Piggy. Whether they are the type to torture, collect, kill, or just admire animals, whether they go on as adults to shoot animals with gun or camera, they likely won't be apathetic about wildlife.

Sharing the belief of wildlife maven Marty Stouffer that the more we know about nature the less we have to fear, I hereby present mini profiles of some of the animals you will see, or wonder about seeing, in the wilderness. I have undoubtedly ignored animals that you might see in your area. I urge you to do the research and fill in the blanks.

BLACK BEAR

Early Americans had a strictly utilitarian view of black bears. Their hides were used for clothing and bedding, their rich meat for food, their fat for frying and healing ointment. Hunting and logging decimated bear populations and habitat until twentieth-century game laws protected them, permitting a partial comeback.

Normally solitary and retiring, black bears live in dense thickets, caves, and tree hollows. In their natural state, they eat nuts, berries, insects, and small mammals. Only recently have they developed a palate for freeze-dried backpacking food.

Excluding polar bears, you can divide the family in North America into black and brown (grizzly or Kodiak) bears. Color is an unreliable guide, as black bears range from black to cinnamon and browns from pale gold to almost black. A better clue is geography. In the United States, if you encounter a bear outside Alaska or Yellowstone or Glacier National Parks, odds are it's a black bear. Black bears are about half as large as browns and a fraction as cranky. In the recorded history of Yosemite National Park, for example, no one has ever been killed by a black bear.

The North American black bear spends the winter in near hibernation, sleeping away the better part of seven months. Female bears rouse themselves long enough to give birth to one, two, or three cubs, each weighing a mere eight to ten ounces. They remain in the den with their sleeping mother, nursing and dozing until spring.

Black bears would no doubt do well in an animal decathlon. They are fast (up to thirty-two miles per hour), powerful (able to break into a car trunk), agile (able to climb a quaking aspen in seconds), and capable swimmers. They are intelligent, curious, and always hungry. Proper food storage is essential to assure the continued wildness of these magnificent creatures. Moreover, because chronically troublesome bears are sometimes exterminated, protecting your food from bears may save their lives.

Yosemite officials suggest the following precautions around bears:

• Use food lockers where available. Keep them closed and latched except when putting in or taking out food. Though bears tend to be most active in the evenings and at night, they may be roaming about at any hour and may even enter your camp when you are present, though that is rare.

• If you are car camping and lockers are not available, all food and food containers should be stored in the trunk of a vehicle. In a vehicle with no trunk, cover food and food containers and keep them out of sight with all windows and vents closed.

Bears occasionally have broken into car trunks, probably driven by strong-smelling food not stored in an ice chest. If you fear such an attack, wipe stove fuel around the edge of the trunk.

• Do not store food in a tent or in the open. Seal it in containers to minimize odors.

• Store toothpaste, suntan lotion, insect repellent, cosmetics, and vitamin C tablets as you would food.

• Keep a clean camp. Deposit all garbage in bear-resistant containers before going to bed or leaving camp. Wash the dishes immediately after use.

• In the backcountry, counterbalance two sacks (sleeping-bag stuff sacks are ideal) containing all food and related items over a branch so that they hang at least fourteen feet above the ground, ten feet from the trunk, and five feet below the branch.

• Do not allow bears to approach you or enter your camp. If one approaches, bang pots, clap hands, throw rocks or pine cones from a safe distance, or yell insulting remarks. Never try to retrieve food taken by a bear.

• Do not feed or approach bears. This may seem obvious, but some parents have tried to put children on the backs of bears for photos.

• Do not get in between a bear and her cubs. Most black bear attacks are motivated by what Mom sees as a threat to her cubs.

Between 1960 and 1980, black bears injured more than five hundred people in North America; 90 percent of these injuries were minor. Grizzly bear attacks accounted for fewer than two hundred injuries between 1900 and 1980. Why such a discrepancy if grizzlies are more aggressive? Because most wilderness recreation takes place in black bear country, and they outnumber grizzlies by more than ten to one.

Camping in Yosemite Valley, as we often did when I was young, our evening entertainment often included a visit to the open dump, where we watched the bears scavenge for dinner. Sitting on our car on a warm summer evening, parked next to other like-minded tourists, the scene suggested the preamble to a drive-in movie. As dusk deepened, about a dozen bears would amble out to begin their nightly ritual.

This desultory prowl over mounds of garbage was an undignified affair, to be sure, but as a kid I didn't see it that way. The dump afforded me the chance to study bears in a way that would have been impossible if I were engaged in panicky retreat. Then one day the government concluded that the dumps were good for neither man nor beast. Today open dumps have been replaced by bearproof dumpsters.

GRIZZLY BEAR

In 1804, as Lewis and Clark moved west through Wyoming, they heard recurring tales—tall tales, they assumed—of a huge bear with a massive head and ferocious manner. They were skeptical because they were well-acquainted with the black bear and found him inoffensive and easily felled with a well-placed shot. They soon had another opinion about the grizzly, with Lewis writing: "The wonderful power of life which these animals possess renders them dreadful. . . . We had rather encounter two Indians than meet a single brown bear."

Besides size—a large grizzly weighs about 850 pounds, a large black bear closer to 400—grizzlies differ from black bears by their longer claws, whitish ("grizzled") hairs on upper parts, and a high shoulder hump, which is actually a knot of powerful muscles that drives the front legs.

The grizzly was given the scientific name *Ursus horribilis*—the "horrible bear"—by a man who had never seen one and who relied on the testimony of another man who, though he too had never seen one, boldly wrote that the grizzly "is the enemy of man and literally thirsts for human blood." This unfortunate hyperbole, along with the fact that people are occasionally mauled by browns, all but doomed the grizzly in the lower forty-eight.

Grizzlies do kill people, about one every other year, but with the possible exception of tigers, there is little evidence of any "man-eating" animals. However, bear attacks are lurid by nature and make good news, infuriating antigrizzly forces. In response to two deadly bear attacks in south-central Alaska in July 1992, seventeen bears were exterminated.

While it was once the most abundant bear, ranging from Alaska to northern Mexico, hunting and habitat destruction have reduced the grizzly's range to Alaska, western Canada, and six tiny enclaves in the West, including Glacier and Yellowstone National Parks. The last grizzly in California went down in 1924. Since Lewis and Clark explored the West, the brown population in the continental United States has declined from about one hundred thousand to fewer than one thousand. Five thousand to ten thousand brown bears still prowl the huge state of Alaska.

> When humans clash with grizzly bears, the bears invariably lose. In the first eighty years of this century, grizzly bears killed fourteen people in the lower forty-eight states. During just five of those years—1968 to 1973—180 grizzlies were exterminated, most within or near national parks.

If you travel to grizzly country:
- Be alert to bear signs, such as scat, claw marks, and prints.
- When selecting a campsite in bear country—especially grizzly country—avoid camping right next to a trail or stream, as bears favor those areas when searching for food.
- Sleep in a tent.
- Do not feed any bears, deliberately or accidentally. The bear you feed becomes a little less self-sufficient, a little more dependent on humans. In the absence of trees or man-made protection, you can place your food on top of a large rock, which may be too slippery for the grizzly to climb.
- Never surprise a bear—they hate surprises. In grizzly country, make noise on the trail. Sing songs, tell stories, recite Tibetan chants or bad poetry, or tell stories. Tie a bell to your pack or periodically blow a whistle. You might try a loud, suggestive rendition of "The Bear Went over the Mountain."

Black bears and grizzlies have quite different temperaments—and tempers—but they both appreciate human food.

• Never charge a grizzly (as if you didn't know).

• If you do spot a grizzly, circle around it in a wide arc, staying downwind, for bears have an excellent sense of smell. (Just assume they do everything better than you do.)

• Consider traveling in a large group. No bear attack has ever been recorded on a party of six or more. Glacier National Park is considering a rule restricting hiking in certain areas to parties of four or more.

In the unlikely event of a grizzly attack, quickly choose one of two alternatives:

• Climb a tree to a height of thirty feet or more. Grizzlies do not climb as well as black bears. Don't worry if you don't climb well; fear is a powerful motivator.

• Play dead and hope the bear stops seeing you as a threat. Recommended dead positions are lying on your stomach with hands behind the head or lying on your side in the fetal position, knees tight to chin.

I once met a graduate student working for a leading grizzly expert. He was a professor, and for years he had preached, "When attacked by a grizzly, don't run. Play dead." Then one day, in Yellowstone, the professor was attacked by a grizzly. He did what came naturally—he ran. The bear also did what came naturally. He caught and mauled the professor. "He's still into grizzlies," said the student.

BEAVER

No animal has had a greater impact on world exploration, history, and economics than the North American beaver. Once extremely abundant (save the deserts of the Southwest and the Arctic tundra), the beaver was exploited to near extinction for its rich, dense fur. History turned against the beaver in 1638, when King Charles II of Britian decreed that beaver fur had to be used in hats. Much New World exploration was fueled by the demand for beaver fur in the late eighteenth and early nineteenth centuries. Today, beaver hats are as passé as muskets, and North America's largest rodent—up to sixty-six pounds—once again ranges far and wide. Beavers are of particular fascination because they display so many human traits, such as family stability, homes (lodges and burrows), food storage, transportation networks (ponds and canals), and complex communication systems.

Still, it is the beaver's habit of building dams that really piques our interest. These torpedo-shaped animals are second only to humans (a distant second) in their ability to alter the environment. They begin by constructing an underwater foundation of mud and stone, then gnaw down trees and drag or float cuttings to the dam site, leaving behind their trademark foot-high cone-shaped stumps. As a pond forms behind the dam, two beavers build a stick-and-mud lodge with underwater entrances and an inside platform above water level. Here they remain much of the day, emerging at dusk to eat plants or to fell some more trees. In late summer or early fall, the cuttings are stored in an underwater food pile to be eaten in winter. Babies, called kits, are born in spring and stay in the home pond until they are two years old. At birth, the kits are mobile, with a full coat of fur and open eyes. Development is swift. The young can swim within hours and build dams within months.

Over the years, beavers continue to add mud and sticks, making their dam higher and longer; some have reached 330 feet in length and 10 feet in height. Dams provide beavers with protection against predators, better exploitation of food resources, and environmental stability. The flooding from their dams creates habitats for other wildlife, including birds, fish, insects, and moose.

The beaver has some fascinating anatomical quirks that permit a semiaquatic life in heavy construction. When the animal dives, its nose and ears close tight and a translucent membrane covers the eyes. The throat is blocked by the back of the tongue, and the lips close around the incisors so the animal can gnaw and carry sticks underwater without choking. A large paddlelike tail provides both steering and power; it can be flexed up and down to produce a rapid burst of speed. The fur is waterproof. Their four large incisors never stop growing; they allow a beaver to gnaw through a sixteen-inch-diameter tree in just one night.

If the desired tree is far from water, beavers have been known to bring the water to the tree. They will dig a canal, sometimes hundreds of yards long, and float the timber out. If the tree is near water, they will try to notch it so that it falls into the water, facilitating transport. Alas, like lumberjacks, beavers sometimes miscalculate and are crushed beneath falling timber.

BOBCAT

This relatively small spotted cat with the Mr. Spock ears is the most common nondomesticated feline in North America. Having adapted well to the presence of man, its numbers are increasing in some places (unlike its close relative, the lynx). Though rabbits and hares are the bobcat's usual food, this cat will also eat other small mammals, reptiles, or birds, and has even been known to capture bats from caves.

Cats larger than a tabby tend to unnerve people, and the bobcat, when cornered, can be ferocious, screaming, spitting, hissing, and lashing out with its sharp claws. A single hunting dog is rarely able to subdue one cat; bobcats caught in steel traps have been known to fight off coyotes. Still, this solitary, secretive animal, the largest of which reach seventy pounds, is no threat to wilderness lovers. Chances are, you'll never even know it's there, but isn't it nice to think that it might be?

CHIPMUNK

A chipmunk is a ground squirrel, distinguished by a bushless tail and stripes on its back that extend to its face. Unlike tree squirrels, which use their bushy tail for balance as they run and leap, chipmunks would find such a tail a liability when diving into burrows.

Although they will climb trees, mostly to escape predators and find food, chipmunks spend most of their time at or below ground level. They dig extensive burrows up to twelve feet long and three feet deep, which usually include a nest, dump, latrine (they are fastidious), pantry, and some concealed entrances and exits. They generally use the same burrow year after year, with regular remodeling. The digging is seldom evident above ground.

The pantry can hold up to half a bushel of nuts and other foods, all carried there in the chipmunk's remarkable cheeks, which hang like saddlebags on both sides of its neck. One patient researcher counted 3,700 blueberry seeds in the pouches of a chipmunk that looked as though it had a bad case of mumps.

When chipmunks get worried, they freeze. They can remain motionless for a long time, relying on acute sight and hearing to escape danger.

Lacking seeds or nuts, chipmunks will adapt. They've been known to eat mushrooms, moles, grasshoppers, small frogs, salamanders, and small bird eggs. Their elaborate grooming may be a clever defense against predators that rely on scent to find prey, or it may be a reaction to the ticks and fleas that bedevil the animal. Indeed, bubonic plague has been found among chipmunks, leading National Park Service authorities to recommend avoiding all rodents.

COYOTE

A member of the dog family, the coyote, with its pointed muzzle, long ears, slender legs, and rhythmic gait bears a strong resemblance to the wolf and the dog. It is distinguished by a long, bushy tail that droops when it runs.

It's rare to see coyotes in the wild but not so to hear them. Their unique howl is a symbol of the Wild West. Their yipping is followed by a long, quavering wail that chills your blood the first time you hear it. Often other coyotes respond, resulting in a group sing that is a lullaby to some and disturbing to others. Relax and enjoy it, and convey that response to your children. There is no danger, it probably won't last long, and it sure beats the caterwauling of alley cats.

Mammals, including carrion, generally make up about 90 percent of the coyote's diet. They also feed on fruit, insects, and barnyard animals. It is the last that provokes the ire of humans. Stockmen hate coyotes with the passion early settlers reserved for wolves. In 1915, the federal government began slaughtering coyotes and wolves. In the next thirty-two years, nearly two million coyotes were exterminated.

A coyote may not get any respect, but it has not only survived but thrived while the wolf has been all but exterminated. One of the few predators to extend its range in the twentieth century, it now roams from northern Alaska to Costa Rica.

Coyotes have many qualities we admire:

They are smart. At bumblebee nests, the coyote will wave its tail until bees swarm out to investigate, then stick in its nose and eat the honey.

They are tough. More than one coyote caught in a steel trap has been known to drag the contraption for miles, even pausing to capture a gopher or two en route. If it cannot pull loose from the trap, it may gnaw off its own paw to escape.

They are fast. Coyotes have been clocked at close to fifty miles per hour in a short sprint, and thirty to thirty-five over longer distances.

They are devoted to family. The male will bring food to its pregnant wife, play with the pups, teach them to hunt, even present itself as a decoy to lure men and hounds away from the family lair.

They are resourceful. Coyotes have been known to work collectively on a deer kill, and some have mated with domestic dogs. They will raid garbage cans if necessary.

Though they are extending their range, they represent no threat to campers, unless you ride into the wilderness on sheepback. As John Muir once said, "Coyotes . . . are beautiful animals, and, although cursed by man, are beloved by God. Their sole fault is that they are fond of mutton."

DEER

The deer is the large mammal that you and your kids have the best chance of seeing in the wild. Say "deer" in North America and you mean either white-tailed or mule deer, although elk, moose, and caribou also belong to that family of hoofed animals that shed their antlers each year.

Dusk and early morning are the best time to see deer; during the day, they lay low and digest their food. In national parks, where they are pro-

(PHOTO BY WILLIAM J. BOGA)

The large mammal you and yours are most likely to see is the deer.

tected, they will often browse for twigs or buds on the edge of your camp. If you wish to prolong their stay, sit still and observe; if you must move, go slowly. Enjoy the quiet grace of these animals.

Only male deer have antlers. Contrary to myth, you can't tell the age of a deer by the size of the antlers or the number of tines. Antler development depends on nutrition, not age.

Deer tend to move to lower elevations before winter and back up to higher elevations in spring. They rut in autumn, when males battle for, and associate briefly with, females. Spotted fawns, usually twins, are born in spring. Young females may stay with their mother for two years, but males leave in the first year.

Don't feed deer. The salt, sugar, and preservatives in human food can make them sick. If deer become too dependent on humans for food, they stop foraging. Also, losing their natural fear of humans can be fatal when they migrate to lower elevations outside of national parks and become easy targets for hunters. Although deer seem tame, they are actually wild and unpredictable. A few years ago a five-year-old boy was killed by a deer in Yosemite. He was feeding the animal with his parents' blessing when it bolted, raking him with its antlers.

FROG AND TOAD

These amphibians lead double lives, typically inhabiting fresh water early on and then changing to forms that can move around on land. As adults, frogs and toads are distinguished by their short, squat bodies, four limbs, powerful hind legs, and lack of tail. Frogs generally have smooth skins and are aquatic; toads generally have warty skin and are more terrestrial. Most true toads have bony ridges on top of their heads and swellings behind their eyes that secrete toxic fluids. Their warts exude a similar toxin but are not poisonous to the touch.

Frogs and toads of the same species may be different colors, depending on environment, temperature, and humidity; the cooler and damper the climate, the darker their color. Female frogs and toads tend to be larger than males. Males attract them with song, then cling to them and fertilize their eggs as they shed them into the water. The eggs hatch into polliwogs—round-bellied, long-tailed larvae. Eventually, in one of nature's most dramatic transformations, tadpole becomes frog or toad. How long a tadpole stays a tadpole varies greatly with species and climate. Desert-dwelling spadefoot toads make the change in about two weeks, but the North American bullfrog may not metamorphose for several years in the coldest parts of its range.

Most frogs and toads are nocturnal, resting during the day in burrows, in trees, or under leaves, undetected until they hop out from under your feet. At night, especially during the spring/summer mating season, males get together for a group croak. Male bullfrogs sing solos. With practice, you can identify species by their calls. You can buy recordings of frog sounds, as you can for birds.

FOX

Say "fox" and most people think "cunning." No wonder. In Aesop's fable, the cunning fox outwits the stork; in the Uncle Remus stories, Br'er Fox is the wily adversary of Br'er Rabbit. The popular tales of many countries portray the fox as sneaky-smart. Indeed, with its sharp eyes and sensitive ears, the fox is seldom surprised. During its waking hours, it is constantly on the alert.

The fox is rarely seen because of its ability to evade detection. It is an intelligent, resourceful animal, arguably the most widely dispersed and adaptable of all carnivores. Its range is enormous, from the arctic to city center, and its diet is diverse. Being a true opportunist, it will eat whatever is available, from fish to rodents and from fruit to plant life. It is smart enough to cache prey and remember where it's hidden.

Foxes communicate by scent and sound. They define territory with strategically placed feces and urine and can distinguish the scent of their own urine from that of strangers. The vocalizations—wild yapping and a resonant howl—are most common during breeding season and when enemies intrude.

Until recently, foxes were the number one transmitter of rabies (now it's raccoons). Millions of foxes were slaughtered in an attempt to control the disease, but neither rabies nor foxes was wiped out. So resilient is the species that populations can withstand 75 percent mortality without further declining; so resourceful that two thousand foxes supposedly roam the streets of London.

INSECTS

Iridescent dragonflies, spectacularly patterned butterflies, and dainty little ladybugs are all fascinating examples of insects. There are 700,000 species worldwide.

Although most insects are neither helpful nor harmful to humans, we waste little love or respect on them. According to a University of Arizona study cited by Sue Hubbell in *A Book of Bugs*, 90 percent of respondents said they were either "acutely afraid of" or "heartily disliked" insects. Excluding the universally loved ladybug, less than 1 percent of Americans say they like bugs. We spend $3.5 billion a year in the United States on chemical warfare against them. How effective is it? Despite their size, there are 300 pounds of bugs out there for every pound of person.

Children are usually fascinated by bugs; they know what it's like to be small. You can help them appreciate their incredible complexity. Share with them the dragonfly's astonishing eyes, each a glittering mosaic of thousands of tiny facets; the defensive odor of the stinkbug; and the camouflage technique of the walkingstick. Marvel at the complex society created by ants and bees and wonder at the metamorphosis of beetles and butterflies, who go through four distinct life stages—egg, larva (caterpillar, worm, or grub), pupa, and adult.

> *"We hope that, when the insects take over the world, they will remember with gratitude how we took them along on all our picnics."*   *—Bill Vaughan*

Some deserving entries in the insect record book:

• Most prolific: There are 17,000 species of advanced beetles in North America alone. If every plant and animal species sent a representative to a convention, one of every five delegates would be a beetle.

• Heaviest: Worldwide, there are 8,800 known species of ants. Weighed on a scale, ants would total 10 percent of the mass of the world's land animals.

• Brightest: Attempting to attract a mate, the firefly converts 95 percent of its available chemical energy into light but only 5 percent into heat.

• Best vision: The dragonfly has huge compound eyes with nearly thirty thousand facets—each a complete eye in itself. It can detect the slightest movement forty feet away.

• Best long-jumpers: Fleas can soar 150 times their own length, the equivalent of a six-foot man leaping nine hundred feet.

• Most tireless: Fleas again, which have been recorded taking off thirty thousand times without pause. (Talk about tireless; what about the scientist who recorded those jumps?)

• Most flappable: The common housefly can flap its wings at more than twenty thousand beats per minute.

• Most persistent: The migration of millions of orange-and-black monarch butterflies to winter shelters in Mexico, California, Florida, and Texas is one of the remarkable feats of nature. The monarchs that arrive are the great-great-grandchildren of the ones that began the migration six months earlier.

• Most insidious defense: The larvae (caterpillars) of the milkweed butterfly feed on milkweed, which makes them toxic to birds and other predators.

• Best hustle technique: The male black-tipped hanging fly attracts a mate by dangling a plump housefly before a female. If the gift is too small, she rejects it, for it must contain sufficient protein to sustain egg production. If it's a go, the flies mate while she dines.

MOOSE

The largest member of the deer family, the moose can weigh up to fifteen hundred pounds and stand seven and a half feet high at the shoulder. Bulls have a mane, a "bell" of skin hanging from their throat, and antlers (shed annually) that may weigh up to seventy pounds and spread seven feet. Cows lack the mane, the bell, and the antlers. Both sexes have an overhanging snout that gives them a cartoonish look.

Unspotted calves, often twins, are born in spring. Weak at birth, these gangly creatures remain hidden and inactive for several days. Calves are vulnerable to wolves and bears, but few predators can overcome a healthy adult moose. They also are adept in water and run well in snow.

Bullwinkle notwithstanding, moose are not party animals; they are solitary or hang in small groups, limiting their population to one or two

(Photo by William J. Boga)

You and your children will never forget seeing your first moose.

per square mile. When they do get together, it's usually for antler-to-antler combat in autumn, when the bulls are searching for mates.

In 1986, a moose wandered onto a farm in Shrewsbury, Vermont, and became infatuated with a Hereford cow named Jessica. For the next seventy-six days, as the world watched, the moose, known as Joshua, nuzzled and mooned over Jessica. The unfulfilled romance came to an end when Joshua's antler's (and his desire) dropped off.

More recently, a moose fell head over antlers in love with a plastic statue of a deer. That affair ended when the statue's head fell off.

MOUNTAIN LION

Also known as cougar, puma, and panther, the mountain lion is moderately plentiful in the West, scarce across the Midwest, and rare as mango trees in the East. The Florida panther is the most critically endangered large mammal in North America.

This lithe cat comes in shades of reddish brown, golden brown, and dull gray. Its throat and chin are white. Weighing up to 120 pounds when mature, it is big because it is the most adept large carnivore in North America (bears, less choosy, are omnivores), a specialized killing machine. The mountain lion's teeth, claws, speed, and elusiveness are designed to bring down fresh meat. Deer really makes a lion drool. Usually solitary and nocturnal, the mountain lion hunts by stalking and rushing or by pouncing from trees and overhanging rocks. Like other large cats, it usually kills by biting the neck of its prey.

Cougar attacks on humans can be serious but are quite rare. During the past century, more than seven hundred people have been killed by lightning for every one killed by a mountain lion. A young girl was seriously mauled in Southern California in 1986, apparently by a lion raised in captivity and released into the wild. In April 1992, a cougar pounced on a Sacramento man dressed in camouflage crouching next to a turkey decoy and blowing a turkey call.

After such attacks, there is a wave of sentiment to wipe out the cougar population. But California biologist Paul Beier, who has examined records of unprovoked cougar attacks in the United States and Canada between 1890 and 1990, brings some reason to the argument. He found fifty-three documented attacks, of which thirty occurred in Canada's British Columbia, and only nine were fatal. Nine human fatalities in a hundred years. Not many compared to the forty or so people who die each year from bee stings, or the eighty from lightning strikes, or the forty thousand killed on the highways each year.

Despite its record for good behavior, the mountain lion has long been viewed as little more than vermin, something to be unthinkingly exterminated. The prevalent attitude was summed up by Theodore Roosevelt, who wrote, "Lord of stealthy murder, facing his doom with a heart both craven and cruel." With such a reputation, an animal that once prowled the entire continent was soon reduced to a few wild spots in the West, usually in rugged high country.

Actually, not only do mountain lions rarely attack people, but researchers have also concluded that they will never overpopulate the countryside (because of their territoriality) and that they do not threaten big-game herds. They prey on the young, the old, and the sick, leaving alone those of breeding age.

Environmentalists and animal lovers have won widespread protection for cougars, and every state except Texas now regulates the killing of the animal. The government thinks cougar numbers are increasing, but many environmentalists believe this is illusory because their increasing contact with humans is due to more homes being built on land where the big cats once lived by themselves.

If you'd prefer not to see any large cats, make noise as you hike in cougar country. Keep your pets and kids close by (better yet, keep your pets out of the backcountry). Control food odors and other enticing smells. Mountain lions are intimidated by height, so get as big and scary as possible. Take off your pack and put it in front of you. Spread out your jacket like wings. Hoist your children onto your shoulders. Speak in a loud, firm voice. Avoid direct eye contact by looking off to the side, monitoring the cat's movements in your peripheral vision.

If the lion continues to threaten, throw rocks, tree limbs, or tent poles, or jab with a walking stick. If attacked, try to stay on your feet. Don't run or play dead, but rather stand firm, yell, and fight back. This would be a good time to use that canister of hot-pepper spray you carry just for this purpose. Above all, be aggressive. Lions aren't used to their prey poking them in the eye or kicking them in the groin. Most people who have resisted a lion attack have lived to tell about it.

MOUSE

North American mice and rats are really an array of 366 species. The largest species are no longer than one foot, not counting tail.

Mice reproduce rapidly, giving birth to some of the few ugly babies in the animal kingdom. They are hairless, pink, and rubbery-looking.

Put a mouse in a cage with an exercise wheel and it will log up to twenty-seven miles a day. Driven by instinct, it does most of its running when hungry or in heat, or as a substitute for its exploratory migrations in the wild.

Enjoy these critters from a distance. They frequently carry disease.

OPOSSUM

The opossum is North America's only marsupial (pouched mammal). Thirteen days after breeding, it bears litters of up to eighteen premature kits, each no larger than a honeybee. Weighing little more than an ounce total, the whole brood could fit comfortably inside a large serving spoon. The young are so immature their skin is translucent, their internal organs visible. Immediately after birth, the tiny creatures begin wriggling up into Mom's pouch in search of a life-sustaining nipple. As Mrs. Possum only has twelve nipples, the race is a textbook case of survival of the fittest.

The twelve winners remain attached to a nipple for a month or two, then move onto Mom's back, which is home for another few weeks. At the tender age of three months, they are sent off to make their way in the world.

As their fifty teeth (more than any other North American land mammal) develop, the young switch from mother's milk to an incredibly diverse diet of insects, birds' eggs, grain, mushrooms, fruit, and carrion. Such versatility permits them to live close to humans and assures the success of the species, if not the individual. While opossums have extended their range almost a million square miles in the past fifty years, the individual in the wild rarely lives to see its third birthday. One reason: They are good climbers but slow afoot and easy targets for cars.

Opossums are distinctive looking, with their pink nose and pointed snout, but they often go unnoticed because they are passive and mostly nocturnal. And, yes, an opossum will defend itself by "playing possum"— curling into a limp heap and entering a catatonic trance that can last as long as six hours. Though an attacker may poke, bite, or pick it up, the opossum will not move. As most predators prefer to eat only what they kill, this tack often saves the opossum's life. Many scientists believe the animal is too stupid to do this deliberately but instead faints from fear, its nervous system overloaded to the point of temporary paralysis.

PORCUPINE

Contrary to myth, porcupines cannot shoot their quills. They don't need to; they are formidable enough as it is. If this nocturnal rodent perceives you as a threat, it will turn its back, raise about 30,000 quills, and rattle them like swords. If you don't get the hint, this twelve-pound walking pincushion will start backing toward you. If you're fool enough to stick around, it will swing its tail with enough force to embed hundreds of quills in your skin. The fight is over and the porcupine has won. Don't feel bad. You were stupid, yes, but quills have even been discovered in polar bears.

Removing the hollow quills is excruciating, but leaving them in can be fatal. Body heat and moisture cause them to expand, and muscle movement forces them deeper into the skin, anchoring each shaft and assuring that if the quills are removed, flesh will be, too.

A few hardy humans regard roast porcupine as a delicacy, but one does not eat a quilled animal without risk. Doctors once operated on a man complaining of severe stomach pains, only to find that his intestine had been punctured by a quill consumed in a porcupine sandwich four days earlier. The man died.

Although porcupines have keen touch, hearing, and smell, they are extremely nearsighted. They supposedly feed on bark, twigs, leaves, and buds, but my brief encounter with a porcupine did not confirm that. One night while sleeping in an open tent in the High Sierra, with my buddy Jeff sleeping outside, I was awakened by movement. I shone a flashlight into the forest, spotlighting an animal about the size of a small dog shuffling slowly away from me. A porcupine! Seeing the light, he turned, cast me a look of utter disdain, then continued on his way. In the morning, I discovered he'd devoured almost a square foot of my foam sleeping pad. "That can't be good for him," I said. "And it's sure not good for me."

"You think you got troubles," said Jeff, with an edge to his voice. "The bastard ate the tongue of my boot."

RACCOON

These cute little ring-tailed, bandit-faced beggars are transcontinental in range and live in rural, suburban, and forested areas from southern Canada to Central America. They are, in short, everywhere.

They usually make their dens in hollow logs or holes in trees, but they may also inhabit deserted buildings. They prefer woods near streams or lakes, which can supply much of their food. This often puts them close to humans, who also like to live near water. That doesn't seem to bother the raccoons. They boldly approach people for handouts in campgrounds and backyards.

Raccoons have long been noted for "washing" their food before eating, but revisionist scientists claim that this behavior reflects the animal's natural habit of finding food in water.

Raccoons are omnivorous in the extreme. When not in search of handouts, they will forage at night for frogs, crayfish, fish, birds, eggs, fruits, vegetables, and insects. Because they are cute and unperturbed by human presence, people go out of their way to feed them. That can be a fatal mistake.

Raccoons, though cute as the dickens, are the number one rabies carrier.

(Photo by William J. Boga)

Though they often appear friendly and passive, raccoons can be surly. Family fights are common, sometimes degenerating into a group brawl, complete with snarling, clawing, and biting. Although the male is polygamous, the female won't take just any mate. Once she has made up her mind, she refuses to have a relationship with another male that season. Raccoons mate in the winter and babies are born about nine weeks later. Dad takes no part in raising the family.

With mother's help, the young quickly learn the art of survival. She leads them to water, where they learn to catch fish and explore for frogs and water insects. They search for grubs in rotting logs and eggs in birds' nests. They learn how to catch grasshoppers and mice. In late summer and early fall, they sample wild grapes, manzanita berries, elderberries, and other fruit. They carry most of their edibles to water and wash or dunk them before they eat.

During the training period, the mother raccoon must be on the lookout for hungry bobcats and cougars. However, she is a fierce defender of her young and few enemies will confront her. Mom stays with her brood through the first winter, after which she goes her separate way.

My friend Tom described an incident with raccoons and children that suggests the risks of overwarning children.

"Jean [his wife] and I were in Missouri, staying with Jean's sister. We decided to take her two kids car camping. Just before dark, we took a walk and saw the first raccoon. The kids had been into playing with the wildlife—catching bugs, stalking chipmunks—and I didn't want them doing that with the raccoons. So I told them, 'Raccoons are dangerous. They have sharp teeth and they can bite. If they're cornered or scared, they can be mean. They could literally tear your arm off.'

"I expected that to take care of the problem of kids playing with raccoons. That night, we were hit with as large a raccoon infestation as I've ever seen. At least a half-dozen of them were coming close to the fire and the tent, running around the cars, running on top of the cars. Courtney, the five-year-old girl, was absolutely terrified. She sat totally quiet, wouldn't answer anybody's questions. She might have been scared anyway, but it's clear my raccoon speech had a big impact."

SKUNK

While rattlesnakes, black widow spiders, and grizzly bears get heaps of hype, far less attention is paid to the unique defense system of striped and spotted skunks.

Skunks generally live in burrows, though spotted skunks might live in deserted barns or hollow trees. Both breeds are nocturnal and employ odor as a defensive weapon. By the time a skunk finally sprays, you have already had several warnings. It begins with a little stamping of the front paws, quickly escalating to hissing and shaking the head from side to side. When at last the skunk raises its tail (the spotted skunk does a reverse handstand with a high degree of difficulty), it is too late for reason. Head for the hills.

If you get a bad jump, the skunk may just hit you between the eyes with a steady stream of mercaptan, a potent glow-in-the-dark fluid that in one form is mixed with natural gas to make it detectable. Up to a dozen feet, it has the accuracy of a Western gunslinger. Once mercaptan soaks into fur, hair, or skin, it not only makes the victim sick but also can cause temporary blindness. Humans typically become teary-eyed and nauseated.

If you or your pet does get sprayed, you can buy an over-the-counter de-skunking solution at a pet store, but nothing neutralizes skunk odor better than bathing in tomato juice. Those stinky clothes, though, will have to be buried or burned; washing will never remove all traces of odor.

This skunk story was sent to *Backpacker* magazine by Bill Dvorak of Dvorak Expeditions: "We were taking a group of city kids from Denver out into the backcountry. For many of them it was their first trip, and they didn't always follow the rules. I told them not to bring food in the tent, but one girl stuck a big bag of M&Ms next to her pillow for a snack. About midnight, a skunk got in the tent and the counselor, still awake next to the girl, froze with fright. She watched it climb over the sleeping girl, tear open the bag of candy, and proceed to sit down on top of her and eat the whole bag. She said later she didn't know if she should chase it out and risk being sprayed or just roll over and hope it went away. She rolled over and, sure enough, it did go away."

My friend Jim had a nasty brush with both raccoons and skunks all in one night. I was there but slept through the action. We were camping together at Bar Harbor, Maine, and Jim and I sat up late one night drinking wine around the campfire while our significant others slept. "I think I consumed a record amount of wine that night," Jim recalls. "Anyway, sometime in the middle of the night, our Afghan hound, Maggie, dived into our tent, barking and madly rubbing her eyes on our sleeping bags. Sheila, who was pregnant at the time, shouted that Maggie had been sprayed by a skunk. Maggie's eyes were burning, my head was splitting, and in the dark and confusion, I tried to shove her outside through the tent window. This provoked several nasty comments from my wife. When I finally got Maggie outside, I tied her to the closest tree. In a couple of minutes, she was barking again. I'd tied her to a tree that had two baby raccoons in its branches. Momma raccoon was nearby freaking out. With the dog and the skunk and the raccoons and the wine, there wasn't much sleep that night."

SNAKE

Nothing provokes the startle response in a hiker faster than the sight of a snake—any snake. Intellectually, we know or should know that most snakes are benign. In North America only the rattlesnake, the copperhead, the cottonmouth (water moccasin), and the coral snake are venomous. Yet slithering reptiles, really legless lizards, are universally reviled.

Snakes are distinguished mostly by what they don't have: legs and eyelids. There are no vegetarian snakes. They are among the most successful creatures on Earth and inhabit every continent except Antarctica. There are more than 2,700 kinds, from the four-inch thread snake to the thirty-two-foot reticulated python. On cool days, many snakes like to warm their cold blood in the sun; when temperatures are high, they seek shade. They are most active when temperatures are moderate.

Even a poisonous snake doesn't always inject its venom. The amount of poison entering a victim's bloodstream can vary from none to a potentially lethal dose. Fifteen percent of rattlesnake bites are not poisonous and another 15 percent are minor.

Like most sensible animals, snakes want no part of man. Except for rattlesnakes, which have an early warning system, most catch your attention only when they are slithering away. When I was nineteen, my hiking partner and I surprised a four-foot rattlesnake on the trail. The snake rattled a warning, but we were upon it before we could react. Even then, the snake sought only escape. Alas, my partner, a macho youth, found a tree limb, beat the snake to a pulp, and cut off its rattle for a trophy.

Chances are slim that you'll die at the fangs of a snake. Of the forty-five thousand snake bites reported in the United States every year (most of which are inflicted on snake handlers), only about eight thousand are venomous. Of those, fewer than twenty are fatal. According to Dr. Findlay Russell, professor of toxicology at the University of Arizona, most venomous bites occur in the South and Southwest, including California.

SPIDER

The spider has never bounced back from the bad press it garnered after frightening Little Miss Muffet away. Even the book and movie *Charlotte's Web*, which elevated a spider to heroine, couldn't undo the damage. Today, spiders are blamed for just about every unexplained bite or swelling.

A dose of reality: Of the estimated 150,000 species of spiders on Earth, only about a dozen are dangerous to man. Of the 3,000 species in North America, only the black widow and the brown recluse produce toxins. The black widow—the more dangerous of the two—is shy and retiring. But with a distinctive red hourglass emblazoned on its belly, it is known to virtually every school kid. Such notoriety helps explain man's irrational hatred of all spiders. As I write this, the movie *Arachnophobia* is a big hit in the video stores.

The spider is a master architect, spinning a web in which to catch prey. With four to six silk glands located in its abdomen, it can produce fibers, dry to sticky, as thin as one-millionth of an inch. Incredibly tough and elastic, the web is stronger than steel wire of the same diameter.

The world's strongest natural fibers are believed to emanate from the body of a golden silk spider.

A spider can do other remarkable things with its silk besides capture prey. Near the end of its life, it spins a sac to hold the eggs that will produce the next generation. In the spring, spiderlings break through the wall of the sac that nurtured them through the winter, then scurry up blades of grass or onto tips of twigs. Standing there with their abdomens tilted upward, they spin little parachutes. Then they float about 200 feet above the ground, traveling miles from their birthplace to begin a new life.

Although black widow venom is drop for drop more potent than rattlesnake venom, the tiny arachnid (the spider, with eight legs, is not an insect) can inject far less than a rattler and does so only when excessively provoked (it hates to have its web jiggled). Only the larger female can produce enough venom to harm humans.

By one account, only four or five of the 1,000 or so black widow bites reported in the United States each year are fatal. Another researcher found that from 1960 to 1969, 344 deaths from bites and stings of venomous animals were reported in the United States, only 4 of which were caused by black widows. By comparison, 122 of those deaths were caused by wasp and bee stings.

Black widows are found in each of the forty-eight contiguous states. They are especially common around abandoned buildings, in piles of debris, and in dark, undisturbed corners of garages and storage buildings. In fact, you are much more likely to run into a black widow in your garage than in the backcountry.

There is much to admire in spiders. The arachnid line goes back four hundred million years to the first land-dwelling invertebrates. Eons of evolution followed, during which spiders infiltrated every ecological niche. They have been found at 22,000 feet in the Himalayas, in below-sea-level deserts, in tropical treetops, and burrowed into the earth. Sailors have sighted them at sea, drifting with the wind beneath silken parachutes. There is even a fishing spider that can run across water and stay submerged for an hour.

Spider numbers are incalculable. Sampling techniques have revealed 64,000 spiders in one acre of meadow and a quarter of a million in an acre of tropical forest. The worldwide count must be somewhere around a google. Which makes sense when you consider that a female black widow carries 300 to 500 eggs that hatch in about thirty days.

Each of those spiders consumes about a hundred insects a year. Think about that the next time you're tempted to squash a spider.

SQUIRREL

You will see squirrels almost everywhere you and your children go. They are diurnal (work and play during the day) and, unlike most animals, make no attempt to hide from humans. In fact, they seem to delight in showing off. They are primarily tree dwellers but also spend time on the ground. Except for the arctic ground squirrel, they do not hibernate.

They are distinguished by an oversized, bushy tail that is more than just ornamental. It serves as a blanket in winter, a sunshade in summer, and is used for balance during acrobatics. Squirrels can convey a variety of messages with their tails:

- Rapid jerks are a threatening gesture.
- Rapid waves (looser than jerks) indicate agitation.
- Holding the tail against the back may mean danger has passed.

Squirrels also communicate with growls, gurgles, purrs, and buzzes that people often assume are made by birds. Some sounds have specific meaning.

- A rapid *kuk, kuk, kuk* signals danger. If a predator is actually in

Squirrels are cute, bold, and pesky. Protect your food.

(Photo by William J. Boga)

pursuit, the squirrel adds a short trill at the end. Still more embellishments are added to identify the attacker, so other squirrels can take appropriate action. If the enemy is a hawk, for example, other squirrels are warned that they are safe in any burrow; if a badger threatens, they must find a burrow with a back door for use as an escape hatch.

• A drawn-out *ku-u-uk*, at two-second intervals, signals less immediate danger.

• A slow *kuk, kuk, kuk* indicates danger has passed.

Like all rodents, squirrels have two pairs of curved incisors, ideal for gnawing on nuts, their favorite food. Those incisors continue to grow five or six inches a year throughout their life. Their habit of grinding their teeth on tree bark, nut shells, and animal bones prevents their looking like saber-tooth squirrels.

Squirrels bury nuts each fall, relying on their excellent sense of smell to retrieve most of them. Because the ones they forget sometimes germinate, squirrels are responsible for planting many trees throughout parks and forests.

Squirrel breeding, usually twice a year, is accompanied by chatter, chases, and fights. Late-winter and early spring litters are usually born in tree hollows; summer young enjoy leafy nests out on tree branches. Males play no role in raising the young, which average three per litter.

Squirrels are well adapted for life in trees. They have sharp claws for climbing and hanging and can turn their paws 180 degrees, so their claws are always in perfect grasping position, even when descending trees head first. They have strong hind legs for leaping from branch to branch. One squirrel's leap was measured at sixty feet. Have your children watch the squirrels near your camp and try to gauge their jumping distance.

WOLF

On a long list of misunderstood animals, none is more misunderstood than the wolf. Western culture has characterized this animal as a red-eyed, saliva-dripping, mean-spirited menace to millions of children. Children's classics like *Little Red Riding Hood, Three Little Pigs, The Big Bad Wolf,* and *Beauty and the Beast* are enough to make a lobophobe out of anyone.

Although the wolf is the largest canine predator—at ninety pounds, three times as heavy as a coyote—it is a cautious, timid animal around people. Says L. David Mech, an internationally recognized wolf expert and author of *White Wolves of the High Arctic*: "In North America, there is not one documented case in modern times of a healthy wild wolf attacking or killing a human."

Like most animals, wolves have far more to fear from us than we do from them. For the past two centuries, irrational fear and a passion for protecting livestock have fueled an appallingly effective wolf wipeout. Though it once roamed freely over most of North America, the wolf was nearly extinct outside Alaska and Canada by 1920.

Federal protection has permitted a partial comeback. The gray wolf (Eastern timber wolf), listed as an endangered species, has been seen in Idaho, Montana, Wyoming, North Dakota, Minnesota, Wisconsin, Michigan, Minnesota, and eastern Washington. Many of these sightings have been on public lands, where wolves are protected.

The largest concentration of wolves in the continental United States is in northern Minnesota, where twelve hundred animals roam. Even there, they are rarely seen and pose no threat to campers, though you may want to leave your dog at home during mating season.

It's unlikely you'll see a wolf, but you may be fortunate enough to hear them. Usually in the evening, wolves howl to keep the pack together, to stimulate the urge to hunt, or just because they feel like it.

"Wolves howl more before a storm because their ears hurt. They're sensitive to low pressure."
—Conrad Nelson, weather expert.

According to Mech, the call of the wolf can carry two to three miles under ideal conditions. Chances are, that's the closest you'll get to this elusive animal.

Farley Mowat, who wrote the book *Never Cry Wolf*, and actor Timothy Dalton, who worked on the PBS documentary *In the Company of Wolves*, have described wolves in essentially the same terms: playful, intelligent, and loving, with good family values. Dalton concludes, "The wolf is neither to be feared or hated. It's not dangerous, evil, or malicious. It's simply the wolf, and that's a smart animal trying to make a living under tough conditions."

ANIMAL WARNING

With the explosion of rabies in the 1990s, there is a greater need than ever to mind the proper relationship between humans and wild animals.

Rabies is a viral disease transmitted by the saliva of infected animals. It attacks the nervous system, producing a frightening array of symptoms in humans: hallucinations, weakness, thirst, irrational fear and furies, and foaming at the mouth (as well as difficulty swallowing food and water, hence its other name: hydrophobia). Since the virus travels through the body inside nerve tissue, rather than through the bloodstream, the disease triggers no antibodies and can't be detected during incubation. Once it reaches the brain, death is virtually inevitable.

Since 1980, only eighteen people have died of rabies in the United States, and ten of those victims became infected in other countries. But the threat is rising. In July 1992, an eleven-year-old girl became the first New Yorker to die of rabies since 1954. Largely eradicated from pets by vaccination, the virus has reemerged with a vengeance among wild mammals, particularly raccoons, skunks, foxes, and bats. Between 1988 and 1992, reported rabies cases nearly doubled, with raccoons (4,311 cases) easily eclipsing skunks as lead carriers. Doctor Charles Rupprecht, head of the rabies section at the National Centers for Disease Control in Atlanta, calls it "one of the most intensive wildlife rabies outbreaks in history."

One reason raccoons account for half of the reported rabies cases is because they are so adorable. You and your children will not be tempted to feed skunks or bats and you won't get near foxes, but those cute little coons will march right into your camp like a horde of trick-or-treaters, and right into your children's hearts.

Without exception, resist the temptation to feed wild animals. Rabies is harder to spot than many people realize. An infected animal may not appear crazed or menacing; instead, it may seem tame or sick, tempting animal lovers to try to help. Your pets should also observe wildlife from a distance. Get them vaccinated, especially the bounding dog likely to encounter wild animals. Protect garbage and pet food from furry intruders.

If bitten or otherwise exposed (at least two victims got rabies in caves by breathing air contaminated by infected bats), wash the wound immediately with soap and water, then get medical help. The rabies treatment, once an excruciating series of fourteen to twenty-one shots in the abdomen, is now a gentler set of five shots in the arm. Even if you test negative for rabies, you may need a tetanus shot.

TWENTY ANIMAL FACTS AND ODDITIES

1. Some spider webs, if straightened out, would extend for three hundred miles. One pound of web would be long enough to circle the globe at the equator.

2. After people, porcupines kill the most bears. If their quills get stuck in a bear's tongue, it can starve.

3. Bald eagles are larger at age two than when fully mature.

4. Ants have five noses, each for a different task.

5. All species of snakes shake their tails when aroused, but only the rattlesnake has a noisemaker.

6. Lizards remain motionless 90 percent of their lives. Nevertheless, they do remarkable work and in fact are far more effective than insecticides in controlling insects and spiders.

7. Hornets and wasps were making paper millions of years before the Egyptians.

8. Birds, proportionate to their size and weight, are 75 percent stronger than people.

9. Reptiles have two lower jaws that hinge, allowing them to swallow food larger than their bodies.

10. Bee hummingbirds weigh in at eighteen to the ounce.

11. Male silkworm moths have a keen sense of smell. They can detect a sexy female six miles away.

12. Red-eyed vireos have perfect pitch and will deliver their two- to six-note call up to 22,000 times a day without variation.

13. Crickets can tell you the temperature. Count the number of chirps in ten seconds, add thirty-nine, and you have the temperature in Fahrenheit.

14. The people of Enterprise, Alabama, erected a monument in honor of the boll weevil in 1919. The weevil, which destroyed much of the cotton crop, forced the farmers to diversify their crops, resulting in a tripling of their income.

15. Moose masturbate.

16. The female praying mantis may swallow her mate during the sex act. The persistent male may continue to copulate even after his head and thorax have been bitten off.

17. Field mice went on trial in Stelvio, Italy, in 1519, for damaging crops by burrowing. They were granted a defense attorney to "show cause for their conduct." He claimed his clients were helpful citizens who ate harmful insects and enriched the soil. The judge ordered the animals exiled but assured them safe conduct.

18. If you put on a raccoon coat, you are wearing twenty to forty dead raccoons.

19. The lovebug spends about fifty-six hours mating, more than half its lifetime.

20. The sapsucker drills little holes into tree trunks, then hides. Sap oozes from the tree, attracting insects. The sapsucker then eats the insects.

TWENTY WILDLIFE-WATCHING TIPS FOR YOUR KIDS

1. Leave perfumes and smelly lotions at home. If you want to see animals, you should smell like an animal.

2. Avoid brightly colored clothes, tents, and packs.

3. Find out which animals live in the habitat you'll be exploring. Start with those likely to pass through your camp, such as squirrels, chipmunks, and deer.

4. Get a good pair of binoculars and practice until you can focus on your subject before it flies, crawls, or swims away.

5. Look for ecotones (areas where two habitats overlap). Ecotones such as forest and meadow edges, streambanks and lakeshores, talus slopes and alpine meadows, and sand dunes and coastal scrub allow you to see animals from two adjacent habitats.

6. Be especially alert at dawn and dusk, when many animals are active.

7. Except in grizzly country, walk softly. Keep that frying pan from clanging against your pack frame. Now listen to nature.

8. Listen with "rabbit ears," a simple technique that improves your

hearing. Place your thumbs against the back of each ear and cup your hands so the fingers bend over the tops, maintain a tight seal around the back of your ears, and turn your head from side to side and up and down.

9. Be alert to shapes and colors. Pay special attention to horizontal lines, which are uncommon in a forest; they may be an animal. Look for birds as oblong shapes high in trees. Objects that appear to be boulders may be bears or bison.

10. Look for tracks and scat. Even if you can't identify the animals that left them, noting animal signs makes you more aware of whom you're sharing the outdoors with. If you want to identify animals from tracks or scat, carry a guide.

11. Take your rest stops off the trail. Animals like trails, too, but they will go elsewhere if they sense humans.

12. When crossing waterways, pause to look up- and downstream. Rushing water hides human noises, so you may be able to spot animals bathing or drinking.

13. If you see something, freeze. You can often prolong the observation, especially if the animal decides you're no threat.

14. Pick a campsite far away from well-traveled animal routes. This may seem backward, but laying your sleeping bag down on an animal trail will not increase your chances of seeing wildlife.

15. Don't build a fire. Animals avoid light and smoke.

16. Make a "track trap" by smoothing out a patch of ground and then checking for tracks later. Make your trap in an area likely to be visited. If you already see tracks, that's a good place to start.

17. You can see a variety of wildlife if you're willing to get down on your belly. Insects and arachnids are abundant.

18. Strive to be one with nature. Backpacking helps achieve this feeling, especially if you avoid large groups of people.

19. Don't interfere in animals' lives. Remember that you are invading *their* space. Above all, do not feed them.

20. Be patient. If you want to see an animal that has disappeared into a burrow, such as a marmot, squirrel, mouse, or chipmunk, find a comfortable place to sit and remain quiet. It usually will reappear, curious about you.

RESOURCES

Books

A Field Guide to Animal Tracks by Olaus J. Murie (Peterson Field Guide Series, 1974: Houghton Mifflin Co., Boston)

Never Cry Wolf by Farley Mowat (1963: Dell Publishing, New York)

Cougar: The American Lion by Kevin Hansen. (1992: Northland Publishing, Flagstaff, AZ)

Mammal Tracking in Western America by James Halfpenny (1986: Johnson Books, Boulder, CO)

Video

"The Bear." (French, 1989) Excellent, realistic entertainment for all ages.

For more information, contact one of the following organizations:

Defenders of Wildlife, 1244 19th St. NW, Washington, DC 20036

National Audubon Society, Education Division, Route 1, Box 171, Sharon, CT 06069

National Wildlife Federation, 1412 16th St. NW, Washington, DC 20036

The Nature Conservancy, 1800 N. Kent St., Suite 800, Arlington, VA 22209

The Timberwolf Alliance, c/o Sigurd Olson Environmental Institute, Northland College, Ashland, WI 54806; (715) 682-1223

Miscellaneous

Scat shirts available from Panagraphics, 1312 North Wahsatch, Colorado Springs, CO 80903; (719) 520-9953

Special thanks to *Backpacker* magazine.

9 How to Stay Healthy in the Outdoors

> *Walking is man's best medicine.*
> *—Hippocrates*

This chapter focuses on several dozen things that can go wrong in the wilderness. Chances are, they won't happen. Also, many of these afflictions are preventible or treatable with an antidote—knowledge. At any rate, the same type of list could be drawn up for accidents around the home. So don't worry; just be prepared. The car ride to the trailhead is the most dangerous part of the trip.

According to Dr. Daniel A. Weinberg, physician and outdoor medicine instructor, "Two common errors of people facing an outdoors emergency are doing far too little and trying to do far too much."

The Boy Scouts have it right. "Be prepared" should be the motto of everyone who ventures into the wilderness, especially with children. That means carrying a good first-aid kit and knowing how to use it. If you plan to spend much time in the wilderness, you should have training in cardiopulmonary resuscitation, setting broken bones, and suturing cuts. It also would help to be familiar with the problems covered in this chapter.

(PHOTO BY WILLIAM J. BOGA)

Don't exaggerate outdoor risks. Hiking and scrambling will generally keep your children very healthy.

ALTITUDE SICKNESS

As you gain altitude, the air gets thinner—the amount of oxygen in a given volume decreases. Cheated of it, the body is plagued with chemical imbalances. The first stage, called acute mountain sickness, is unpleasant but not life-threatening. Temporary symptoms, usually a throbbing headache and nausea, can be endured. Susceptibility to AMS seems to be greater in those under forty. Not everyone feels sick at modest altitude, and there's no way to predict someone's highest comfortable altitude. Few people have trouble below 8,000 feet, but two-thirds of those who summit 14,410-foot Mount Ranier suffer some symptoms.

Everyone needs time to adjust to such conditions, no matter how often they have been to high altitude. Afterward, when they descend to sea level, this is lost in a few days. At very high altitudes (14,000 to 18,000 feet above sea level), pulmonary and cerebral edemas—water accumulation in the lungs or the brain—are more likely. They are less common than AMS but far more serious. Early symptoms may include a hacking cough, shortness of breath, and coordination problems. Later may come a bluish skin color and a phlegm-producing cough. In some cases, an edema victim can lapse into a coma or die without warning.

Prevention

• Ascend gradually. If ascent is less than a thousand feet per day, altitude sickness is unlikely to occur.

• Maintain a high-carbohydrate, low-fat diet.

• Make intermediate stops to allow the body to adjust and minor symptoms to pass.

• Drink lots of water.

• Avoid alcoholic beverages.

• Don't try to overpower altitude.

• Descend immediately if you feel particularly ill.

Treatment

• If the symptoms are mild, rest and wait. Induce vomiting if it feels as though that will help. Once when I was deep in the throes of mountain nausea, I caught and cleaned a brook trout; scrutinizing the inner workings of a fish was enough to make me throw up.

• If the symptoms are severe, including a cough or a loss of coordination, descend a couple of thousand feet.

BEE STINGS

What can attract bees and increase the likelihood that you'll be stung? Brightly colored clothing, floral prints, perfumes, skin lotions, and sweet foods at a picnic. Still, if you treat honeybees and bumblebees with respect, they will return it. In four decades of outdoor life, I've never been maliciously stung by a bee (I have stepped on a couple), though more than once I have been dive-bombed by their aggressive cousins—yellow jackets, wasps, and hornets.

If you are hypersensitive to bee venom, one sting can cause nausea, irregular heartbeat, massive swelling (a sign of circulation problems), a lump in the throat (breathing problems), faintness (a drop in blood pressure), and, for about forty people a year, death. Fortunately, most people suffer only swelling, pain, and itching that disappear after a few days.

The risk of a serious reaction naturally increases with multiple stings. That can happen if you disrupt a nest or hive, some of which are close to the ground. Also, one sting can make you more vulnerable to a second, as it releases a chemical that attracts subsequent attackers.

Brothers Rich and Rob White had a memorable childhood encounter with bees that shows how seldom animals threaten people if we don't threaten them. "I was twelve and Rich was ten," Rob said. "One day we were hiking and came upon a swarm of bees right in the middle of the trail. No easy way around. I remembered hearing that bees won't sting you if you don't move too fast, so we tried it. I led and Rich followed, inching our way through the swarm, and didn't get stung."

"We weren't as lucky another time," Rich put in. "We were picking berries and reached into a place we couldn't see, a bees' nest. We got stung plenty."

Treatment

• Quickly remove the stinger. A bee's stinger is barbed, meaning the bee can't pull it out after stinging you. Don't use tweezers or your fingers to try to remove a bee stinger; it has a sac at the exposed end that can pump more venom into you if squeezed. Instead, scrape the sac away with a fingernail or knife blade, then remove all the stinger.

• Wash the site thoroughly. Apply ice, then some itch inhibitor like calamine lotion or, a favorite of mine, Derma Pax. According to a University of California at Berkeley Wellness Letter (August 1993), a paste mixture of meat tenderizer or baking soda and water may offer relief. Others say that meat tenderizer is useless and that you should rub a cut clove of garlic on it.

• A more traditional treatment includes an ointment containing an anesthetic, such as benzocaine, and an over-the-counter antihistamine, such as Benadryl or Chlortrimaton to help reduce swelling.

• Emergency bee-sting kits are available that include a syringe of epinephrine (adrenaline). The device has a spring mechanism that automatically triggers the injection when pressed against the skin. If you know you or your children are allergic to bee stings, carry a kit whenever you go outdoors. Long-term treatment for the highly sensitive includes regular desensitizing shots.

A re children at greater risk from bee stings? Apparently not. Life-threatening reactions usually occur in people over thirty.

BLISTERS

A hiker's feet are often his weak link. On a seven-mile hike, your feet will pound the ground about fourteen thousand times, often on rough, uneven terrain in unfamiliar boots. Such an effort will expose the slightest chink in your first line of defense against blisters.

Foot blisters are caused by friction. The movement of skin against a sock, for example, sends thick outer skin back and forth over a thin inner layer. The layers separate, and fluid rushes into the space between the layers. If untreated, the skin covering the fluid may break, exposing highly sensitive skin and increasing the risk of infection.

Prevention

• Have your children toughen their feet before a big hike by walking a lot. They should wear the boots in which they will hike, especially if they are new. Better yet, have them go barefoot; they will probably like that.

• Make sure the boot fit is snug but not cramped (see chapter 2 for fitting boots). Check them each time you put them on for dirt and rocks.

• See that your children wash their feet every day on the trail.

• Wear the correct kind, number, and thickness of socks to assure proper fit. Smooth out any wrinkles before putting on shoes. Watch for hikers whose socks are slipping into their boots.

• Keep feet dry with sock changes and foot powder.

• Everyone should carry at least one change of socks. While hiking, hang the damp pair from your pack to dry.

• At rest stops, prop your feet up higher than your heart to reduce swelling and increase circulation.

• Upon arriving at the campsite, remove boots, massage feet, and slip into a pair of soft shoes.

• Be alert to the first signs of rubbing. Stop early and check "hot spots."

Treatment

• A hot spot is the first sign of trouble. Tender to the touch, it is the early stage of a full-blown blister. Treat with tape (some people swear by duct tape), Second Skin, Moleskin, or Newskin, which can be used to coat the friction area and protect it against further rubbing.

• If the rubbing is in the toe area, put a thin lining of adhesive felt inside your boots so your feet don't slip forward. You can also stuff in a small piece of foam to help absorb impact.

• Do not open a blister unless it is the size of a nickel or larger and there is danger of it rupturing or interfering with walking.

• If you plan to open a blister, wash your hands and wash the skin with soap. Sterilize a pin or needle over a flame, holding the end of the pin with a cloth, then let it cool. Puncture the base of the blister, not the center, and let it drain. Gently massage the remaining fluid out. Apply an antibiotic ointment, then cover with a light bandage, a piece of gauze, or a thin foam pad with a hole in the center.

• Leaving the blister uncovered and going barefoot, if practical, speeds healing.

• Check daily for signs of infection—reddening, swelling, or pus. See a doctor if infection occurs.

BLOODY NOSE

Children are more susceptible to this when camping, especially at higher elevations. As the air turns dry and dusty, the urge to pick your nose increases. The result is tissue irritation and, often, a bloody nose.

Prevention
A damp handkerchief or bandanna regularly dabbed in the nose keeps things moist and manageable. Persuade children to gently blow, to rinse out the nostrils, and to avoid picking their noses.

Treatment
Tilt the head back and stop the blood flow with a damp, clean cloth, paper towel, wad of toilet paper, or whatever is available. If the bleeding doesn't stop in a few minutes, plug the nostrils with any of the above and get to a doctor.

BROKEN BONES
Use gentle, persistent traction to set the bone in its proper alignment and minimize soft tissue damage. Immobilize the set bone with a splint or sleeping pad. If the fracture is compound (bone poking through the skin), immobilize but don't try to set. See a doctor.

BURNS
In the wilderness, burns can be caused by stoves, pots, boiling water, or falling in the campfire (sunburn will be treated separately). The severity of such burns depends on the intensity of the heat and the length of exposure. For example, water at 120 degrees F. will burn skin in five minutes; water at 140 degrees F. will do the same damage in five seconds.

First-degree burns injure only the outer skin, causing it to turn red, as in most sunburns. Second-degree burns result in blisters and may be swollen for several days. Third-degree burns make the skin look charred, leathery, gray, and dry, but may not be painful if nerve endings are destroyed.

Treatment
If necessary, remove the source of the burn. If clothing or hair is on fire, stop, drop, and roll. Remove clothing and jewelry, which can hold heat and continue to burn.

Next, cool the burn. Treat minor burns with cold-water applications. Weather permitting, a cool, wet T-shirt or clean cloth can be applied to a burn in which there is no broken skin. Clean the area with soap and water, and apply a topical anesthetic. Also, you can reduce pain by blocking the burned area from air with plastic wrap or plastic bags. Remove the block after three hours.

Second- and third-degree burns mean broken skin; do not use ointments, sprays, or any home remedy on these. In case of a third-degree burn, do not remove adhered particles of clothing. Instead, bandage over the burns and cover with a clean (sterile, if possible) dressing. Elevate burned hands, feet, or legs. If the face is burned, maintain an open airway with the patient sitting up. You may apply cold packs to cool the body, but not directly to third-degree burns.

Victims of severe burns often go into shock from fluid loss. If the victim is conscious and not vomiting, you may give water or a sports drink. Seek medical help as soon as possible.

CUTS

Cuts are an integral part of growing up; they're badges of courage for children. As a parent, you have to decide which wounds can be treated with a chuck on the chin and which are genuine first-aid matters.

Level 1: No blood, no foul. Chuck on the chin.

Level 2: Slight bleeding. Apply pressure to the injured area with a gauze pad, paper towel, or clean cloth and, if necessary, elevate the injured area above the heart. For a cut foot or leg, the patient can lie down and prop his leg against a tree; hold a cut hand above the head.

Level 3: Larger cut, more blood. Draw the edges of the wound together with fingers before applying pressure. If bleeding persists, squeeze the pressure point for the blood vessel feeding the cut. Elevate the wound. If that doesn't stop the bleeding, tape the edges of the wound together with a butterfly bandage.

As soon as bleeding is under control, wash the wound with soap and water or irrigate. Once cleaned, blot the area with a clean cloth and bandage. If the wound is minor, especially on a protected part of the body, leave it unbandaged. Larger wounds may require a gauze pad held in place with adhesive tape.

Those antiseptics our moms gave us—mercurochrome, iodine, merthiolate—are no longer recommended. They tend to trap bacteria in the wound. The drier the wound, the less chance of infection. A wet bandage inhibits healing by providing an environment favorable to bacteria.

DEHYDRATION

Humans are reservoirs of water. The brain is cushioned by fluid, joints are lubricated by fluid, blood is 90 percent water, and every biochemical reaction requires water.

Dehydration is the cause or a complication of many mountain ailments. It contributes to hypothermia, heat illness, altitude sickness, and frostbite. It worsens fatigue, decreases the ability to exercise, and reduces alertness. End-of-the-day headache, weariness, and irritability are often preliminary signs of dehydration.

We can survive much longer without food than without water. As effort increases, so does the need for water. Exercise causes water loss through sweating, breathing, and metabolism. If it is not replaced, a fluid deficit results. With a 2 percent fluid deficit, we experience mental deterioration, nausea, loss of appetite and energy, an increased pulse rate, and a 25 percent loss in efficiency. A 12 percent fluid deficit means a swollen tongue, inability to swallow, sunken eyes, and neurological problems. A fluid deficit of 15 percent is potentially lethal.

Prevention

• Drink, drink, drink—especially water. Force fluids before a big hike. Even if you're not thirsty, drink because you know you should. During a long hike, sipping frequently is preferable to gulping vast amounts during long rest stops. Drink after hikes, too. Urine color is an indicator; darker urine is an early signal of dehydration.

• Early in your children's lives, give them water when they say they're thirsty. Avoid the excessive consumption of soft drinks. Two quarts of water a day should be the minimum, and three or four are better.

Treatment

Force fluids. In severe cases, you may have to evacuate the victim.

DIABETES

Diabetes should not keep you or your children from enjoying the wilderness. It does, however, require care and planning. If you're going to overexercise, then overeat. Fill your pockets before a long hike with nuts, trail mix, and dried fruit. Munch frequently. If the diabetic loses consciousness, sprinkle sugar under the tongue or use one of the commercial gels made for this purpose.

I n the 1970s, I backpacked a lot with my friend Jay, who is diabetic. As he was young, lean, and fit, the disease didn't prevent him from hiking twelve mountain miles with forty pounds on his back. But more than once, usually after we had reached camp, he descended into insulin shock. He eventually came to understand that backpacking burned more calories than he was replacing. The result could be frightening.

One drizzly afternoon, after a long hike, I was building a fire while Jay was digging a trench around the tent (trenches were in vogue then). After nursing a tentative blaze to life, I turned to speak to Jay and found him eating . . . dirt. Like a drunk, he wore a goofy grin on his face and had only spasmodic control of his limbs. I'd seen the symptoms before, so I quickly administered a candy bar and two cups of sugary lemonade. Thirty minutes later, he was shaky but recovered.

FISHHOOK IN SKIN

My friend Tom, who has done most everything, once accidentally buried a fishhook, barb and all, in his index finger. He said, "It occurred to me and my two friends that none of us had the slightest clue what to do. We tried digging it out with a knife, but that didn't work too well. Then another fisherman came by who knew the trick. It took him maybe ten seconds to get it out."

Treatment

• Tie a short piece of fishing line around the hook, near the skin surface.

• Grasp the eye of the hook with one hand and press down about an eighth-inch to disengage the barb.

• While still pressing the hook down with one hand (barb disengaged), grasp the end of the fishing line with the other so that it runs parallel to the skin surface. Then begin gently tugging on the fishing line and jiggling the eye, until the hook shaft leads the barb out of the skin.

• Wash the wound thoroughly, with soap if available.

FROSTBITE

Unlike hypothermia, which affects the whole body, frostbite acts on local areas such as fingers, toes, and ears. It happens when tissue is frozen. Severe tissue damage from frostbite can lead to gangrene and amputation, although this is not as prevalent as it once was because clothing is now better.

The following can contribute to frostbite:

• Low temperatures
• Windchill
• Moisture
• Poor insulation
• Constriction of blood flow from tight jewelry, boots, gaiters, or cramped position.
• Dehydration

There are three categories of frostbite: simple (frost nip), superficial, and deep.

Treatment for Frost Nip

Gently warm the affected area. Place your hands under your armpit. For other parts of the body, place your hands over the affected area, blow warm air on it, or immerse it in warm (100- to 108-degree) water. A burning sensation during recovery is normal. Never rub snow on frost-nipped areas—this promotes further chilling and can damage tissue. Never expose frost-nipped skin to direct heat, such as a campfire or stove.

Frost nip is physiologically similar to a first-degree burn. Upon rewarming, the layer of frozen skin becomes red. After a few days, the dead skin will peel, just like a sunburn.

Treatment for Superficial Frostbite

Superficial frostbite affects deeper tissues, injuring a partial thickness of skin, similar to a second-degree burn. The skin, which appears white and waxy, will feel frozen on the surface but have a normal pliant texture. As long as there's no chance of refreezing, immediately begin rewarming the affected part by immersing it in warm (100- to 108-degree) water. If bath water is unavailable, cover the victim's body and keep it warm during and after treatment. Handle the affected area carefully. Blisters likely will appear within twenty-four hours.

Treatment for Deep Frostbite

The most serious frostbite is deep, or third-degree. The skin has the feel of frozen meat. Its surface changes from blotchy white to grayish-yellow to grayish-blue. Deep frostbite should not be treated in the field. Walking out on frozen feet does less damage than partial rewarming followed by refreezing. Try to keep the area frozen until rewarming can be carried out correctly. Act quickly, though, for the longer tissue is frozen, the more damage it sustains. Don't break the skin; that increases the chance of infection. As the tissue thaws out, it is further prone to infection, which usually calls for antibiotics.

"It was so cold I almost got married."   —*Shelley Winters*

GIARDIA

Contaminated water is believed to account for most infectious diarrhea in the wilderness. This is a remarkably recent phenomenon. When I first started backpacking in the late 1950s, one of life's great pleasures was drinking straight from a cold mountain lake or stream. As recently as 1977, the Sierra Club backpacker's guide lauded drinking directly from wilderness water as one of the special pleasures of backcountry travel. No more. Today, primarily because of a protozoan called *Giardia lamblia*, that is a type of wilderness Russian roulette.

Children are generally harder hit by giardiasis (the parasitic disease) and suffer symptoms more severely than adults. Giardia is shed in human feces that find their way into water that finds its way into a new human host. Infection can occur from swallowing as few as six microscopic cysts.

Giardiasis used to be called "beaver fever," which almost certainly misplaced the blame for the problem. After all, beavers were around long before giardia, and today the disease is prevalent in areas that have never been home to beavers. Humans are the more likely villains. I support the theory that cross-country skiers who relieve themselves in the snow are at least partly to blame. In the spring the snow melts, forming giant sluiceways that carry the parasites into the water supply.

Before about 1978, water that looked good and was moving fast was considered safe. Today, according to the Centers for Disease Control in Atlanta, no surface water is guaranteed free of giardia. It has been discovered in mountain headwaters and at Vasey's Paradise in the Grand Canyon, close to where water springs forth in utter purity from ancient aquifers deep in the limestone. Technically, as soon as water falls from the sky or bubbles from an underground spring, it may be unsafe.

Slow to heed the warnings that began cropping up in national parks in the late 1970s, I contacted giardia in 1980. Although I lived, there were times when I wondered whether it was the right thing to do. It was an unpleasant, at times debilitating, disease that produced the following symptoms:

• Chronic diarrhea, commencing seven to ten days after ingestion.

• Abdominal distention, flatulence, and cramping, especially after meals.

• Symptoms lasting seven to twenty-one days, followed by periods of relief, then relapses.

Prevention

• In addition to giardia, there may be viruses or bacteria in water. Always assume wilderness water is contaminated and use one of the three basic methods of disinfection.

• In the wild, away from established toilets, dig an environmentally sound toilet hole six to eight inches deep, well above the high-water line of spring runoff, and far enough from surface water—two hundred feet is usually recommended—to prevent feces from washing into any surface water.

- Educate children and newcomers to the wilderness on the importance of proper toilet holes.
- Ritualize hand washing after squatting and before handling food.
- Teach children not to swallow the water when swimming.
- If possible, use only tap water for drinking. If not, carefully boil, filter, or chemically treat your drinking water. Years ago, the choice was chemicals—iodine or chlorine—or boiling. Both have serious drawbacks.

Boiling takes time and fuel and leaves you with hot, flat-tasting water. It is, however, highly effective. Contrary to previous thinking, boiling immediately kills all diarrhea-causing microorganisms. According to Dr. Howard Backer, a lecturer at Berkeley, any water is adequately disinfected by the time it reaches its boiling point, even at twenty-four thousand feet, where it boils at 135 degrees Fahrenheit. One strategy is to boil your water just before bedtime, then pour it into drinking bottles that you can use as hot-water bottles in your sleeping bag. Secure the tops.

Chemical treatment means adding halogens to water. Chlorine is the choice for municipal water, and iodine has been used by the military since the beginning of the century. For backpackers, the choice has long been between Halazone (chlorine) or Aqua Potable (iodine). Chlorine doesn't kill giardia, but iodine kills viruses, bacteria, and protozoa cysts. However, it tastes bad and is not recommended for babies, small children, or nursing mothers.

Filtration removes all microorganisms except viruses, which are really not a threat in North America. Filters are expensive ($40 to $250), but they last a long time, don't weigh much, and are, in my opinion, the best solution. There are many models, some smaller than your water bottle. Filter pores must be five microns or smaller to remove giardia.

Filters can clog. Make sure the one you buy can be easily cleaned or has a replaceable filter. When treating cloudy or debris-filled water, first strain it through cheesecloth or coffee filters.

Treatment

If untreated, giardiasis can last for years. If you think you have been infected, see a doctor for a stool test. Unfortunately, diagnosis can be elusive and drug treatment can be hit or miss.

If you do have giardiasis, three prescription medicines are available for treatment: Atabrine, Furozone, and Flagyl. Flagyl is the most effective, but it can be hard on the stomachs of small children. No one medicine is 100 percent effective, so it may be necessary to try a second course of treatment using a different medication.

If diarrhea is a symptom, drink lots of fluids.

HEAT ILLNESS

In a temperate climate, a person loses two to three quarts of water per day, half of it in urine. In the desert, water loss climbs to eight to twelve quarts in sweat, one in urine, and almost a quart exhaled. Since much of this lost fluid was concentrated in the blood, the blood becomes abnormally thick unless the water is replaced.

Drinking plain water is the best way for the average person to replace lost fluids. Excessive loss of sodium and potassium (electrolytes) occurs only after a severe and prolonged sweat. Otherwise, a normal diet will replace the minerals lost in sweat. Remember, though, when you're exercising hard, your thirst mechanism lags behind your need for fluids. In other words, by the time you're thirsty, you're already dehydrated. Always drink before, during, and after exercising.

The three stages of overheating are, from bad to worse, heat cramps, heat exhaustion, and heatstroke.

Treatment for Heat Cramps

Cramps, characterized by severe, spasmodic contractions of one or more of the large muscles of the legs, is caused by sweating away body minerals during heavy exertion. Try rest, gentle massage, stretching, and lots of drinking. Now is the time to replace minerals with a sport drink. Ice comforts painful muscles and reduces the inflammation. For the common calf cramp, straighten out and support the affected leg, grasp the foot at the toes, and pull slowly and gently. Never pound or twist a cramping muscle.

Treatment for Heat Exhaustion

Heat exhaustion is caused by the body's inability to dissipate heat. It too involves the loss of minerals during strenuous exercise, usually in a hot, humid environment. Symptoms include dizziness, faintness, fatigue, nausea, and vomiting. The victim's skin becomes pale and moist, but heart rate and temperature are normal.

Treatment includes rest, mineral replacement, and water. Apply wet cloths to the victim and fan vigorously. When the victim feels better, activity can be resumed.

Treatment for Heatstroke

This most serious heat condition is also caused by the body's inability to dissipate heat. The onset of heatstroke symptoms can be rapid, with the victim quickly losing the ability to help himself. Complaints are weakness, fatigue, headache, vertigo, thirst, nausea, vomiting, muscle cramps, and faintness. Body temperature is between 102 and 104 degrees F., and the skin is hot and usually dry. Pulse and respiration rate are elevated, while urine output is nil. Altered brain function—confusion, delirium, even loss of consciousness—is a sure sign that heat exhaustion has degenerated into heatstroke. Shortness of breath, diarrhea, and seizures may also arise.

Treatment must be immediate. Stop all activity and protect the victim from the heat source, usually the sun. If no shade is available, make some. Remove the victim's clothing, apply wet cloths, and fan vigorously. If water is limited, sponge the victim, especially around the armpits, groin, and neck. Give liquids only if the victim is conscious and able to swallow. Continue cooling until body temperature returns to normal. Do not administer aspirin or stimulants. After the condition has stabilized, get the victim to a doctor as soon as possible.

HYPOTHERMIA

This is a dangerous cold-weather condition in which the body can no longer generate enough heat to compensate for heat loss. It is one of the two risks (frostbite is the other) of exercising in the cold. You are most susceptible to hypothermia if you are wet, injured, or not moving about enough to stay warm. It can happen in minutes or take hours. Children and the elderly are at greatest risk.

It doesn't have to be freezing for hypothermia to strike; in fact, it's most common when the temperature is between thirty and fifty degrees F. Far more insidious than temperature are wind and moisture, which can penetrate clothing and remove the insulating layer of warm air next to the body. For example, a fifteen-mile-per-hour wind makes thirty degrees feel like ten degrees. This is the wind-chill factor.

Hypothermia can strike on even the sunniest summer day. Fifteen minutes in water as warm as sixty degrees can turn lips blue and cause uncontrolled shivering, symptoms that kids tend to ignore but parents should not. If your child's skin begins to look bluish, towel the tot off, put clothes on, and set place him the sun until toasty.

Mild hypothermia generally involves little loss of acuity or coordination, though the victim may have difficulty managing buttons, zippers, or laces. Profound hypothermia alters mental status. The victim may become belligerent or uncooperative and dispute your diagnosis of his condition. Muscle rigidity replaces shivering. Movements become erratic and jerky. If untreated, the victim will die from cardiac arrest or other complications.

My friend Tim had a frightening brush with hypothermia: "We were two couples, camping at about 8,000 feet in the Sierra. It wasn't that cold—maybe fifty degrees—but there was a storm moving in. I suggested to my friend Jeff that he move their tent to higher ground, near ours. I went back to our tent to wait, but he didn't show. It started to hail, so I ran down to see what was wrong. Jeff was basically out of his mind, wandering around in a daze. We had to lead him back to the car. It was only a half-mile away, but it occurred to me that he would have died if I hadn't been there. He's six-foot-two and 185 pounds, and his wife couldn't have helped him out by herself. Back at the car, we changed his clothes and turned on the heat. He was all right in about thirty minutes, though pretty depressed. It was scary."

Prevention

Hypothermia is easier to prevent than to treat. Preventatives include a balanced diet, plenty of fluids, controlling sweat, and dressing for the weather—that is, covering head, neck, and hands, and wearing clothes that insulate even when wet.

Treatment

Treatment should begin immediately. Insulate the victim from the ground up—have him lie on a sleeping pad or bag. Get the victim out of the elements and remove any wet clothing. Protect him from any further heat loss, especially from the head and neck. Give warm, nonalcoholic beverages.

To accelerate warming, place wrapped warm rocks or hot-water bottles around the victim. Treat gently when removing clothing and giving care; sudden movement may force cold blood from the limbs into the core of the body. Do not rub or squeeze the extremities to stimulate circulation; it can damage tissue. If possible, place the victim in a sleeping bag between two warm people. Continue warming until you can get the victim to a doctor.

LIGHTNING

> *"Lightning is especially attracted to people on golf courses, but if it cannot find a golf course, it will attack anyone wearing loud clothing."* —Dave Barry

Thunder is impressive, but lightning is the real show. It streaks across the sky at sixty thousand miles per second, lasts but a few thousandths of a second, and withers anything in its path. Every year in the United States alone, hundreds of people are killed by lightning, more than by snakes, spiders, bears, bees, and mountain lions combined. Three times as many are injured, and untold numbers have the bejesus scared out of them.

Getting hit by lightning has become a standard of comparison, as in, "Bernard, you've got a better chance of being hit by lightning than meeting a girl who likes you." Actually, the risk of being struck by lightning exceeds most other outdoor risks. That's because there are about 16 million annual thunderstorms.

That's an average of 44,000 storms building up, exploding, and dissipating daily, which works out to 360,000 lightning streaks every hour, or about 8,640,000 per day. As you read this sentence, about 1,800 lightning strikes are hitting Earth. That seems incredible to denizens of the temperate zones, but probably not to the people of Java, who hear thunder 231 days a year.

With such pervasive distribution, lightning has been seen by almost every person on the planet—past and present. Columbus called it "holy fire" and regarded it as a good omen. Martin Luther said his decision to become a monk originated with a lightning strike. He considered it a call from heaven.

"Thunder does all the barking, but it's lightning that bites."
—*Art Linkletter*

Prevention

• Here's a guide for estimating how far away lightning is: When you see a flash, start counting until you hear thunder; every five seconds equals about a mile. Next calculate how fast you can run.

• If you are indoors, stay there and get to the center of the room. Don't venture outside unless absolutely necessary.

• Don't handle metal objects like fishing rods or tent stakes.

• Don't handle flammable materials in open containers.

• Get out of or off the water and out of small boats.

• Seek shelter. If no buildings are available, take refuge in a cave (but not near the mouth), ditch, canyon, or cluster of small trees.

• When there is no shelter, avoid the highest object in the area. You're better off crouching in the open than near an isolated tree.

• Avoid hilltops, open boats, fields, wire fences, exposed sheds, and any electrically conductive objects, like transmission towers or transmitters.

• In a grove, stay away from the tallest trees.

• Get off your bike or horse.

• If you are caught in the open, crouch. Better, stand or sit on something dry and nonconducting, such as a foam pad or sleeping bag.

• If you begin to feel an electrical charge—your hair stands on end, your skin tingles, or you glow in the dark like a black light—immediately drop to the ground.

• Watch the weather for cloud buildup. In the mountains, the afternoons are generally more dangerous than the mornings. Get below the timberline if you see a storm building.

Treatment

A lightning bolt can create heat up to fifty thousand degrees for up to a tenth of a second. With such a short duration, severe burns are uncommon; more likely, a victim will suffer ruptured eardrums, cardiac or respiratory arrest, or brain or spinal cord damage. Breathing may stop while the heart keeps beating. Artificial respiration may be necessary. Be prepared to commence CPR immediately, even if the person appears to be dead. People frequently survive direct hits of lightning.

Some, like Roy C. Sullivan, the Human Lightning Rod, have survived more than one. Roy was struck seven times during his thirty-plus years as a ranger in Virginia's Shenandoah National Park. The first bolt hit him in a lookout tower in 1942, the second while he was driving a truck. One incident cost him an eyebrow; others ripped off a toenail, knocked him unconscious, set his hair on fire, and tossed him from his vehicle.

At one point, Sullivan had twelve lightning rods surrounding his home but no sense of security. "Lightning has a way of finding me," he said. "I have a feeling I'm going to be struck again someday."

All things being equal, your chance of being hit by lightning in any year is about one in six hundred thousand. Sullivan is a reminder that all things are not equal.

A Canadian couple camped north of Toronto had a shocking experience. They were hugging in their tent, waiting out a thunderstorm, when a lightning bolt hit. It struck a gold medal lion around the man's neck, then emerged through his eyes, ears, and nose. Amazingly, both survived. They suffered only first-degree burns and, no doubt, a barrage of ribbing about their "hot date."

LYME DISEASE

Lyme disease, so called because it was first identified in Lyme, Connecticut, in 1975, is transmitted by certain species of ticks. Worldwide, only the mosquito transmits more disease than the tick.

Before a tick becomes engorged with blood, it looks as innocuous as a mole or a blood blister. The male is black and the female is dark red and black. While an adult is about one-tenth of an inch long (three times that when filled with blood), an immature tick (nymph) is about the size of a pinhead.

Tick eggs hatch into larvae that are nearly invisible. The larvae become infected by feeding on white-footed mice in the East and lizards or jackrabbits in the West. The larvae molt and become infected nymphs; the nymphs are the chief threat to humans—70 to 90 percent of all cases of Lyme disease are caused by nymphs.

Nymphs and adults like to hang out on low vegetation and transfer to whatever or whomever brushes by. They don't fly or jump. Dogs or cats can carry ticks. According to the game Trivial Pursuit, the hardy tick can live for twenty-five years and survive starvation for five.

Lyme disease poses a double bind for doctors; many people who have it don't know it and many others are convinced they have it but don't. The disease is hard to diagnose because its symptoms vary from person to person. No symptom appears in all cases, and there's no sequence of symptoms. The blood tests for Lyme disease are only about 60 to 70 percent reliable. Still, three general phases have been identified:

Phase one: Three to thirty days after the bite, a white-centered red ring may appear, possibly at the site of the bite, possibly somewhere else. You may also develop classic flu symptoms, such as headache, fatigue, muscle and joint aches, chills, and low fever. You may skip the rash and just get the flu symptoms, or you may have none of these symptoms but still carry the disease. If you do have symptoms, they may disappear after phase one or more severe symptoms may develop, sometimes months later.

Phase two: About 20 percent of untreated victims develop neurological or cardiac disorders within weeks or months of the bite. These range from heart rhythm abnormalities to impaired motor coordination and even partial facial paralysis.

Phase three: About half of untreated people develop chronic or recurring arthritis after a dormant period of up to two years. The knees are almost always affected.

More and more cases of Lyme disease are reported each year. The Centers for Disease Control reported 4,574 cases in 1988 and 7,400 in 1989. Nevertheless, there is no reason to panic or avoid the outdoors. Instead, take precautions.

Prevention

• If you're in tick country, wear a long-sleeved shirt with buttoned cuffs; tuck the shirt into your pants and your pants into your socks. Sure, you'll look like a geek, but Lyme disease makes you *feel* bad, not just look bad.

• Wear light-colored clothing. It's easier to spot ticks on white or gray pants than on black ones.

• Use insect repellent with DEET on your body and clothing (see section on mosquito bites).

• In an overgrown area, try to stay near the center of the trail.

• Do an occasional body check for ticks. Have someone check your back and head.

Treatment

Lyme disease is treatable and almost always curable, especially in its early phase.

• If you find an embedded tick, use forceps or tweezers to grab the tick's head close to the skin and gently pull it straight out. Do not burn the tick off, do not use Vaseline, and do not break the head off in the skin.

• If you want to know whether a tick was infected, preserve it (dead or alive) in a moist paper towel or cotton ball (so its body fluids don't dry out) and put it in your freezer until you can take it to a lab. Tests can now determine whether a tick was infected. If so, you should immediately commence antibiotics. If caught early, treatment lasts about six weeks and is virtually foolproof. Waiting can cause treatment to last more than a year, and even then it's not always effective.

• If you develop the characteristic ringlike rash, see your doctor, who should prescribe antibiotics. If you have only the flulike symptoms, a blood test may or may not reveal Lyme disease. You may want to shop around until you find a doctor who will prescribe antibiotics, but the medication can have physical side effects and overuse of these drugs can produce resistant organisms.

MOSQUITO BITES

"Mosquitoes were using my legs for filling stations."
—*Cornelia Otis Skinner*

No member of the animal kingdom regularly causes greater discomfort and misery on camping trips than the mosquito. It is numerous, voracious, and willing to sacrifice its own life for one last shot at your juicy self.

Prevention

• Learn the enemy's habits. In the mountains, mosquitoes breed in pools formed by melting snow; below four thousand feet, most prefer to breed in the water-filled nooks of trees. Obviously, snow melts earlier in the lower elevations, so expect mosquitoes earlier there as well.

The mosquito's life span is short; in any area, the mosquito problem seldom lasts more than a few weeks. Call ahead to park or tourism officials to find out if the area you intend to visit is under attack.

• Know your limitations. You can't kill them all or outrun the little beggars; lured by your warmth and expired carbon dioxide, they move in for the attack. Even if they don't strike (only the females bite), their incessant whining in your ears may drive you to the nearest Holiday Inn.

• Wear lots of clothes. Most heavy nylon is mosquitoproof, as are loose-fitting thick cottons. Keep head, neck, and ears covered with hats, bandannas, and hoods. Don't forget gloves and thick socks. If the problem is serious, wear head netting.

• Use a chemical repellent containing DEET (diethyl metatoluamide). Apply it sparingly to skin and liberally on clothes. DEET is absorbed through the skin—48 percent of an application is absorbed within six hours. The most common side effect is a rash, but occasionally anxiety, behavioral changes, lethargy, and mental confusion have been reported. If using a spray repellent, aim the spray at your hands, then rub it on your face. After applying DEET, wash your hands or keep them away from your eyes and mouth. With young children, don't use a repellent with more than about a 30 percent concentration of DEET. If you prefer an alternative to DEET, try Natrapel, which contains citronella.

If your timing is bad, repellent can go quickly, but one four-ounce bottle per person per week is usually more than enough.

• Take advantage of rain, wind, and cold. Mosquitoes take shelter in inclement weather.

• Look on the bright side. While mosquitoes are merely annoying in the United States, elsewhere they are downright deadly. Thousands of people die every year in Africa, Asia, and Central America from such mosquitoborne diseases as malaria, yellow fever, and dandy fever.

• Go camping with someone who is more attractive to mosquitoes than you are. Mosquitoes, like humans, seem to like some people better than others. Body temperature, skin color, personal odor, and levels of lactic acid in the blood all may be factors. So may karma. As a kid I was on every mosquito's hit list. I tended to take it personally, lashing out in a fury, keeping a running tally of my kills. Now, older and calmer, I have more of a live-and-let-live attitude, and insects seem to return the favor.

• Consider bringing along a pig. In Italy, it is said that he who sleeps with a pig in the room will be free of malaria. Perhaps the pig's higher body temperature makes it more attractive.

Treatment

• Don't scratch. I can offer no better outdoor advice. I used to be a mad scratcher, which resulted in quarter-size welts followed by hideous scabs followed by scars. Eventually, I learned that if I can get through the first hour without scratching, the welt goes away.

• Anti-itch medications like Campho Phenique, Afterbite, or calamine or cortisone lotions may help reduce itching.

OVERUSE INJURIES

Wilderness hypothermia, dehydration, and lightning hits are fairly rare compared with the number of stress or overuse injuries. They are brought on gradually by the wear and tear of a repetitive activity, say, hiking with weight on your back. In one survey of athletes, overuse injuries outnumbered acute injuries in every sport except basketball and skiing.

An acute injury is almost always caused by one incident. An overuse injury may have no obvious cause apart from a sudden increase in activity. A perfect candidate for an overuse injury is the fifty-week-a-year worker who embarks on an ambitious two-week backpacking trip. The result, too often, is a dull pain in the knees or ankles that recurs intermittently, then more frequently. You have pushed your body beyond its abilities. Tissue has developed microscopic tears that cause pain and swelling.

The most common overuse problem is tendinitis—the inflammation of the cords that anchor muscles to bones. Tendons are especially vulnerable because the force of muscle contractions is transmitted through them. People who exercise regularly actually are more at risk because of the powerful forces transmitted by their well-developed muscles. Perhaps that's why children seem to suffer less. Tendon inflammation is characterized by pain, swelling, warmth, and redness.

Tendinitis can be deceptive. It may hurt at the start of exercise, diminish, then return sharply once you've finished. For hikers and backpackers, knees, feet, and Achilles tendons at the back of the ankle are most at risk.

Prevention

Start slowly and build up. Apply heat to vulnerable parts of the body before exercise and ice afterwards.

Treatment

• The standard therapy is RICE—rest, ice, compression, and elevation. Apply ice to the tender area for twenty minutes right after you finish your hike; repeat every two waking hours. Cooling decreases nerve conduction and pain, constricts blood vessels, limits inflammation, and reduces cellular demand for oxygen. Don't exceed the twenty-minute limit lest you damage skin and nerves. If you are car camping, put cubes or crushed ice in a towel or plastic bag and press gently on the affected area. If you are backpacking, use a chemical cold pack or immerse the injury in a cold lake or stream.

Make your own frozen gel pack by filling a heavy-duty plastic freezer bag with a mixture of one part rubbing alcohol and three parts water. Double-bag it, then freeze. The gel will remain soft (the more alcohol you use, the slushier it will be), making it gentler on injuries than ice cubes. On the other hand, the alcohol makes this colder than regular ice, increasing the risk of frost nip.

Outfielder Rickey Henderson suffered a case of frostbite by falling asleep with an ice bag on his leg.

• Stay away from heat, especially at first. It may relieve symptoms, but it will increase the inflammation.

• Regularly take an over-the-counter anti-inflammatory drug, such as aspirin or ibuprofen (Advil).

• Rest or at least reduce your workout. Actually, research suggests that "active rest" is better than stopping. Besides, if you are midway through a hundred-mile backpacking loop, you can't very well stop; you can, however, slow the pace and reduce the stress on the affected area.

• Massage the tender area to increase blood flow and promote healing.

POISON IVY/OAK/SUMAC
My mother asserts that when I was five, I fell into poison oak but never

got a rash. I grew up believing I was immune. Turns out, just about any-body will get the rash if exposed enough times. Poison oak, ivy, and sumac contain an irritant called urushiol, a sap found in the roots, stems, and leaves. The plant must be touched—bruised slightly—to release urushiol; you can't get a rash from just being in the neighborhood. Urushiol doesn't affect dogs and cats, but they can bring it home in their fur.

Prevention

• The best way to escape the wrath of poison oak, ivy, and sumac is to know what the plants look like and stay away from them. Keep in mind the ditty "Leaves of three, let it be" (though if you take that too literally, you'll miss out on some good berries). The poison plants may cling to the ground or grow up the trunks of trees or along fences. They may look like shrubs, bushes, small trees, or vines. Leaves may be dull or glossy with sawtoothed or smooth edges. In autumn, the leaves may turn orange; in summer, poison ivy has white berries.

• The big three haven't taken root in Nevada, Alaska, or Hawaii. California has no poison ivy but does have plenty of western poison oak, which is rampant from Mexico to Canada. The rest of the United States and southern Canada has poison ivy and eastern poison oak. Poison sumac is found in bogs and swamps in the eastern United States.

• If you think you've touched poison plants, wash the area. If you have urushiol on one hand and scratch your back or touch your face, you can spread it.

• Beware of vines entangled in your firewood; they may be poison ivy, which can elude identification when the leaves are gone. Even touch-ing dried-out poison ivy can cause a rash. Inhaling fumes from a burning plant can cause extreme respiratory irritation (a major hazard for firefighters).

• If you are in heavy poison plant country, wear gloves and other heavy clothing. Lightweight garments are inadequate, as urushiol can penetrate them.

• Don't eat a poison ivy or oak leaf to "desensitize" your skin; it won't work and may make you sick.

Treatment

• If you believe you have brushed up against urushiol, put on clean gloves and carefully remove your clothing. Wash everything in strong detergent; wipe off your shoes.

• Wash your body with soap and water, ideally within fifteen minutes.

• If you become rashy, try not to scratch. Scratching won't cause the rash to spread, though it can lead to infection. The blisters don't contain urushiol, so you can't pass the rash to another person. However, if you have the oil on your body before the rash develops, you can pass it by touching someone.

• Cold saltwater compresses, cool baths, calamine, baking soda, and over-the-counter cortisone cream offer relief. The best product I've found for drying up the blisters is Derma Pax. Even if you do nothing, you'll probably be rid of all traces in less than three weeks.

• Be happy. With thousands of plant species in North America, it could be worse.

SHOCK

Shock is the body's response to injury, serious illness, overwhelming blood loss, infection, or dehydration. It occurs when the blood supply to the vital organs, skin, and muscles is decreased. When the blood flow to the intestines, kidneys, heart, and brain falls far enough, collapse follows. Severe shock leads to death when the heart stops. Symptoms of shock include pale, cold, clammy skin; shallow, irregular breathing; rapid but weak pulse; dilated pupils; beads of perspiration; weakness; nausea; and thirst. Loss of consciousness may follow.

Treatment

Shock demands immediate medical attention.

• Have the patient lie down. In case of vomiting, turn the head to one side to keep the victim from inhaling the vomit.

• Loosen tight clothing, particularly near the head.

• Keep the victim warm but avoid sweating.

• Speak soothingly, striving to instill confidence and keep spirits up.

• Light, rhythmic massaging is comforting; holding the hands or feet can be reassuring.

• Do not give water if the victim is unconscious, nauseated, or if medical help will arrive within thirty minutes. If medical help is more than thirty minutes away, give sips.

• If the victim stops breathing and the heart stops, cardiopulmonary resuscitation should be started immediately. CPR should be learned by everyone. Classes are available through the American Heart Association and the Red Cross.

SNAKEBITE

The risk of snakebite is greatly exaggerated by most people. Although there are about eight thousand bites from venomous snakes in the United States each year, many are inflicted upon professional snake handlers, and only twelve to fifteen people die each year from these bites, mostly the young, the old, and the infirm. Most snakebites occur when a snake is antagonized or inadvertently stepped on.

There are only four poisonous snakes in North America: the rattlesnake, copperhead, cottonmouth (water moccasin), and coral.

Prevention

• Stay away from snakes and they will stay away from you. Like most wild animals, they want no part of people.

• If practical, wear long pants, a long-sleeved shirt, and gloves, especially when gathering firewood.

• Be careful when turning over a rock or fallen branch.

• Don't reach or step into dark places.

• Don't gather firewood at night in snake country.

• Don't alarm a sleeping snake or tease an awake one (they hate being called "legless lizards").

• Shake out sleeping bags and clothing before use.

Treatment

• Carry a snakebite kit. Read the instructions at the time of purchase rather than waiting for an emergency.

• If you are certain the snake that bit you was nonvenomous, treat the bite like any other wound.

• If bitten by a poisonous snake, symptoms usually appear within minutes: a metallic, rubbery, or tingling taste in the mouth and possibly a burning sensation at the bite site. Within one hour: swelling, pain, or tingling at the bite. After some hours: skin discoloration, blood blisters, chills, fever, muscle spasms, decreased blood pressure, headache, and blurred vision.

• If those symptoms arise, seek medical help as soon as possible. In the meantime, immobilize the bitten body part and keep it below heart level.

• If a foot or leg has been bitten, the patient should be carried.

• If the bite is on the hand, remove rings. Most snakebite wounds will cause swelling.

• Don't apply ice. This can drive the venom deeper into the body and damage tissue if left in place too long.

• Avoid tourniquets. They shut off arterial blood and can result in loss of the limb.

• Cutting a wound and sucking out the poison should be done only if you are the star of a TV western or if you are hours away from medical help (and only then if you have a suction cup, can start treatment within five minutes, and are trained in the procedure).

SPIDER BITES

There are over 30,000 spider species in the world. All are carnivorous, but there's nary a one that wouldn't choose a juicy fly over your fleshy arm. The most dangerous spider in North America, the black widow, kills only four to six people a year in the United States despite its sinister name.

Spiders are blamed for a lot of bites they don't commit. Shy and retiring by nature, they decline the opportunity to hang out with people and will bite only when brushed against or when someone blindly reaches under a log or into a dark hole. The bite of a venomous spider is barely noticeable, but it is usually followed by redness and swelling, then numbness, then large-muscle cramps. The abdomen may become hard and painful. Weakness, nausea, breathing difficulties, vomiting, and anxiety are common. The pain generally peaks in one to three hours and symptoms begin to regress after several hours. Poisoning is more likely to be fatal to children or to people with hypertension or coronary problems.

Often the victim has not seen the spider and does not realize the cause of his illness (though two tiny red marks identify the bite). That can mean the occasional blown diagnosis, the most common of which is appendicitis. If doctors suggest taking out your appendix, raise the possibility of spider bites.

Prevention
Don't brush against spiders or reach blindly into dark holes.

Treatment
- Clean the wound with antiseptic soap.
- Ice (or clean snow) may be used on the bite.
- Keep the victim quiet.
- If symptoms develop, get the victim to a doctor. Antivenin is readily available.

SPRAINS
The most common ankle problem is a sprain. Sprains are partial or complete tears or ruptures of ligaments, the elastic cords designed to prevent excessive motion. The sprained ankle is to the backpacker as the knee injury is to the football player—common and debilitating.

The severity of sprains varies greatly. Most amount to nothing more than a fleeting twinge. The worst ones require the victim to be immobilized.

Prevention
- Wear good hiking boots and socks for ankle support. You may feel as light as Mercury in running shoes or sneakers, but they offer no protection when your ankle decides to move sideways on uneven terrain. There are hiking boots for toddlers.
- Watch your step. If you miss one, keep your balance, shift your weight slightly forward, and seek a safe landing zone for the next step.

Treatment

• To limit swelling and permit healing, the standard treatment is rest, ice, compression, and elevation. Aggressively treating a mild sprain with RICE for a day or two might keep you from having to cut short your trip. When you do start walking again, provide support for the injured joint with tape, elastic brace, or Ace bandage.

• If you suspect a severe sprain or fracture—the area becomes black and blue—immobilize the injury.

SUN INJURY

A sobering 600,000 cases of skin cancer are diagnosed each year in the United States, almost all due to overexposure to the sun's ultraviolet rays.

Sun protection can be a big issue when you're camping. First, you tend to spend more time outdoors; second, if you're in hills or mountains, the air gets drier and thinner as you climb, making you more susceptible to sunburn. The thin atmosphere at, say, 10,000 feet above sea level, does a poor job of filtering out the particular UV rays that tan and burn.

Because I tan easily and rarely burn, I have long shunned sunscreen. It may have been the biggest mistake of my life. Scientists now tell us that a golden tan is prima facie evidence of skin damage.

Prevention

Exposure to UV rays is cumulative. The exposure your daughter gets at age ten can harm her at forty. The damage accumulates and can't be undone. A tan protects her from sunburn but not necessarily from skin cancer.

The most important time to defend against skin damage from the sun is during childhood. Research indicates that the more sunburns you had as a youth, the greater the chances of skin cancer. So protect your children. The following tips will help you accomplish that:

• The first precaution is to minimize the amount of time your skin is exposed to the sun. Shade yourself with a hat; many skin cancers involve the lips, nose, and the top of the head. They now have scalp screen— for young and old.

• Keep infants and toddlers out of the sun as much as possible. If you use a carriage or stroller, make sure it has a hood; if you're backpacking a child, consider an umbrella clamped to your pack frame.

• Try to schedule your children's outdoor activities before or after midday. The sun's rays are most intense from 10 A.M. to 3 P.M. Intensity also increases as you gain altitude or get closer to the equator.

• If your child is on medication, consult your doctor about possible adverse reactions to sunlight. Antibiotics can make a sunburn worse.

• Some sunscreens may cause allergic reactions. Try out a new product before taking it to the backcountry.

• For children and the fair of skin, use a sunscreen with a sun protection factor (SPF) of 15 or higher. Sunscreens are oils, lotions, or creams containing compounds that filter out UV rays. Because sunscreens are regulated by the Food and Drug Administration, you can trust the labels. The all-important SPF tells you how long a sunscreened person can stay in the sun compared with that same person with no sunscreen at all. Each person's base figure depends on location, time of day or year, and skin type. In the tropics, a fair-skinned person who freckles can endure only about ten unprotected minutes; sunscreen with an SPF of 15 will extend that safe time to two and a half hours (15x10).

An SPF rating measures only a sunscreen's ability to block the rays, that burn. Ultraviolet light also contains nonburning rays that penetrate deeply and are now believed to cause cancer. The most commonly used ingredients in sunscreens—PABA (para-aminobenzoic acid) derivatives such as padimate O—effectively absorb UVB rays but let through the longer-wavelength UVA rays. Look for products containing dibenzoylmethane compounds, which offer the fullest protection against such rays. Because no SPF rating exists that speaks to UVA protection, two sunscreens with the same SPF can offer markedly different protection against UVA rays.

• Apply the protection thirty to forty-five minutes before going out to allow it to soak in.

• Apply it generously and often. Studies have shown that people tend to apply only about half the sunscreen the FDA used to determine SPF.

Thus SPF 14 effectively becomes SPF 7. It takes at least an ounce to cover the average adult.

• If you swim or sweat, use waterproof or water-resistant sunscreen. By law, products labeled "water-resistant" must protect at their SPF level even after forty minutes in the water. Those labeled "waterproof" must protect after eighty minutes in the water. Bring a watch.

Waterproof sunscreens are also sweatproof. That's a huge plus, especially when hiking with kids. It means when they exercise, the stuff doesn't run into their eyes and mouth.

According to a study in *Pediatrics*, only 9 percent of teenagers always use sunscreen and 33 percent never do. Those with family histories of skin cancer are no more likely to use sunscreen than other teens.

• Have a bottle of sunscreen of undetermined age? Toss it. Unless the label says otherwise, sunscreens last about three years.

• Don't forget the lips. They don't tan but they burn. Lip balm with SPF 15 or more is available. Blistex 30 doesn't melt in a hot car or pocket.

• If you or your kids have fair skin, red or blond hair, and light eyes, cover up with long pants, long-sleeved shirts, and hats.

Fabrics, too, can be rated for SPF. In clothing, tight, opaque weaves are better protection than loose weaves and dyed fabrics are better than undyed. One researcher rated a cotton T-shirt as having an SPF of 5 to 7.4, lower if it's wet. According to the UC Berkeley Wellness Letter of August 1993, another researcher rated a cotton-polyester T-shirt at 12 to 20. On the upside, dark blue denim, according to an English study, has an impressive SPF of 1,000.

Clothing with SPF ratings is coming on the market. Because such products are classified as health devices, claims must be approved by the FDA. Such garments are intended primarily for people with conditions like lupus or melanoma that make them especially sensitive to the sun, but if the ozone layer continues to deteriorate, they may someday become the height of fashion.

• Long-billed hats can halve the eyes' exposure to UV rays. Lawrence of Arabia–style neck drapes attach to some hats to protect vulnerable ears and neck.

• Wear sunglasses. Even on cloudy days, 60 to 80 percent of UV light can reach your unprotected eyes. Around bright granite and snow, you risk burning your cornea, an affliction known as snow blindness. Symptoms typically don't appear until eight to twelve hours after exposure. The eyes, red and painful, feel like a sandbox. Sunglasses with side blinders decrease the UV radiation received by the eye and prevent snow blindness. If someone loses a pair of sunglasses, you can improvise with two pieces of cardboard with slits cut in them.

Manufacturers are not required to reveal how much UV protection sunglasses provide, but many do. Look for shades that block 100 percent of UV light and, unless you plan to cross a glacier, transmit 75 to 90 percent of visible light. For kids, plastic lenses are more practical than glass; they're lighter, cheaper, and shatterproof. Glass is more scratch-resistant and offers greater clarity. What's the best? Consider glass lenses that darken with increased visible light.

Young children may resist wearing sunglasses while others think they look cool. Infants will usually brush glasses off their face; for older kids, getting a good pair that fit well may be the key to cooperation.

Treatment

Just because your skin isn't red while you're outdoors doesn't mean you're not sunburned; a sunburn is most evident six to twenty-four hours after exposure.

• If you do get sunburned, the best remedy is to soak the affected area in cold (not iced) water or to apply cold compresses. This is the same treatment for first-degree burns. This removes heat from the skin, provides some immediate pain relief, and eases the swelling. If you or yours are sunburned all over, try an oatmeal bath. If you're backpacking, you might actually have the oatmeal; you're on your own for the bathtub. Sprinkle a cup of dry instant oatmeal (or cornstarch) in a tub of cool water and soak for a while. The oatmeal soothes the skin and reduces inflammation.

• If the burn is severe, try a first-aid spray containing benzocaine, a topical anesthetic. Benzocaine can sensitize the skin, leading to allergic reactions to other medications in the "caine" family. Don't use other "caine" anesthetics for sunburn, for they are readily absorbed into the bloodstream if the skin is broken and may cause a toxic reaction.

• Greasy substances such as butter, baby oil, or after-sun creams seal in heat. Cooling lotions containing menthol or camphor can ease symptoms, but they can also cause allergic reactions, especially in children.

SWIMMER'S EAR

Among young children today, ear infections are rife. Swimming just increases the risk. But just as you needn't be an athlete to get athlete's foot, you needn't be a swimmer to get swimmer's ear. It's an infection brought on when water containing bacteria or fungi gets trapped in the outer ear canal. Swimming is the most common cause, but you can get water in your ears from showering or washing your hair.

Prevention

The longer water remains in your ear, the likelier it is that any microorganisms will breed. There are simple steps to prevent swimmer's ear:

• After swimming or washing your hair, shake your head to remove trapped water.

• Dry your outer ear well with a towel or soft cloth.

• Still feel that bubbling sensation? Tilt your head, cup your hand over your ear, and gently press on the ear until the pressure forces the water out.

• If you are prone to ear infections, use antiseptic eardrops, especially after swimming in a lake. You can buy them at any drugstore, or you make them yourself by mixing equal parts of white vinegar and rubbing alcohol. Put one or two drops into each ear with a dropper. This will restore the natural acid balance of the ear canal and kill the bacteria. If alcohol irritates your skin, use vinegar diluted with water. If your ear continues to itch, use the drops three times daily.

Treatment

Ordinarily, antibiotic drops and irrigation of the ear canal will cure the problem. However, if the ear swells and becomes painful, if the triangular piece of cartilage becomes sore to the touch, or if you have a discharge, seek medical care.

Buck Tilton's Ten Biggest Medical Myths

1. Use a tourniquet to stop serious bleeding.
2. A shot of liquor will warm a cold or hypothermic person.
3. Rub snow on frostbite.
4. Put butter on burns.
5. Cut and suck a snakebite.
6. Immediately soak a sprained ankle in warm water to speed healing.
7. Someone "struck dead" by lightning is ready for the undertaker.
8. Never let someone with a head injury fall asleep.
9. Clear water tumbling over sun-washed rocks is naturally purified.
10. Since the brain dies after being deprived of oxygen for four to six minutes, someone under water that long is beyond resuscitation.
11. God protects the ignorant.

—Buck Tilton is coauthor of *Medicine for the Backcountry*, ICS Books

---

RESOURCES

NOLS Wilderness First Aid by Tod Schimelpfenig and Linda Lindsey (1991: Stackpole Books, Harrisburg, PA)

A Sierra Club Naturalist's Guide: The Deserts of the Southwest by Peggy Larson (1977: Sierra Club Books, San Francisco)

First Aid for the Outdoors by William W. Forgey (ICS Books, Merrillville, IN)

10 How to Survive in the Wild

*In the fight for survival, a tie
or split decision simply will not do.*
—Merle L. Meacham

I once interviewed a sixty-year-old woman, Audrey Sutherland, who was an inveterate sea kayaker. She thought nothing of going off for weeks on solo expeditions to Alaska, Canada, or some other potentially threatening environment. A seagoing backpacker, she would paddle her rubber kayak and camp, content in her self-sufficiency.

She told me once that she had been able to embark on her solitary adventures because her children had been brought up to be self-reliant. "We have no television, so they read omnivorously," she said. "There have never been many other children living nearby, but there is plenty of life in the tide pools in front of the house. We have a list posted of the twenty things every kid ought to be able to do by age sixteen. It includes fix a meal, splice a cord, change a tire, change a baby, listen to an adult with empathy, see work to be done and do it. That last one will take about five years more."

Sutherland is a survivalist of the first order. Not the kind who stockpiles a bunker with three years' worth of food in readiness for some holocaust, but rather the kind who hones impressive survival skills. She's the person I'd most like to be stranded with if survival were at stake.

It seems to me there's no more valuable skill you can teach your kids than how to cope when things go wrong. Think of it as an insurance policy, an antidote against ignorance, because a lack of knowledge can be fatal. The misguided have died of hypothermia less than a mile from help, the misinformed of dehydration with water still in their canteens, the ignorant of starvation with food growing all around them.

> *"If you want to see what children can do, you must stop giving them things."*   *—Norman Douglas*

These are the skills necessary to survive alone in the wild:
- Wayfinding
- Making shelter
- Finding water
- Making fire
- Signaling for help
- Finding food

WAYFINDING

> *"I take my kids everywhere, but they always find their way back home."*   *—Robert Orben*

It would be nice if everyone carried a compass and knew how to use it, but it won't happen. That's why using nature to find your way is such a handy skill. Being a skilled wayfinder means being alert and tapping into all five senses. That takes concentration and practice. Try some of the games at the end of this chapter to massage your senses.

Infants generally cannot move fast enough to get lost, especially when their every move is watched by doting, hawkeyed parents. As kids grow older, however, their legs mature faster than their brains, parents relax a notch, and the risk of becoming lost increases. Dress them in bright colors and put a whistle around their neck. Insist that there be no whistle blowing except in an emergency.

Put a survival kit in your kids' day packs. Here's a complete kit; some of these items will be added as children get older.

- Butane lighter
- Matches
- Plastic whistle
- Signal mirror
- Compass
- Coins for a phone
- Map
- Toilet paper
- Sunscreen
- Lip balm
- Water bottle
- Swiss army knife
- Sunglasses
- Nylon rope
- Fishing line

- Rescue blanket   • Garbage bag   • First-aid kit
- PowerBars or trail mix   • Plastic cup and spoon
- Flashlight (with headband and fresh batteries)
- Hackey Sack (a footbag for keeping warm and passing time)

There's an amazing survival kit available from Hunter (P.O. Box 164, Rough & Ready, CA 95975). It contains fifteen items—everything from whistle to matches to fishing equipment—in a film canister and weighs less than an ounce.

This survival kit is light, so kids can routinely carry it whenever they go off day hiking. Most children love having their own day pack, and having their own survival kit makes them feel so-o-o-o grown up. Talk with them about the items so they understand the purpose and value of each one.

Even well-equipped children need to be alert to the signs of nature. Teach them to study the countryside as they hike. Note how it looks going the other way, keying on dramatic and unusual features. Known as "taking a back bearing," this should be done routinely.

Note your position relative to landmarks. Talk to your kids about it. As you hike around a ridge or peak, take mental photographs of how it looks from different angles; remember the route you've taken in relation to it. After you set up camp, walk a circle around it, noting how it looks from all angles.

Involve your children in route finding, even if you're just following a trail. Pull out the map at rest stops and discuss the route. Ask them to show you where you are on the map. Help them by comparing real cliffs, rivers, and trail junctions with those depicted on the map.

Direction

Sometimes determining direction is easy. For example, most people standing on one coast or another with the sun low in the sky can roughly gauge east and west merely by recalling that solar verity, "The sun rises in the east and sets in the west." Having established west, face that direction. North is on your right, south on your left.

Of course, most of the time the sun doesn't rise due east nor set due west. Moreover, you might be a thousand miles from a coast, misplaced in the wilds of, say, Nebraska, with the sun high in the sky. If so, would you be able to tell north from south? If the answer is no, try the "stick-and-shadow" method. It's easy and kids enjoy it.

Find a flat, clear piece of ground. Drive a three-foot-long stick into the ground. Cut two other sticks about a foot long and drive one into the ground at the tip of the shadow cast by the three-foot stick. Come back twenty minutes later. Insert the remaining stick at the tip of the new shadow. It will have moved from the first mark. Now find or cut a direction-pointer stick and mark one end with tape or knife marks. Lay it against

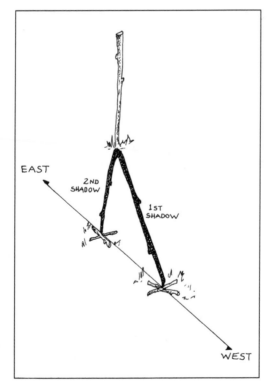

Even if you don't know up from down, the shadow-and-stick method is a simple way to tell north from south.

the two small sticks with the marked end against the second stick. The marked end points east (as the sun moves west, the shadow it casts moves east); the unmarked end points west.

Need to know how long before sunset? Extend your hand at arm's length, thumb up (as though shaking hands). Count the number of fingers between horizon and sun. Time until sunset is ten to twelve minutes for each finger.

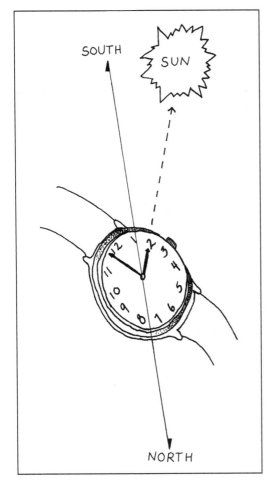

If you wear a watch with hands, you can tell direction on a sunny day.

If you're wearing a watch with hands (kids, don't try this with your digital), hold it flat and point the hour hand toward the sun. South will then lie midway between the hour hand and the number twelve. (This works because the sun moves fifteen degrees in an hour, while the hour hand moves thirty degrees.)

If you can determine the approximate time, you can figure direction by noting the path of the sun and knowing the following: At middle latitudes of the Northern Hemisphere, the sun always lies toward the south at midday. Thus, your shadow points north at approximately noon standard time (1 P.M. daylight savings). On the summer solstice (late June), the sun rises roughly in the northeast, passes high overhead in the south at noon, and sets in the northwest. The path of the winter sun lies far to the south, rising south of east and setting south of west. During the equinoxes (late March and September), the sun rises due east and sets due west.

When stars are visible, teach your children to find Polaris, the North Star, which is never more than one degree from true north. It's at the tip of the handle of the Little Dipper, a constellation high in the summer sky. The easiest way to locate it is to start at the Big Dipper. The two stars located on the outer edge of the cup (farthest from the handle) are called pointers. They point upward to the nearby North Star. Thus the North Star is opposite the open side of the dipper.

Actually, any star can teach you direction. Like the sun and the moon, stars move east to west across the sky. That's because the Earth is revolving beneath them; the North Star, directly over the North Pole, does not appear to move at all.

To confirm that stars move, drive a stick into the ground, then back up and drive another stick into the ground. Sight along the tops of the two sticks at a star. Keep watching the star. Which direction does it move? If it moves left, you are looking north; to the right means you are looking south; a rising star means east, a falling star west. Of course, you only have to remember that a rising star means east and left means north—the opposites will take care of themselves.

Nature provides plenty of other directional clues:

• Snow is generally more granular on southern slopes.
• Evergreens are bushiest on the eastern side.

• The tops of pines and hemlocks point east.

• Vegetation is larger and more open on the northern slopes, smaller and denser on southern slopes.

• Many plants orient themselves toward the sun. Others, like the compass plant, align their leaves north-south to shade themselves.

• The smell of a wind blowing off the ocean can lead you to shore.

• The path of migrating birds (flyway) offers directional hints. The ancient Polynesians traveled thousands of miles in open waters using flyways to guide them.

• Birds build nests in the most protected places. More nests on one side of an area's bushes or trees suggests which way the wind blows. If you know the prevailing winds, you have a shot at figuring direction.

Distance

It may help to know how far you have walked. Unless you are wearing a pedometer, an instrument that straps to your leg and measures the distance walked, this figure will be an estimate. Try to make it an educated guess.

Knowing how fast you walk will help you estimate how far you've walked. A young, well-conditioned adult walking swiftly on level ground carrying not too much weight can do about four miles per hour (mph). In mountainous terrain above six thousand feet, the same backpacker will do well to average three mph. The average city-bred backpacker will be closer to two mph. Add kids to the mix and that figure can drop to one mph or less.

You can measure distance by counting footsteps and multiplying by the length of the hiker's stride. All you need to figure stride is a tape measure and a place to walk. Children will enjoy doing this.

Lay out the tape measure in a straight line. Have everybody start at the beginning of the tape and walk along it with a natural pace, counting their steps. To figure stride length, simply divide the distance walked by the number of steps. (I take eighteen steps to walk fifty feet. Fifty divided by eighteen equals a stride of 2.77 feet, or 33.24 inches.)

Urge your children to make a list in their journal of some places within walking distance of home. Have them guess the distance. They can then check their accuracy by counting their steps and doing the arithmetic. Hint number one: Count only the right footfall and multiply by two. Hint number two: There are 63,360 inches in a mile.

> *"There is hardly a wilderness you can't walk out of in a*
> *few days, provided you walk in a straight line and avoid*
> *danger."*   —Tom Brown, Jr.

Compass

Buy your children a compass and show them how to use it. A cheap floating-dial model will suffice on well-marked trails or in familiar country. If you plan to engage in even semiserious navigation, get an inexpensive orienteering compass with movable dial and transparent base. The magnetic needle of a quality compass is contained in a sealed, fluid-filled, clear vial. The purpose of the fluid is to slow down the spinning action of the needle and provide a true reading.

Whole books have been written on land navigation, but you can learn the basics in about thirty minutes. Here are a few tips for happy compassing. First, determine which end of the needle points north. It is usually painted red. Keeping the compass flat, move it until the painted end of the needle points to the *N*. Congratulations. You have found north. The unpainted end of the needle points south. East and west will quickly fall into place.

Declination. Your compass needle is actually pointing toward magnetic north. For reasons unknown, our planet has a magnetic north pole that is near, but not precisely at, the geographic north pole. The difference, or error, between these poles is called magnetic declination. It is read as an angle measurement, expressed in degrees. For North America, declinations range from about twenty-one degrees east (northern Washington) to twenty degrees west (northern Maine). If that seems backward, consider this example: A zero declination line runs through Wisconsin and then curves slightly southeast through the Florida Panhandle. As you go east of this line, your compass needle, locked on magnetic north, will move to the west of true north. Conversely, as you move west, your compass needle will move east.

Since the magnetized needle in your compass will always point to magnetic north, you must compensate or your readings will not correspond accurately to map coordinates, which are based on true north.

How far off course will you be if you ignore declination? Farther than you might think. For each degree of declination error ignored, you will be off almost eighteen feet per thousand feet traveled, or about ninety feet per mile. Consider the example of a group of hikers in central Maine, where declination is twenty degrees. For each mile they hike without adjusting their course for declination, they will deviate from their final destination by ninety (feet) times twenty, or eighteen hundred feet. If they hike three miles, they will be off by more than a mile.

Bearings. A bearing is the direction of travel from your present location to another location, expressed in degrees. If a mountain peak were directly east of your position, the bearing of the mountain relative to your position would be 90 degrees. If the peak were directly south, the bearing would be 180 degrees; west, 270 degrees; north, 360 degrees.

To take a bearing, hold your compass level in front of you with the sighting line (line-of-travel arrow) pointing directly at the object upon which you wish to take a bearing. Turn the compass housing until the orienting arrow (on the bottom of the liquid-filled vial) lines up directly under the painted end of the magnetic needle. The bearing to your object can now be read at the index line.

Maybe you already know the bearing, say sixty degrees, but you need to determine your line of travel. That is, which way to go. First, rotate the housing until the known bearing on the index line (sixty degrees in this case) is lined up with the front sight. Then hold the compass level in front of you and pivot your body until the orienting arrow lines up with the painted end of the magnetized needle. The front sight (line-of-travel arrow) now points the way to your destination.

Map. All maps have three things in common: They are representations of some place, they use symbols, and they use some kind of scale.

Your children must acquire map skills. You can start by pulling out state and city maps, which show the terrain as though it were all one level (planimetric maps). Eventually, you will want to graduate to topographic ("topo") maps, which use contour lines to show the shape of the land, or topography. If topo maps are too complicated for young children, consider drawing them simple maps for a while.

Begin by reading the map's fine print. Find the arrow that indicates north. All topo maps are printed with the direction of true north toward the top of the map. Now find the scale, which usually looks like a ruler. It shows you how many inches (or centimeters) represent a mile (or kilometer) on that particular map. The scale of a map depends on how much area it covers. On a U.S. map, one inch can equal more than one hundred miles; on a small topo, an inch might equal only a mile.

C arry pipe cleaners. They are good for tying bags, playing games, as zipper tab extensions, and for measuring trail mileage on a map. First bend the pipe cleaner to the shape of the trail you intend to hike, then straighten it over the map scale and note the mileage. If you forget pipe cleaners, you can use bread twists, string, thread, matches, twigs, or green pine needles.

Next, look for the legend, which tells you what the symbols on the map mean. Pretty soon, you'll be able to distinguish between a ranger station and an outhouse.

For hikers, backpackers, fishermen, hunters, skiers, and other adventurers, topo maps are essential. You can find them in camping stores or order them from the United States Geological Survey.

At first glance, a topographic map looks like an incomprehensible jumble of squiggly lines, but it's really quite easy to read. Consider the ice cream cone example. Imagine that you place an ice cream cone upside down on a piece of paper. You want to draw a map of it, looking straight down, that will show its cone shape.

Draw a line around the base of the cone. That circle is the outside perimeter of the cone. Then measure all around the cone one inch up from the table and slice the cone along that line. Put the partial cone back on the paper and draw around the new base. You now have a circle within a circle. The inside circle represents all the points on the cone exactly one inch up from the table.

If you repeated the process, each time measuring another inch up from the table, you would have several concentric circles. Any point on a line is the same elevation as any other point on that line.

Each of those lines is called a contour line. Contour lines connect points of equal elevation, so they never touch or overlap. You gain or lose elevation when you travel from one line to another. Lines close to one another indicate steep terrain, while lines far apart show the opposite. Walk along a single contour line and you will be on level ground.

Some other topographic truths:

• The vertical distance between contour lines—the contour interval— is given in the lower map margin. For Sierra topos, fifteen-minute series, the contour interval is eighty feet. That means if you walk from one line to the next, you are climbing or dropping eighty feet. The larger the contour interval, the less detailed the map.

• Where contour lines are close together, you will find an abrupt drop, a falls or canyon.

• The closed or V end of a contour line always points upstream.

• U-shaped contours indicate an outjutting ridge of a hill or mountain. The closed ends of the U's point downhill.

• Elevations are given periodically on many of the lines. The actual height of many objects—mountain peaks, settlements, trail junctions—is also noted, often marked with an X.

• Topos are commonly available in fifteen-minute series, which covers an area of about thirteen by seventeen miles, and seven-and-a-half-minute, which covers about 6½ by 8½ miles. Map minutes are measures of distance, not time. There are sixty minutes in a degree, and one degree covers about seventy miles of latitude or longitude at the equator.

Topo Skills Quiz

    I. (Multiple choice) Contour lines that are

        1. Evenly spaced indicate _____.

        2. Closely spaced indicate_____.

3. Widely spaced indicate_____.
4. Irregularly spaced indicate_____.

a. Gentle slopes
b. Varied terrain
c. Steep slopes or cliffs
d. Uniform slopes

II. True or False
1. Contour lines crossing a stream form V's that point downstream.____
2. Contour lines sometimes split, intersect, or cross._____
3. The farther apart contour lines are, the steeper the hillside._____
4. An intermittent stream is portrayed as a broken blue line._____

Answers

I.
   1. d   2. c   3. a   4. b

II.
   1. False. Contours crossing a stream valley form V's that point upstream.
   2. False. Contour lines never split, intersect, or cross. However, they may be so close together as to appear to converge, which represents a vertical, or nearly vertical, slope.
   3. False.
   4. True.

MAKING SHELTER

The biggest outdoor killer is hypothermia (see chapter 9), a condition in which the body loses more heat than it produces. If your children get lost, making shelter is the most important skill they can have, since they can survive for days with only water and adequate shelter. Besides physical protection, shelters offers a sense of security that is so important in calming frightened children.

The first step is to pick an emergency campsite. The ideal site has:
• Protection from weather
• Protection from rockfall, flash floods, high tides, insects, harmful animals, and poisonous plants
• Level ground for a bed and fireplace
• Materials for making shelter and bed
• Firewood
• Food and water supplies

The ideal shelter should retain heat as well as protect from wind, rain, and snow. Surviving means getting out of the wind, which chills and dehydrates. Natural features, such as caves and hollow logs; the leeward side of ridges, boulders, and overhangs; and deadfalls may offer temporary refuge, but they can also be dangerous. Given wildlife's own fondness for natural shelters, you may just barge in on a sleeping bear, a nest of bees, or a coiled snake. Moreover, some natural shelters are naturally unstable and may collapse. An added problem is that they offer camouflage, making search and rescue more difficult.

I n a pinch, a beaver lodge may offer shelter. After a beaver leaves, his dam often washes away, leaving his house high and dry. Enlarge the opening and you have a tight, waterproof shelter for sleeping. Abandoned beaver ponds usually have a good supply of dead trees lying around for firewood and shelter repairs.

In order to assure survival, teach children how to construct at least a rudimentary shelter. Have them do most of the work. Most people learn better by doing than by watching, and the finished product will give them a sense of pride and accomplishment.

Teach them the concept of how dead-air space warms the body, using examples from their lives: fluffy blankets, down jackets, or the loft of a sleeping bag. Birds fluff their feathers to create dead-air space for warmth. Make a pile of forest litter—soil and leaves—and show your children how it holds dead-air space. Have them make their own litter pile, bury their hands in it, and feel the warmth.

The simplest man-made shelter, effective against rain but less so against cold, can be made from one decent conifer. Look for a spruce or pine with branches growing nearly to the ground. Break off enough lower limbs (this is an emergency) to allow room to sit against the tree. Use the broken boughs as insulation against the ground or weave them through the other branches to make a tighter canopy.

If caught in blizzard country with night falling and weather worsening, find the leeward side of a ridge, boulder, or gully. Dig through the snow, if necessary, to hollow out a burrow. Line with vegetation; if not available, use sticks and logs (dirt gets very cold).

If no natural windbreaks are available, make a trench shelter. Dig a rectangular hole in the ground, about eight feet long and three feet wide, with the length of the hole at a right angle to the wind. If vegetation is available, use it for both bedding and roof. If snow is available, build a windbreak, piling it high on the windward side of the trench.

With time and sufficient materials, your children can construct a decent shelter. Many survival books advise building wickiups or lean-tos, but debris shelters are easier. Pick an area that won't get washed out in a hard rain. It should be free of rock and tree fall, with good drainage, far from poisonous plants, and not over an anthill or animal hole. Keep in mind that the air temperature under a thick stand of evergreens is up to ten degrees warmer than that in open areas and that thick trees help break the wind, reducing the windchill factor. On the other hand, a thick forest is shielded from the sun and may be perpetually damp. The best place for a shelter is usually the transition area between forest and field.

Now help your children find a boulder, a fallen tree, a stump, or some other object about three feet high. Congratulate them. They have just completed one wall of their shelter. Next, they should find a stick several inches in diameter and five or more feet long. Lean one end of the stick on the object and rest the other end on the ground. That's the shelter's center ridge pole.

Next, have them collect a few bushels of smaller sticks to lean on both sides of the ridge pole, perpendicular to it. This forms the roof of

Building a survival hut is easy, fun, and great for kids' self-esteem.

the structure, with the ridge pole at the peak. Near the boulder, stump, or log, on the side away from the wind, leave a small opening for a door.

At this point, have your children crawl inside their shelters to make sure they are large enough. They should permit movement without kicking out the sides. If so, finish the outside by piling on a thick insulating layer of twigs and dried leaves. Add another layer of small branches to hold the insulation in place. Finally, taking a lesson from animals, stuff the inside with dried leaves, pine needles, or ferns, loosely filling the shelter from top to bottom. Need more insulation? Evergreen boughs make a comfortable bed.

With the shelter complete, your child should be able to crawl inside feet first and, if need be, survive warm and dry for days. If this is a practice run, let your kids play with their shelters for a while. They can crawl in and out, pretending it's home. After you're done, show them how to restore the environment to its natural state by breaking down the shelter and scattering it.

Building a shelter is strenuous work, and it's easy to move so quickly that you perspire heavily. Then when you stop, your body gets badly chilled, which can be life-threatening without a fire. Work at a moderate pace and minimize sweat.

> The proper attitude can make you warmer. If you are cold, relax and think hot thoughts, like, say, running through the desert in the summer.

FINDING WATER

Most children will think of finding food first, then water. That's because they have the metabolism of a hummingbird and are probably not in the habit of drinking water. In truth, humans can live much longer without food than without water.

> According to the Backpacker's Law of Threes, you will die if you go longer than:
> Three minutes without air
> Three hours without shelter from a storm
> Three days without water
> Three weeks without food

Water is critical at any time of the year. Dehydration, which can strike even in the winter, worsens other outdoor ailments, such as hypothermia and frostbite. Lack of water also makes us more susceptible to the cold. On the other hand, water weighs more than two pounds a quart, so we don't want to carry more than necessary. Store it in your body by drinking a quart or two before you set off on foot.

The water table is often close to the surface and can be located by digging in the following places:

- At the base of cliffs where more than a little vegetation is thriving.
- At the base of large sand dunes on the steep or shady side. If you hit wet sand, cease digging; if conditions are right, water will seep out of the sand into the hole you created. The primary water should be fresh; if you dig deeper, the lower water may contain salt.
- In dry mudholes, sinks, and at the outside bend of riverbeds.
- Anywhere the ground is damp or muddy.

• In low spots favored by indicator plants, which grow only where they can obtain water. These include sycamores, cottonwoods, cattails, salt grass, greasewood, willows, hackberries, and elderberries.

Obtaining water from the soil is possible if you do the following:

• Dig a hole in damp or muddy sinks, allowing water to seep in.

• Wring mud through a shirt or cloth to force out water.

• Construct a solar still, which requires a little equipment but almost no building skills. You need a container (usually a bucket), a plastic drinking tube, and a six-by-six-foot piece of clear plastic.

Dig a three-foot hole and place the container at the bottom of it. Stretch the plastic sheet over the hole and hold it in place with dirt, which seals the hole off from outside air. Place a rock in the center of the plastic to weigh it down until it sags to within two inches of the container. Ar-

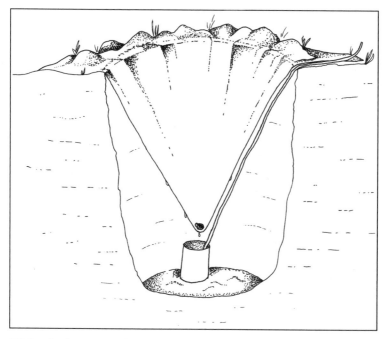

With a bucket, some plastic, and a drinking tube, you can create drinking water. Isn't condensation wonderful?

range the drinking tube so that one end sits in the container and the other end extends outside the still.

The sun's warmth will penetrate the plastic and warm the soil in the hole. Moisture from the soil evaporates, then condenses on the underside of the plastic, where it runs down the cone and drips into the container. The water can be sucked right through the plastic tubing without disturbing the still.

Green plants placed in the pit will augment water production. It is best to locate stills in damp areas, lowlands, at the base of hills, in dry riverbeds, or in rich soil at the bottom of gullies.

Other sources of water include these:

• The dew from rocks and plants. In many arid parts of the globe, primitive peoples arise before dawn to collect dew. The easiest way is to mop gently with a handkerchief or shirt, then wring it into your mouth or a container. If cloth is not available, you can use a handful of dry grass. It is possible to mop up more than a pint an hour using this technique. Though generally dew is one of the safest water sources, don't mop from poisonous plants or chemically sprayed vegetation.

• If you're desperate (why else would you be mopping up dew?), you can cut and peel a cactus and suck out the moisture. This slakes thirst but the taste is vile.

• In the Southwest, much of the desert is dotted with uplifted sandstone ridges that divide the land into valleys and drainages. These exposed areas of stone absorb little moisture, and even a skimpy rain can cause water to collect in tiny rock pockets. To find it, you must abandon your instinct to look in low land; instead, seek high ground. Check side canyons, narrow clefts, and white sandstone ridges. Such pockets can sometimes hold water for months after a rain.

More Water Tips

• Animal tracks may lead you to water.

• Birds can sometimes be seen circling over, or heading toward, water holes, especially in the morning and evening. Listen for their calls and watch their flights.

• When you find water, mark it on your map with the date. Build a valuable history of water sources in favorite areas.

• Beware of stagnant water bearing no signs of life. If the water has crawling or wriggling creatures, it probably is not deadly poisonous, though it may harbor harmful microorganisms. Animal tracks near water holes are a good sign, unless there are a lot of skeletal remains.

• Consider all water polluted, even if it looks good. Giardia does not discolor the water; it just makes you sick. Simple diarrhea or vomiting can dehydrate a body quickly, leaving the victim worse off than if he had stayed away from water altogether.

• Water polluted by animals or debris tastes bad, but it is harmless if purified or treated.

• Let muddy water stand overnight. Run it though a grass filter or several layers of cloth, or allow it to seep through the soil into a hole dug about a foot away.

• If the water supply is limited, walk slowly and avoid the midday heat. Eat little or not at all, as digestion depletes the body's water reserves.

• Sucking on pebbles and chewing gum slake thirst but do nothing to stave off dehydration.

• Drinking blood or urine increases dehydration, although soaking clothing in urine will cool the body and stem sweat loss.

• Store water in the stomach. People have died from dehydration with water still in their canteens.

MAKING FIRE

Besides providing light and heat, a fire can aid in cooking, signaling, purifying water, and feeling more secure.

You must determine when your children are ready to acquire fire skills. Outdoor author Tom Brown believes that a child of eight should be able to make a primitive fire. Whatever the learning pace, here is a logical order for earning merit badges in fire skills:

• Wood Gatherer
• Careful Observer of Adults Building and Maintaining Fires
• Assistant Fire Maintainer
• Chief Fire Maintainer

• Assistant Fire Builder
• Chief Fire Builder

Over time, you should teach your children all of the following and more:

• How to use matches safely. Stick matches are best for teaching kids.
• When it is appropriate and legal to have a fire. If possible, take your children to the site of a forest fire and show them the destruction.
• How to find dry wood under logs or around the base of trees.
• How to use a knife to find dry wood inside of wet wood.
• How not to find it—except in emergencies—on live trees.
• How to find the best wood for kindling.
• How to break wood against rocks or stumps so it fits in the fire.
• How to avoid burning poison oak, ivy, and sumac.
• How to construct a tepee fire.
• How to position wood in the flames to maintain the fire.
• How to moderate the flame and create proper coals for cooking and roasting marshmallows.
• How to select a fire site that is distant from trails, waterways, standing rocks, and overhanging limbs, protected from the wind, relatively free of ground vegetation, neither beneath tree branches nor too close to a shelter, and, except in emergencies, in an established pit.
• How to put out a fire and camouflage the remains.

When it's time for your children to build a fire from scratch, have them use a stick or rock to scratch out a fire hole about twelve inches deep by two feet across. Clean the immediate area of vegetation (I once had a fire travel several feet through rich, loamy soil). Ring the hole with rocks to contain the fire. Use dirt, rocks, or wood to build a wall on the windward side of the fire. That will protect the flames from the wind, reflect heat, and conserve wood.

For weightless, no-fail emergency tinder, carry cotton balls rolled in petroleum jelly. Store them in a film canister,

It's never too early to teach your children how to collect firewood.

(PHOTO BY JIM HAMILTON)

which will hold at least thirty. Show your children how you can web two or three together and lay a tepee of twigs over them.

Here's another no-weight, no-cost fire starter: dryer lint. Pack it in plastic bags and use it as a fire core as needed.

Everyone who is old enough should have in their survival kit a means of starting a fire. Matches are a terrific invention. They consistently beat striking rocks or rubbing two sticks together, two very challenging friction methods for starting fires. Most people forced to rely on friction for a flame will do better waiting to be struck by lightning.

I f you insist upon mastering a primitive friction technique for starting fires, practice the hand-drill method. First fashion a hand drill and a fire baseboard out of dry wood. The drill is a stick usually eighteen to twenty inches long, tapering at one end. The tapered end is the upper end; the larger end rests on the fire board, which is placed flat on the ground. Place the palms of your hands together over the tapered end of the drill and rub them together with a constant downward pressure. Place dry tinder around the friction point of the fire board. Your hands will tend to slide down the drill; move them back to the top. With practice and patience, friction should build enough heat to ignite the tinder.

No matter where you get your spark, you will need tinder. This can be last night's math homework, but if you want to perfect fire skills, practice with nature's own. It can be found in many forms, including dead grass or dry twigs (shredded between the fingers), the inner bark of dead trees, dry moss, evergreen needles, downy feathers, abandoned nests, dried animal dung, cattail fluff, and oily birch bark. Other tinder includes paper, clothing, bandannas, and burnable trash. Ideally, tinder should be finely shredded but not powdered.

Over a carefully placed ball of, say, shredded twig mung, pile tiny dry twigs, tepee style. A tepee's flame is hot and efficient and holds up well in rain. The twigs should be close enough to feed off one another, but not so close that oxygen fails to reach the core. Light the tinder in more than one place. If a prolonged flame is needed, try lighting a well-placed candle stub.

If rain threatens the life of your young fire, have your children cover it with bark slabs, being careful not to smother the flame.

As the fire builds, gradually increase the size of the sticks. Teach your children not to drop or throw sticks on the fire—it sprays sparks and hinders air flow—but to lay them on the fire carefully, maintaining a cone shape. After branches an inch or so in diameter are burning, you can hunt for bigger pieces. Increase the size of the fire until it will burn logs six inches or more in diameter. Those will hold a fire for hours. If they can't be cut short enough, push the ends into the pit as they burn.

Know your woods. Softwoods, like pine and fir, start a fire more easily than hardwoods, like oak and birch. But they burn more quickly and, being full of pitch, have a tendency to spark.

Once a fire is made, it must be maintained. You can keep it going through the night by building up a deep bed of coals and banking them with ashes and a thin layer of dirt. You can also lay two green logs across the fire bed so that flames dart up between them. If they get a good start before the other wood burns out, they will smolder through the night. The key is to keep the wind from the coals. If it rains, cover the banked fire with bark, a flat stone, or something waterproof.

The Paiute Indians used to transport fires over long distances by ingeniously wrapping coals in a core of finely shredded bark, around which they wrapped more shredded bark, then several layers of bark strips. The finished package, resembling a cigar two feet long and six inches wide, could hold a spark for up to twelve hours.

Some more fire tips:

• You can buy waterproof matches at an outdoor store, waterproof them yourself by dipping the tips in wax, or carry two dozen wooden ones (break and alternate ends) in a plastic 35mm film canister. This handy little container will keep matches dry even if you fall in a lake. Damp wooden matches can usually be dried by stroking them twenty to thirty times through your dry hair.

• Candle stubs can be a big help, especially if the wood is wet. They can sit in the fire tinder for a long time, drying out the wood.

• You can direct sunlight through a magnifying glass, or any convex lens, to start a flame in tinder.

• Soft woods give more light than hard woods.

• Use reflectors for added warmth.

Especially if conditions are less than ideal, stay with the basics when building a fire.

• Use flames for boiling and baking, coals for frying.

• When leaving a fire for good, douse it with water, then douse it again.

• When using something other than a permanent fire site, scatter ashes and work them into the soil to remove all traces.

• Before building a fire on bare rock, put down a two-inch layer of sand or soil to prevent charring the rock. Scatter the protective layer when you are done. Archaeologists have found rocks still smudged from fires that burned thousands of years ago.

Some wet-weather fire tips:

• Matches must be kept dry not just from water but from dampness, too.

• If it looks like rain, gather tinder and kindling for several fires and stash them under something waterproof.

• Split open wet logs to get to the dry wood inside.

• A disposable butane lighter should be good for a thousand lights even in wet weather.

• Use a fire starter (a petroleum gel) to prolong the flame so that the tinder has a chance to catch.

• If the damp tinder is slow to ignite, blow gently on the spark until it bursts into flame.

• In some parts of the country, you can find pitch wood—dead pine that is warted with dried sap. The sap burns easily, making it a natural fire starter.

SIGNALING FOR HELP

Pose this exercise in creative thinking to your children: "If you were lost in the wilderness, how could you signal rescuers?" Here are a few ideas; there are no doubt others.

• Build a smoky fire, taking special care when fire risk is high. Clear an area and burn green boughs, which create a lot of smoke and are less likely to spread. If you can't keep a fire going, set it up but wait to light it until you hear a low-flying aircraft (a 747 at thirty-eight thousand feet won't be much help).

• Lay out bright-colored clothing or camping gear on a hilltop or in a clearing.

• Rearrange the natural features of the landscape into some unnatural geometric form, if it doesn't require too much energy.

• Blast your whistle three times. Three of anything (gunshots, lip pops) is the universal signal for distress.

• Use a mirror to reflect sunlight. A regular hand mirror will do, but a signal mirror with a sighting hole in it is best. Used by the military, they are available at surplus stores.

If you do use a regular mirror, hold your hand in front of it and catch the reflected light. This will give you a rough idea of the direction of the most intense flashes and allow you to adjust your aim.

No mirror? Improvise. A piece of broken glass covered on one side with dark mud will make a usable mirror; a can lid can be polished until it is like a mirror, and it's easy to punch a sighting hole in the center. A wet log slab can be a signal mirror, as can a slab of ice.

Even though it may seem futile, flash your mirror repeatedly throughout the day. It takes little effort, and in open areas the flashes can be seen for long distances. Flash toward the sound of an aircraft, even though you cannot see it.

• Aircraft in sight? Flash a flashlight three distinct times. If not, especially at night, wave it around. Someone may see it.

• Wave a bright-colored jacket on the end of a stick.

• Climb a tree or mountain and tie something eye-catching up high so it will wave in the wind.

• When snow covers the ground, stamp out "SOS" and fill the depressions with leaves and branches to make the message more visible. Try to make the letters at least twenty feet long.

• Pile rocks or logs in the pattern of a cross at least twenty feet long.

• Stand with both arms raised, palms open. In football, this means touchdown; in search and rescue, it means, "I need help." Don't go halfway: Holding up one hand means, "I don't need help."

• Pound on a hollow log, a rock, or a metal object with sticks. It will make quite a ruckus and can be kept up for a long time to guide rescuers.

• Use international ground-air emergency signals. Make the following symbols large, using whatever is available: aluminum foil, clothing, rocks, or tree limbs.

Unable to proceed:	X
Require doctor:	I (single straight line)
Need food and water:	F
No:	N
Yes:	Y
All is well:	LL
Am going in this direction:	use arrow

Audio signals will be the most effective for the first day or two; after that, when aerial rescue is more likely, concentrate on visual signals.

FINDING FOOD

Although most of us get irked if we miss a meal, you can survive weeks without food. On the other hand, if you are physically, stressfully involved in staying alive, you'll be burning a lot of calories and survival time may be reduced. Foraging alone can be a full-time job, carrying the risk that the hunt will burn more calories than the meal provides. Always consider the physiological costs of the search for food.

If water is scarce, eat nothing, for digestion requires extra water. Normally, someone fighting a water deficit does not feel hunger.

For someone desperate for food, almost every animal may be considered edible if properly prepared. He who concentrates solely on large game will starve, so exploit as much of the food chain as possible. Adaptability is important, as are certain skills. There is a telling moment in the movie *Jeremiah Johnson* in which Robert Redford is making a futile attempt to snatch a fish with his hands while a skeptical Indian looks on. He was finding out what Hollywood had kept secret for so long: Obtaining food in the wild is hard.

The pursuit of edible animals is a special challenge. Slow-moving beasts tend to be small, perhaps requiring dozens to make a meal. Larger, meatier game tends to be too fast or powerful for easy capture.

Even insects can provide an important emergency source of food. Found in profusion after hatching, they have high nutritional value and can add substantially to a meager meal. They must always be cooked, though, as they carry parasites. Insects can be roasted, dried, ground into meal, and served in soups and stews. Consider grasshoppers, locusts, crickets, katydids, cicadas, and ants. Grubs and caterpillars can be added to soups and stews, but avoid fuzzy ones, as some are poisonous.

Audrey Sutherland, who could give the Boy Scouts lessons in being prepared, said, "I ought to be able to eat anything that anyone in the world finds edible, but there are still some prejudices to overcome. Cockroaches have a greasy, bland flavor and a repulsive crunch. Ants are crisp and acid flavored, and cling to my tongue even after being chewed."

Of the reptiles and amphibians, frogs are probably the best food source. They are easily caught and are sometimes numerous in marshy areas. Lizards may require too much effort for the return, though a capable slingshotter can have some success. A well-thrown rock can also stop small game. The best tool for snake hunting is a sharp, fire-hardened stick. Like all reptiles and amphibians, snakes should be skinned and eviscerated before they are cooked. That should take care of your appetite for a while.

Jeremiah Johnson notwithstanding, you can catch fish by hand, spear, trap, or hook. Hooks can be fashioned from twigs, bones (including fish skeletons), nails, or thorns. Fishing line can be adapted from plant fibers, wire, the inner bark of some trees, a leather belt cut into strips and tied together, or unraveled clothing. Before you start taking apart your clothes, however, search the area for discarded fishing line. Ten feet on a long pole should suffice.

If you're trying to grab a fish, move your hand slowly through the water until it is below the fish's belly, then quickly scoop it onto the bank. Watch grizzlies to improve your technique.

Some animals, such as rabbits and deer, are quick but lack endurance and can be run down and caught by hand. Prefer to outthink your animals? Make a noose out of string, rope, or fishing line and place it around an animal's hole or burrow. When the animal begins to emerge, jerk the string and tighten the noose around its neck. You also can put bait under a box propped up by a stick. Tie a line to the stick. When your prey goes after the bait, pull the string, drop the box, and trap the animal.

Pay attention to birds of prey. Sometimes you can scare them away from their catch of the day. As for preying directly on birds, the small ones usually require more effort than they're worth and the larger ones require unusual dexterity or a sophisticated knowledge of traps and snares. Occasionally, by using fishing line, birds can be caught at a water hole or where seeds have been scattered. Attach one end of a very fine line to a fixed object and place the rest of it in a loose tangle on the ground. The hope is that a plump, tasty bird will become entangled in the line, permitting capture by hand. Once in a new moon, you might bring down a distracted, possibly retarded, bird by throwing a stick. Quail and chuckers, which prefer to scurry rather than fly, can sometimes be herded, especially in narrow canyons.

If you seek animals for food, consider the following:

• Bird eggs, regardless of the stage of embryo development, are good to eat.

• Lizards are all edible, although you should be careful of the gila monster's bite.

• Snakes of all species are good to eat.

• Tortoises and porcupines are slow afoot, easy to kill, and good eating (if you remove the shell or quills).

• Meat may be cooked on a stick over a fire or wrapped in green leaves, aluminum foil, or mud, then nestled in coals and baked.

• Any extra meat can be preserved by making it into jerky. Take lean meat, cut it into thin strips several inches long, then hang it in the sun for two or three days until completely dried. The jerky will keep indefinitely as long as it is dry and may be eaten soaked, cooked, or as is.

If you seek animals for food, beware of the following problems:

• Some animals, particularly rabbits, have been known to carry tularemia, a disease transmittable to man. If an animal acts sickly or its liver is spotted, do not eat it.

• Rabies is another concern. Beware of wild animals that seem abnormally fearless, though not all animals that fail to run have rabies.

• Skin a frog before eating it (and you thought you'd never use tenth-grade biology); avoid toads, which have glands in their skin.

• Rodents may harbor plague-carrying fleas.

• A few animals, like skunks and peccaries, have scent or musk glands that will taint the meat unless removed immediately after killing.

• Don't allow the hair of an animal to contact the meat; it may give the meat a strong taste.

Edible Plants. People have died amid plenty because they couldn't "stomach" wild foods, a bad trait if there ever was one. There are plenty of edible plants in the wild; unfortunately, there are also a bounty of inedible ones and some poisonous ones. You must know plants to tell the difference. In other words, before you can know edible plants, you must know plants in general.

Make botany a fun family project. Stock your library with field guides

You might begin plant-identification lessons with these two represent-atives from species Toxicodendron.

in plant identification. Take a class on the subject. Each time you take your children into nature, open your guides and key out some plants.

When your children have improved their identification skills, teach them about wild edibles. Focus on one plant at a time. Identify it, compare it to look-alikes, harvest it, take it home, and prepare it with a regular meal. In order for children to truly know a plant, they must participate in every step.

Unless you are experienced, stay away from mushrooms; also avoid plants that secrete a milky sap, for they are often poisonous.

Consider concentrating on four species of wild, edible plants and branching out only after you and your children have achieved some expertise. Acorns, cattails, grasses, and pines are pervasive in North America and are easy to identify, with almost no poisonous look-alikes.

Acorns. Oaks, which produce acorns, are everywhere. They range from scrubby plants to huge trees and are easy to identify. Young children tend to call lots of nuts "acorns," so be careful with identification.

The acorns of all North American oaks are edible, though some are bitter. You can remove the bitterness by leaching. Have your children shell the nuts and mash the meat. Soak the paste in water for two hours, drain, and soak again and again. The paste is ready when it has lost its bitter taste.

Cattails. One need not starve where cattails grow. They are edible from root to top. In fall and winter, the rhizomes (thick root) can be peeled and cooked like potatoes or dried and pounded into flour. In spring and early summer, the young shoots can be eaten raw or cooked and the immature flower spikes can be boiled and eaten like miniature ears of corn.

It is hard to confuse the cattail with any other plant, so eating it is safe. However, children should be cautious harvesting these bog-loving plants, as survival often demands staying as dry as possible.

Grasses. New shoots of grass, up to six inches, can be eaten raw. Mature grasses contain cellulose, which is difficult to digest. You can chew these grasses and spit out the pulp or steep them in hot water for thirty minutes and make a tea. That way you get the nutrition without the cellulose. Most grass seeds are edible, but because a few are toxic, cook all seeds.

Pines. Widespread throughout North America, pines are easy to recognize and supply nutritious food. To make a tea high in vitamins A and C, break the needles into tiny pieces and steep them in warm water for thirty minutes. Pine nuts are found within mature cones; a delicacy in many cuisines, they are edible raw, roasted, or ground into flour. You can open cones by placing them near a fire. Even the inner bark and tiny rootlets of a pine tree are edible in a stew or soup.

Several evergreens are toxic, so it's important that your children learn to identify pines.

LOSTPROOFING

If you want to minimize the chances of losing your children, teach them:

- To wear a whistle and a survival pack
- To develop direction awareness
- To look at prominent and unusual features

- To turn and look at features as they will appear on the return trip
- To use all their senses when traveling in the wilderness
- To STOP—sit, think, observe, plan—if they think they're lost.

If you accomplish this, you will notice quite a change in your children. They will be more confident, both of their own abilities and of their place in nature. This is a priceless insurance policy against panic, the lost child's greatest enemy. With survival skills and a positive outlook, children will feel at home in the wilderness. When that happens, they are never really lost, only misplaced.

An organization called Hug-a-Tree and Survive puts out a list of the eight things to do to reduce the chances of your children becoming lost:

1. Take their footprints. Have your children walk across a piece of foil on a soft surface, like a rug or towel. Mark the foil with the child's name. With this print, searchers can separate your child's print from others and quickly determine direction of travel.

2. Have your children carry a trash bag and whistle. The bag can be an emergency shelter/poncho (a hole must be cut for the face to avoid suffocation), and the whistle carries farther than the sound of a child's voice.

3. Try to keep children oriented. Point out landmarks, terrain changes, and the direction of the sun.

4. Assure them that you won't be mad if they get lost. Children have actually avoided searchers because they feared punishment.

5. Assure them that there will lots of people searching for them and that they should stay put rather than wander.

6. Assure them that there are no animals that will hurt them. If they hear a noise at night, they should yell at it. If it's an animal, it will run; if it's searchers, they will be found.

7. Teach your children to make themselves big for possible

(Photo by Jim Hamilton)

When you finally make it back to camp, there's nothing like that first root beer.

aerial rescue. Wave or wear bright-colored clothing. Spell out "SOS" using shrubbery or rocks or by rubbing a foot in the dirt.

8. Teach children to hug a tree if they think they are lost. It will ground them, help avert panic, and keep them in one place.

If Someone Is Lost

Parents and guardians must also avoid panic in the face of a lost child. When you first suspect a child is lost, take a couple of deep breaths, then yell until you turn red in the face.

Stop and think, "Where did I last see him?" Return to that spot. Yell and blow your whistle. If there is no response after a search of the immediate area, send for help. Include the following information about the lost child: description, clothing, type of footwear, and when and where last seen.

I t's not always kids who get lost. My wife's hairdresser, Marlena, told this story: "One afternoon, my friend Paul and I went to Armstrong Woods (a California state park). We just started walking, no real aim in mind. I had Devon [her one-year-old son] on my back in a kid carrier. We walked a couple of hours up a dirt road, toward Bullfrog Pond, but then we realized it was getting dark. So we headed down a trail that we knew would take us back to the parking lot.

"As we dropped into the forest, it got very dark very fast. No moon. Suddenly, we couldn't see our hand in front of our face. It got so bad we had to get down on our hands and knees and feel for the trail. At one point, I could feel that we were right on the edge of a cliff. Then Paul rammed right into a tree and bent his glasses. I was right behind him and I dropped the baby bottle. I couldn't see it, but I could hear it rolling way down the hill. That was the low point.

"Finally, we'd had enough. I was ready to spend the night. We found a leafy area and lay down with Devon in between us. It was probably midnight, cool but not freezing. I fell asleep, but I don't think it was too long before I heard someone yelling, 'Hey, are you out there? Hey!' I sat up and yelled back, 'Hey! Here we are!'

"It was a ranger. Turns out, we were about twenty feet from an outbuilding with a telephone in it.

"The lesson for me was—is—be prepared. It's one thing to be spontaneous, but when you have a child, you have to plan ahead. I was hiking in a skirt and cowboy boots."

Marlena was telling me this story in my backyard. We were miles from the nearest trail, with no intention of hiking that day. She wore her hiking boots—just in case.

SURVIVAL ACTIVITIES

One way to teach children about direction is to have them make a simple compass. For both of the examples below, you will need a needle and a fairly strong magnet (a strong refrigerator magnet should work). Tape one end of the needle to the magnet and leave it overnight. The next morning, test your new magnet by trying to pick up another needle.

Floating Compass

Skewer a small piece of cork with your new magnet-needle, so that the cork is balanced roughly in the middle of the needle. Carefully float the cork in a cup of water. Move the cup around the room or take it outside. The needle should continue to float in the same direction.

Swinging Compass.

This is even easier to construct. Just tie a long thread around the middle of the magnetized needle and let it hang. Move the thread back and forth on the needle until it hangs parallel to the ground. The needle will turn back and forth until the kinks are out of the thread, after which it should always point in the same direction.

In both cases, the needle will align itself north-south. But which is which? Take your homemade compass outside. Face the sun and stretch your arms straight out to your sides. If it's before noon, your left hand is pointing north; if it is afternoon, your right hand is pointing north. Once you identify north, you can link it with either the pointy end of the needle or the eye end.

GAMES

Fun is a better motivator than fear. Make learning fun and children may better remember the lesson. In teaching survival skills, emphasize the adventure-play part. Games can help.

These games can be modified for individual or group play or for different ages. They can be made more or less competitive. As always, make any local rules necessary to assure safety. Later, devise games yourself. Better yet, encourage your kids to invent their own games.

Fast Shelter Game

The object is to see which child can build a debris hut the quickest. Divide into groups or play as individuals. Tell your charges that upon your signal, they are to move quickly out of camp, find the best location, and build a debris hut. While they are working, adults can roam from hut to hut, offering help, correcting big mistakes, and letting little ones go.

Once everybody has returned to camp, go as a group to each hut, stopping to discuss the good, bad, and ugly of each one. Don't offer too many opinions; let the children do most of the analysis. When you do offer criticism, find positive things to say. Afterward, have the children return their debris huts to nature.

Fast Fire Game

Like the Fast Shelter Game, this one can be played by individuals or groups. Have each person or group dig a fire pit, clearing a safe area around it. All the children should build their pits in the same general area so that you can see all fires at once.

Once the pit has been dug, have the children hammer two stakes into the ground, one on each side of the fire. Tie a string between the stakes, about two feet above the bottom of the pit. Upon your signal, the children should go collect firewood, build a tepee fire, and light it. The first one whose fire burns through the string wins.

Fast Water Game

Supply each group or child with a cup and a four-by-four-foot piece of clear plastic. Upon your signal, have them pick a suitable location and build a solar still. When everyone is finished, go to each still as a group and discuss the pros and cons. The winner is the child or group whose still produces a pint or so of water. Thus, the game rewards the most effective, not necessarily the quickest, construction.

Natural Shelter Hide-and-Seek

Play this game only after a detailed group discussion on natural shelters. When you give a signal, the children should move from camp and find a natural shelter in which to hide—not only from you, but from the weather. They can choose brush piles, deadfalls, lightning-carved tree caves, rock outcroppings, or other natural shelters. As always, encourage a discussion on the good and bad points of each shelter.

The next two games permit children to see the world through the eyes of animals.

The Crawl: Children crawl slowly through the backyard or the city park, peering into brush, pulling back blades of grass, looking under stones, and scanning all around them like an animal alert to danger and food.

Limited Vision: Cut toilet paper tubes in half and tape them to each lens of an old pair of sunglasses. Use more tape to block all peripheral vision, then have your children walk or crawl around outside, discovering an animal's perspective, one without stereoscopic vision.

RESOURCES

Books

Land Navigation Handbook by W.S. Kals (1983: Sierra Club Books, San Francisco)

The Sierra Club Wayfinding Book by Vicki McVey (1989: Sierra Club Books, San Francisco)

The Boy Scout Handbook (Boy Scouts of America, Irving, TX)

Wilderness Basics by the San Diego chapter of the Sierra Club (1993: The Mountaineers, Seattle)

Tom Brown's Guide to Nature and Survival for Children by Tom Brown, Jr. (1989: Berkley Books, New York)

Organizations

Project Hug-a-Tree and Survive
6465 Lance Way
San Diego, CA 92120

11 How to Do the Outdoors with Babies and Small Children

Now I see the secret of the making of the best persons,
It is to grow in the open air,
and to eat and sleep with the earth.
—Walt Whitman

Having a baby is no reason to stop camping and hiking. All it takes is some special gear and a thorough checklist. Both parents should list the items they think are important, then decide what goes and what stays. Besides special foods, toys, and practical clothes, you may need diapers and bottles, which are bulky. There are also regular items, such as insect repellent, sunscreen, and medicine, that take on special importance when a baby is along.

Although you certainly won't need all of these items, your checklist might look like this:

DIAPER BAG
- Bottles
- Baby spoons
- Bibs
- Baby powder/diaper rash cream
- Diapers (cloth or disposable)
- Damp towelettes without alcohol
- Formula
- Blankey/lovey
- Garbage bags for used diapers
- Baby food and juice
- Washcloths

Diapers. Let's face it, the monster issue here is diapers—cloth or disposable? Camping with diapers causes environmentalism to run smack into convenience. Both cloth and disposable types are bulky and must be packed out. Both cause environmental problems (disposables create trash; cloths require water and fuel to wash). Cloth diapers are reusable and thus cheaper in the long run. They pack better than disposables and can play other roles, such as towels, bibs, and washcloths. On the other hand, cloths are heavier, less convenient, and less absorbent than state-of-the-art disposables. Also washing cloth diapers in the wilderness is no small hassle.

Many parents who do take cloth diapers refuse to wash them until they get home. The alternative is using time and precious fuel to heat water, dumping feces and wastewater at least two hundred feet from waterways, then scrubbing diapers in hot, soapy water, rinsing twice, and trying to dry them, perhaps in wet or chilly weather. My advice: Take disposables.

If you plan to do a wilderness diaper wash, consider carrying a plastic bathtub in which to soak and wash them. Get one that fits in your backpack. Stuff gear in and around it and it won't take much room. You can also use it for bathing baby or soaking your feet.

Whether you carry cloth or disposable diapers, include plenty of plastic bags, big and small, for transporting dirty diapers. An ammonia-soaked sponge kept in the diaper bag will help control odors.

Food. The nursing infant is the easiest person to feed on a camping trip, as long as you don't lose Mom. Bottles present more of a problem, as the formula and paraphernalia are heavy and bulky, and cleanliness is essential. For a day trip, fill bottles with boiled water at home or camp, then add formula powder to the bottle on the trail.

For camping, the lightest and least bulky method is to carry powdered formula, a couple of special plastic bottles, and plenty of their disposable plastic bag inserts. Because this method demands boiling water in camp, it requires the most time and fuel. An alternative is to carry ready-to-drink bottles. This is much less work, but you must deal with the weight, bulk, and expense of all those bottles.

Other options fall between those two extremes. One possibility for short trips is to reduce the amount of formula baby gets. This won't be a problem as long as she gets lots of fluids and other healthful foods. If you rely heavily on juices, provide a variety of flavors.

Most bottles you make up in camp will be clean but not sterile. Bacteria love warm formula; don't mix it until feeding time. If you are worried about keeping formula fresh, bring "terminally" sterilized bottles from home. This involves cooking filled, loosely capped bottles in a sterilizer for twenty minutes. After the bottles have cooled in the sterilizer, the caps are tightened. These bottles can be stored without refrigeration, for you have effectively canned the milk.

The baby's solid foods in camp can be the same as she gets at home. Cereals can be stored in plastic bags, juices in plastic bottles. Store-bought baby foods should not be opened until ready to use. Pack them so the glass jars don't bang against one another.

There is a wide range of dried baby foods—cereals, fruits, dinners, and deserts. With snap-on lids, you reconstitute only the amount you need, saving the rest.

When you pack the little nipper's meals, include her plastic Peter Rabbit bowl and spoon, her Aladdin bib, and her Winnie-the-Pooh washcloth.

Take the same precautions camping that you would at home. Beware of inappropriate foods. According to surveys from Johns Hopkins University, the following foods were most likely to be involved in the fatal choking of children under five.
- Peanut butter/peanut butter sandwiches
- Grapes   • Hard cookies/biscuits • Round candy

• Peanuts	• Apple chunks/slices	• Meat chunks/slices
• Raw carrots	• Hot dogs/sausages	• Popcorn

CLOTHING

• Booties	• Socks	• Hats
• Sweater	• Hooded sweatshirt	
• Rain jacket/poncho	• Jumpsuit	
• Mittens (they're warmer than gloves but reduce dexterity)		

Clothing. When evaluating clothing needs, remember that babies are not just miniature adults; they have their own special needs. They are especially at risk during their first year, when they have less insulating fat, a smaller reservoir of heat, no concept of cold, and an inability to communicate specific discomfort. If they are being carried, they also have less opportunity to produce heat.

Dress babies and toddlers in warm, nonbreathable layers and moni-

Be vigilant about keeping the nonhiker warm.

(PHOTO BY BRUCE MAXWELL)

tor their condition for signs of cold or overheating. Check telltale extremities like nose, ears, toes, and fingers. Footed sleepers, hooded sweatshirts, and balaclavas all warm cold extremities. One-piece baby bags cover most of the body and won't ride up in a kid carrier.

Layering works for the hands, too. A synthetic, moisture-wicking liner beneath wool gloves or mittens gives added protection. The world's best mittens won't be any good if they're lost or dropped in a puddle. Some parents fasten them to the jacket sleeve with clips, buckles, or Velcro. Or you can use the traditional method of making sure mittens stay attached to a coat: Thread yarn or string through the sleeves and across the back of your young one's garment, then tie a mitten to each end.

You can adapt adult clothing for babies. Adult wool socks, for example, can be pulled up past the knees over a young child's shoes and pants; use safety pins to keep them in place. Bandannas can provide much-needed sun protection. Adult ponchos can be trimmed to fit smaller bodies.

Protect yourself and your children from skin cancer with sunscreen and wide-brimmed hats.

(PHOTO BY KEN YAGER)

Rainwear worn by children who are not walking does not have to be breathable. On the other hand, kids three and older tend to be energetic in short bursts, which creates perspiration and a need for an inner moisture-wicking layer of clothing. Once babies are out of diapers, they will need easy-on-and-off clothing for toileting.

Like adults, children lose a disproportionate amount of body heat through their uncovered head and neck. Wear hats and hoods to reduce heat loss and protect skin and eyes from the sun.

FOR EXPLORING NATURE
- Small pack
- Magnifying glass
- String
- Red cellophane
- Notebook/pencil/crayons
- Kitchen strainer   • Trowel
- Lightweight flashlight
- Rubber bands

Exploration. If you race through nature, it will be little more than a blur to young children. If you stop and investigate some of the micro-mysteries of life, you will share some spectacular discoveries with your children.

Bring paper and crayons. Most children will enjoy doing interpretive drawings of nature. A kitchen strainer is handy for sifting through dirt, sand, and even water. A plastic trowel is a search-and-don't-destroy tool. You can turn over scat, construct a makeshift pond for a wriggling tadpole, move stubborn rocks, dig up wild onions, and perform myriad other tasks. String can be used for bundling vegetation and as a measuring device. Attach red cellophane to the lens of your flashlight to search for animals at night. Mirrors and magnifying glasses are fun and educational for young children.

CARRYING BABY
When Madeleine was only three months old, my wife cleverly rigged a sling out of a sweater and hiked a couple of miles with baby cradled against the front of her body. For bigger kids and longer hikes, however, baby should be on your back.

A good child carrier will fit and ride like a backpack. It will have a hip belt for you and safety straps for the baby. It will be so comfortable that sometimes you may have to remind yourself that there's a child back there, not gear. There is good reason to stay alert. To avoid problems:

• Duck when you walk beneath low branches.

• If you bend over to pick something up, bend at the knees, not the waist.

• If you sit down, don't crush baby's feet.

• Check baby frequently for diaper needs and for signs of chafing where her skin might be rubbing against the pack.

• Periodically, help her change positions to avoid circulation problems.

• Stay off steep snow slopes with baby on board. In fact, stay away from any place where you might fall.

• When baby falls asleep (riding is soporific), cushion her head with a shirt or towel.

• Reduce facial glare by wearing dark clothing and wrapping the shiny parts of the baby carrier with black tape or bandannas. Don't forget sunglasses and sunblock.

• Stuff something—a pillow, towel, diaper, or magazine—between baby and the back of the carrier for support and insulation.

• Most child carriers have an extra metal bar that swings out to allow the pack to stand alone as a seat. It's convenient in camp for feeding and keeping track of baby, but beware of the contraption tipping over.

• The adult not carrying a child will probably be burdened with a heavier load than usual. Take advantage of the compartments available on the child carrier.

12 How to Get Home Again

There are only two lasting bequests we can hope to give our children. One of these is roots; the other, wings.
—Hodding Carter

Returning home from a camping trip with Madeleine, I am forced to conclude that nature brings out the best in my daughter. Compared to her paved, plastic, electronic world at home, the outdoors makes her more alert, inquisitive, sensitive, adventurous, enthusiastic, and respectful of life.

Examples of this are everywhere. One day in the wilds of Yosemite, Madeleine and a playmate discovered a slew of ladybugs. Wouldn't it be neat, the other little girl suggested, to smash them into ladybug dust? Madeleine, who at home has been known to snuff the life out of ants, voted against capital punishment, and the ladybugs lived. Later she wanted to pick a wildflower but accepted with relative calm my explanation that it was illegal and wrong to pick flowers in a national park. In the shadow of El Capitan, with three groups of climbers visible high on that mammoth stone, she imitated them by scaling her own miniature rock wall.

Which, of course, is another outdoor benefit—increased exercise. Lord knows kids today need it. I just read a scientific study that said children in 1988 ate the same amount of calories (and even less fat) than their 1973 counterparts, yet weighed an average of 11.4 pounds more. An ominous trend showing no sign of reversal, it must be blamed on the increasingly sedentary, vicarious life our children lead.

Inhabiting a world dominated by TVs, cars, and video games, many kids see hiking and climbing as something the pioneers did. As parents, we have to seize the day. Draw a line in the dirt. Pull the plug. Kick the young off the couch and out the door. Climb a rock. Hike a trail. Touch the earth.

> *"If I were to name the three most precious resources of life, I would say books, friends, and nature; and the greatest of these . . . is nature."*   —*John Burroughs*

We can no longer rely (if indeed we ever could) on schools to secure children's ties to nature. They may study ecology, but by and large the school curriculum has a "city" bias, an emphasis on the skills supposedly needed in an increasingly urban world. Many students are required to take shop; few are required to take nature walks, build a shelter, or find their way through a wilderness.

It is left to parents to turn kids on to nature. Even city dwellers should teach their children the outdoor ethics and survival skills detailed in this book. Whether or not young people make use of the techniques, the added knowledge will build self-confidence and resourcefulness that will spill over into everyday life. Thus young people learn to rely on themselves, to overcome fears, to take control of their lives, and to seek solutions and shun excuses.

> *"I am glad I shall never be young without wild country to be young in. Of what avail are forty freedoms without a blank spot on the map?"*   —*Aldo Leopold*

If kids avoid nature, our species' ties to the planet will continue to fray. Those who confront nature only on TV and movie screens tend to see it as a dangerous, alien place (take, for example, the wolf scene in *Beauty and the Beast*). The result is us-versus-them thinking, an alienation from other life so profound as to threaten our very existence. It is also a damn sorry way to live. Henry David Thoreau spoke to this point in his

(Photo by Ann Brice)

If you start your children on nature trails, they'll soon have you climbing mountains.

book *Walden*: "I went to the woods because I wished to live deliberately, to front only the essential facts of life, and see if I could not learn what it had to teach, and not, when I came to die, discover that I had not lived."

> *"The wild places are where we begin. When they end, so do we."*   *--David Brower*

So get out there and live. And relive. As you head home from your next nature excursion, keep the trip alive by reviewing some of the poignant moments. This may even endure beyond the car ride. When we arrived home from Yosemite, Madeleine asked me to help her write down the highlights of the trip so she could share them with her preschool pals. The list looked like this:

Waterfalls	El Capitan	Half Dome
Coyote	Deer	

I urge you to routinely expand your children's minds by asking questions. What did they see? How did they feel? What do they know? Probe. Don't let them get away with this:

"What was it like?"

"Fine."

"What did you do?"

"Nothing."

By rehashing experiences, you will engrave events in their impressionable little minds.

> *"In wilderness is the preservation of the world."*
> —*Henry David Thoreau*

Below are some sample questions for your kids. Most of the topics have been discussed in this book. Unless your charges love taking tests, don't pepper them with all thirty at once. Be patient. Work them into the conversation or play games. Twenty Questions works well for questions that aren't yes-or-no. Asking questions will promote focused, logical thinking.

1. What animal was found at twenty-two thousand feet on Mount Everest, making it the highest land creature ever documented? (spider)

2. How many noses does an ant have? (five, each with a different purpose)

3. What poisonous snake bites the most North Americans? (copperhead)

4. Do beavers' teeth ever stop growing? (no)

5. Can porcupines climb trees? (yes)

6. When does a diurnal animal usually sleep? (at night)

7. Do tarantulas spin webs? (no)

8. Are birds warm-blooded? (yes)

9. What fraction of a beaver's life is spent swimming (one-half)

10. Do bees fly in the rain? (no)

11. What are the only vertebrates that outnumber birds? (fish)

12. What literary animal's first words every day are, "What's for breakfast?" (Winnie the Pooh)

13. What's the only North American mammal with a grasping tail? (opossum)

14. What does a blue jay do after eating a monarch butterfly that had milkweed for breakfast? (it vomits)

15. Do female crickets chirp? (no)

16. There is a sign in the Bronx Zoo that reads, "The only creature that has ever killed off entire species of other animals." Under what does the sign hang? (a mirror)

17. Can fish smell? (yes)

18. Do bears' claws retract? (no)

19. What do bees make honey from? (nectar)

20. What kind of bath should be 2½ inches deep? (birdbath)

21. What's the primary cause of forest fires? (lightning)

22. What kind of tree is most often struck by lightning? (oak)

23. Toward what direction does a west wind blow? (east)

24. What direction is halfway between east-southeast and south-southeast? (southeast)

25. Which kind of clouds float higher, stratus or cirrostratus? (cirrostratus)

26. What's the primary shaper of landscape? (water)

27. What's the most common form of cancer? (skin)

28. What is classified as forked, ribbon, sheet, and ball? (lightning)

29. What part of a fisherman's equipment features an eye and a shank? (hook)

30. The longest spider webs, if straightened out, would span ____ miles. (300)

One last word about motivation, because it is so critical. Children are rebellious by nature. You cannot force-feed them wilderness. Do it in baby steps. Take a walk at night. Sleep in the backyard. Be enthusiastic, patient, perseverant, and tactical.

What I have discovered is this: If you introduce children to Mother

Nature early and often, teach them right from wrong, and make it fun, chances are they will grow up with an abiding respect for natural life and a willingness to put themselves on trails.

It's worth sleeping on the ground for that.

Nature can be very restful.

(PHOTO BY KEN YAGER)